MUSTANG

MUSTANG

PETER HENSHAW

CHARTWELL
BOOKS, INC.

Published in 2004 by
Chartwell Books Inc.
A division of Book Sales Inc.
Raritan Center
114 Northfield Avenue
Edison
NJ 08837 U.S.A.

ISBN 0-7858-1782-4

Printed in China by Sino Publishing
House Limited

Acknowledgements
*We thank photographer Gary Stuart, who
helped to make this book possible;
also Lawayne Matthies of Dallas, Texas, for
setting up photo shoots; Berry's Motor Cars
of Arlington, Texas, for allowing their
showroom cars to be photographed; the
Cowtown Mopar Club of Fort Worth, Texas,
for turning out in zero temperatures for a
photo shoot; and Elite Cars of Dallas,
Texas.
    We also thank the kind owners who
allowed their classic cars to be
photographed.*

Mustang represents the personal view of
the author and is not an official Mustang
publication.

CONTENTS

MUSTANG PRECURSORS:
THUNDERBIRD, MONZA & FALCON

Three cars had a profound effect on the Ford Mustang, and without any one of them it is possible that the revolutionary 'personal car' would never have happened. The original two-seater Ford Thunderbird appeared a decade before the Mustang, while the Chevrolet Corvair, and in particular the Monza, was a svelte four-seater coupé that convinced Lee Iacocca that Ford would benefit from something similar. Finally there was the Ford Falcon, whose low-cost

components made it possible to produce the sporty-looking Mustang at a low price. None of these cars is usually associated with the Mustang, but they all played a vital part in the story of its life.

The Thunderbird
The similarities between Ford's first 'personal car' – the Thunderbird – and its second – the Mustang – are striking. Both were conceived as sporty yet comfortable

cars with a range of options, set almost halfway between a spartan sports cars, such as an MG or Porsche, and the traditional American sedan. Both were aimed at two-car families, not intended to replace the big sedan, but to supplement it, and both were designed to appeal to a wide audience. They were not speciality sports cars aimed at enthusiasts used to suffering for their pleasure; they were intended for a wider market that while it might be attracted to a car that looked special, was loath to dispense with comfort and convenience.

The crucial difference, of course, was that the original Thunderbird had just two seats (though the bench could accommodate three), whereas the Mustang always was a four-seater, a factor that was crucial to its phenomenal success. In 1958, however, the Thunderbird also became a four-seater, but in the process lost that magic combination of low price and sportiness, which Ford did not regain until the Mustang appeared six years on.

It was 1951 when the idea of a personal car first presented itself. At the time, Lee Iacocca (later regarded as the father of the Mustang) was just beginning his career at Ford, where he had a relatively lowly sales job in Philadelphia; it is unlikely that Ford Division general manager Lewis D. Crusoe and styling chief George Walker even knew

A 'Battlebird' Thunderbird at the Daytona Beach Speed Week Trials, Florida, 1957. This was a highly modified Thunderbird 312 with V8 supercharged engine.

also made of fibreglass, a new material that General Motors was eager to test (steel was cheaper for high-volume cars), but Chevrolet wasn't interested in that either. To underline the Corvette's position as a desirable exotic, the company at first deliberately produced it in tiny numbers. Barely 300 were built in 1953, many going to selected customers, and it was only in 1954 that production was boosted to 500 a month as dealers began work on their long waiting lists. By then, of course, much of the excitement of the launch had died down, and many prospective buyers had changed their minds in the meantime, making the Corvette a very limited-production car by Detroit standards.

LEFT
1955 Ford Thunderbird with the top down.

BELOW
The 1957 Thunderbird was the last of the 'classic' two-seater T-birds. Restyled for the new model year, it had tail fins, opera windows, a new grille and a choice of five V-8 engines. The last was built on 16 December 1957.

of his existence when, strolling through the Paris Salon that year, the idea came to them, later described by Mike Lamm as 'a cross between a factory sports car, a factory hot rod and a factory personal car'. As it happened, Ford's design department was already working on a two-seater, though it wasn't until February 1953 that the project was given the official rubber stamp. By then, of course, work had been progressing well, and only 19 months later the first production Thunderbird rolled off the line.

Later that same year, Chevrolet had begun production of the Corvette, and the two cars were destined to be arch-rivals for the next three years. On paper, they certainly looked similar, being open two-seater sports cars with some sedan components. But in actual concept they were completely different, just as the Corvette's successors would remain worlds apart from the Mustangs of the 1970s, '80s and '90s. The Corvette was a sports car that made few compromises, aimed head-on at the exotic foreign imports. Chevrolet was well aware that it would not sell in large numbers, but that didn't matter. It hoped, in fact, that the Corvette would be an image-builder for the whole marque, and that some of its glamour would rub off on the lowlier models. It was

A 1958 Thunderbird – bigger, fatter and with four seats.

The Thunderbird couldn't have been more different. Like the Mustang, 10 years later, it was not aimed at the sports car enthusiast, and was not without its creature comforts, having a three-person seat, wind-up windows and generous luggage space, plus an adjustable steering wheel. A soft top was standard, but buyers could also specify a solid, weatherproof fibreglass hardtop which could be clipped on or off very quickly. Decent fenders came as standard, an essential for most American motorists but a flimsy afterthought on most imported sports cars, as

well as the Corvette. Options included power steering, automatic transmission, power windows and a four-way power seat, while the suspension was tuned for comfort rather than outright handling. Instead of the Corvette's tuned three-carburettor straight six, there was an easy-going V8 offering 160 horsepower, with the option of Fordmatic or three-speed overdrive stickshift. Moreover, the bodywork was steel – heavier than the Corvette's glassfibre, which took longer to get into production but was cheaper if high-production volumes were required.

This was a new sort of sports car (if it could be categorized as such) that Americans had not seen before – sleek and different enough to turn heads, but practical for everyday use. If someone accidentally reversed into a parked Thunderbird, the fenders could take it, whereas the same thing happening to a Corvette would result in a complicated and costly repair. If it rained on the way home, the hardtop would keep the interior dry where a Corvette's might not.

Ford's hunch was that it was exactly what many Americans were looking for.

There was no market research industry in those days, but the company had discovered that 17 per cent of American families owned two or more cars, one of which, naturally, would be a large and prestigious sedan, while the other could be something like a Thunderbird.

The advertising was unequivocal, describing it as 'a new kind of sports car', and 'custom-designed for the American road' (probably a dig at those small-engined imports, not really suitable for long-distance American motoring). 'Introducing a completely new kind of sports car … a truly fine car … with low-silhouette styling … road-hugging stability … and high performance … plus the conveniences and all-weather protection of today's modern automobile.' And this was the punchline. Early magazine reports had suggested that the Thunderbird would be in the $3,500–4,000 price range, in other words, maybe the same or a little more than a Corvette. When it was announced in early 1955, the car's basic price was just $2,695, and that included the hard top! As with the Mustang, Ford decided that price would be a major part of the Thunderbird's appeal.

Consequently, it cost the same as a very ordinary low-range Detroit convertible, but it looked a million dollars.

It was not surprising, therefore, that it was an instant hit. In its first year it sold over 16,000, which was tiny by Detroit standards but significant for the U.S. sports car market; moreover, it outsold the Chevrolet by a massive 24 to 1. Even in subsequent years, with the Corvette up to full production, with more power, wind-up windows and better weatherproofing to meet the Thunderbird challenge, Ford sold around five Thunderbirds to each Corvette.

By 1964, the Thunderbird had strayed far from its sports car origins.

The question was, how did it compare with the Chevrolet? Different as the two were in concept, it was inevitable that they should be seen as close rivals. *Motor Trend* tested the two cars back to back in June 1956, driving them over Mount Wilson, across the Mojave Desert and in city conditions. There seemed little between them where performance was concerned, though the Thunderbird was slightly quicker off the mark, its extra power making up for nearly 600lb (272kg) of extra weight. But what really set these two all-American sports cars apart was their handling.

Motor Trend thought the general feel of the Thunderbird was not what one would have expected, given the car's size and appearance. In short, the Thunderbird may have looked like a sports car, but it didn't corner like one. It rolled into corners like a softly-sprung sedan and would let go into a four-wheel-drift. On one test corner it even ran off the road several times. The Corvette, by contrast, 'feels much more like a sports car', and cornered flatly, with quicker steering and better road-holding. The upside of the Ford's soft suspension, however, was that it gave a quieter, more comfortable ride. As *Motor Trend* points out, by 1956 several sedans could out-accelerate the Thunderbird, and cornered just as well, though that didn't lessen its appeal to those who wanted a good-looking, feel-good car but weren't too concerned about outright performance.

In England, *Motor Sport* magazine tested the T-Bird in 1957, describing it as 'a gentleman's high-performance coupé', as well they might, with power boosted to

245hp from a four-barrel carburettor 312-ci (5.1-litre) V8; this came with the optional overdrive or Fordmatic transmission, the basic V8 being a 202-hp two-barrel 292-ci (4.8-litre) unit, and there were 270- and 285-hp options as well. But even the 312 failed to give stunning performance, especially when compared with the Corvette's latest fuel-injected 283-ci V8. Ford's answer was the rare F-Bird of 1957, supercharged to offer 300hp, which many considered a modest claim on Ford's part, as up to 340hp was allegedly available with only a little fine tuning.

However, the supercharged T-Bird was shortlived. True, Ford had sold over 21,000 two-seater T-Birds in 1957, comprehensively outselling the Corvette, which could manage only 6,246 sales that year; in Detroit terms, however, these were still tiny numbers. With its low price and unique body, the two-seater T-Bird simply wasn't turning a big enough profit, and Ford decided to axe the car forthwith.

Its replacement for 1958 was bigger and heavier and had four seats. In fact, the concept of a larger four-seater Thunderbird had been broached by Lewis Crusoe barely a month after the two-seater had gone into production, when it was realized that it wouldn't have a sufficiently broad appeal to satisfy the Ford mass-production machine. So the two-seat Thunderbird died, and with it the concept of Ford's sporty personal car. However, a few years later, Lee Iacocca (by then general manager of the Ford Division) decided it was time to respond to all the letters pleading for the return of the sporty

Thunderbird. His reply was a car that looked good, had a wide range of options, but was easy to drive – rather like the original T-Bird. Its name? The Mustang.

The Falcon

At first glance, the Ford Mustang and Ford Falcon couldn't be more different. The former is lean and lithe, the latter upright and sensible, the kind of car a bank clerk would own, one who preferred to invest his savings in a decent pension or a fine house rather than a flashy car.

Yet the two were intimately connected for the reason that, under its shapely skin, the Mustang used many Falcon components: the 170-ci (2.8-litre) straight six came straight out of Ford's value-for-money sedan, which was also offering the 260-ci V8 as an option before the Mustang went on sale. The Mustang's rear suspension was Falcon-derived, while that of the front was transferred complete. Six-cylinder Mustangs used Falcon brakes and rear axles too, while transmissions were also shared, as was the instrument panel. One magazine went as far as to describe the new Mustang as a rebodied Falcon, and it wasn't far wrong.

There was good reason to use all these utilitarian parts in the svelte four-seater coupé. The Falcon had been carefully designed to be a low-cost car – cheap to build and cheap to run – and after four years of production its tooling costs were probably close to being paid for. This allowed Ford to advertise the Mustang at its seductively low basic price. Indeed, without the Falcon, there's reason to believe that the Mustang

would never have happened at all; the whole point of the car, according to Lee Iacocca, was that it offered sporty looks at a low price.

The Falcon also gave a hint of what was to come in the Futura coupé derivative of 1963. After their initial huge success, Falcon sales were beginning to flag, and it was Iacocca who hurried through the Futura. He was well aware that Ford needed to capture a share of the growing youth market, and as a stopgap while the Mustang was under development, fitted bucket front seats, a centre console and more upmarket trim to upgrade the basic Falcon. All of these were crucial feel-good items designed to optimize the Mustang's showroom appeal, but the Falcon had them first.

Lee Iacocca, of course, could rightly be termed the father of the Mustang. The Falcon also had its own progenitor, though he

OPPOSITE
The Falcon later caught the attention of customizers.

BELOW
1964 Falcon Sprint.

couldn't have been more different from the brash salesman, Iacocca. Robert McNamara was an intriguing figure in Detroit. Many of his colleagues were car men through and through – enthusiasts with gasoline running through their veins. McNamara was the archetypal incorruptible public servant, whose every decision was careful, considered and thoroughly weighed. He was a liberal by instinct and a Democrat in practice, when most senior managers were Republicans. In fact, he was invited to join the first J.F. Kennedy administration, an offer he declined, though he later went on to become Secretary of Defense.

So Robert McNamara was a far cry from the usual Detroit top executive, and his background explains why. He was one of the famous Whiz Kids, the ten young Air Force officers brought into Ford in 1945 to improve its tottering finances. All had performed wonders of cost-efficiency in the Air Force, and in the late 1940s/early '50s did exactly the same for Ford. Finances were brought under control by making every department financially accountable, and the company subsequently recovered. Fifteen years on, McNamara had risen to become president of Ford. Though he was cool and aloof, it is clear that Lee Iacocca had a lot of time for him, describing him in his later autobiography as 'a very kind man as well as a loyal friend'. He also considered McNamara's intelligence so formidable and his actions so disciplined that his true personality tended to be obscured.

Rather than glamorous objects, McNamara regarded cars as simple, basic

transportation, tolerating upmarket, luxury cars only because of their higher profit margin. This was almost heretical as far as Detroit was concerned, though in the late 1950s there were good reasons to heed his words. The American public was leaning towards small imported cars – the VWs, Volvos and MGs, which in 1955 made up a mere 1 per cent of the U.S. market, but by 1960 would reach 10 per cent. The American auto industry finally fought back with its own 'compacts' – Chrysler's Valiant, the radical Chevrolet Corvair and McNamara's baby, the Falcon.

All three were different: the Valiant was a conservative, scaled-down big car, while the rear-engined Corvair was avant-garde and daring. The Falcon lay somewhere between the two, at first sight ultra-conventional, even

dull, but in effect rather spacious. In fact, one of the Falcon's first design objectives had been to provide much the same interior space as a standard American sedan, with seating for six.

The other objectives were light weight, low initial cost, low running costs, the same performance as a full-sized six-cylinder Ford, and good fuel economy. It met almost all of these criteria: at 2,425lb (1100kg) it was remarkably light, while at less than $2,000 for the basic four-door sedan it was cheaper than both its home-grown rivals. The 170-ci (2.8-litre) six could average 30mpg (10.6km/litre), unheard of in a U.S.-made car; moreover, the detail design also ensured that it would be cheap to run, service and repair. Only in performance did it lag behind its objective, and the early sedan in two-

OPPOSITE
Only a little over 3,000 1965 Falcon Sprints were made.

BELOW
1960 Chevrolet Corvair.

speed automatic form could only wheeze up to 84mph (135km/h), and took 25 seconds to reach 60mph (97km/h), though the three-speed manual was quicker.

But to many American buyers, this didn't seem to matter. Here was an American-made car that combined the space of a full-sized sedan with something akin to the economy of a VW. It may have been lacking in glamour, but the Falcon was an outstanding achievement and the public seemed to agree, buying 417,000 of them in its first year: never before had a new model out of Detroit sold so fast.

Of course, the car that broke that record was the Mustang, and it's worth reiterating just how much Iacocca's 'personal car' owed to McNamara's 'sensible' one. As well as sharing engines, transmissions, brakes, suspension and axles, the two were almost identical in size, every major dimension being within an inch or two of one another. The only exception was height, the low-slung Mustang being 3.5in (8.9cm) lower.

Of course, not everyone liked the Falcon, and those that didn't seem to have been motoring journalists raised on a diet of hot-rod V8s and the dream of the open road. According to one, it had all the luxury of the men's room at a Greyhound bus depot with the performance of a love-sick mud turtle. But in the end most had to admit that the Falcon made sense – especially as it wasn't that bad to drive. With a manual gearbox, the 0–60 time was less than 18 seconds, while the high top gear combined restful high-speed cruising with good economy. *Road & Track* described both ride and handling as

'superlative', with less roll and float than in other, heavier Detroit sedans.

If Robert McNamara's ideas had continued to hold true, Ford would possibly have gone on selling the sensible economical Falcon in huge numbers for year upon year, with barely a change. Unfortunately, the consumer car market has never worked like that: to sustain customer interest, manufacturers have to introduce something new almost every year, and in the Falcon's case it meant bigger engines and a more luxurious trim. In other words, the original idea of simple, basic transportation was being gradually eroded.

The first sign of this was a 170-ci (2.8-litre) six-cylinder option on top of the standard 144-ci (2.3-litre) unit. This was the same motor that would power the basic Mustang in 1964, and here it came in the same state of tune, offering 101hp and 156lb ft, up from 85hp/123lb ft from the 144. It was usefully faster, with a 0–60 time of 14.3 seconds for the manual car, though it used more fuel in the process. The Falcon range was also expanded, with two- and four-door station wagons joining the line-up.

Soon afterwards, the Falcon Futura appeared, a version of the basic two-door sedan, but with 'personal' touches to take it upmarket. Reflecting the latest Thunderbird influence, there were two individually adjustable bucket seats, with a central console with storage space between. European cars had been offering separate seats for years, but in Detroit, where the bench seat still ruled supreme, they seemed exotic and unfamiliar. There was full

carpeting, with a choice of colours to match the vinyl upholstery – even the steering column and instrument panel were colour-keyed. Externally, so that the neighbours would be immediately aware that this was no ordinary Falcon, were polka-dot wheel covers, whitewall tyres and 'teardrops' on the rear wings. There was no Futura station wagon, but buyers could opt for the Squire, with simulated wood panelling along its flanks. A convertible Falcon joined the range for 1963 – heavier and less fuel-efficient than the original, perhaps – but was what the public wanted.

There was big news at the end of 1962, when *Car Life* was permitted a test drive in a modified Falcon with Ford's 260-ci (4.3-litre) V8. Officially, this was a privately modified car, Ford maintaining that it had no plans to do the same itself. However, the car turned up at Ford's official unveiling of its 1963 cars, and a 164-hp V8 soon became a regular option. Performance drivers could finally begin to take an interest in the Falcon. With the high-revving Fairlane V8 under the bonnet, the Falcon could sprint to 60mph (97km/h) in 9.3 seconds, and top 123mph (198km/h). It made its debut as the fastback Falcon Sprint Coupé, complete with more rakish roofline, whitewall tyres and 'rally' stripes. In fact, these turned out to be most appropriate, as Ford eventually entered Falcons in the Monte Carlo Rally.

In fact, once the Mustang had been successfully launched, sporting versions of the Falcon seemed to undergo a sort of 'Mustangization'. The Sprint already had the bucket seats and floor-mounted four-speed gearchange, but 1965 saw the option of Ford's 195-hp 289-ci (4.7-litre) V8, another engine shared with the Mustang. As was pointed out at the time, it represented a 230 per cent power increase over the original 144-ci six. That was dropped, however, and a new 200-ci (3.3-litre) six-cylinder option was added, this being yet another Mustang/Falcon crossover. For 1966, the Futura coupé even began to look a little like a Mustang, with a shorter rear trunk and slightly kicked-up waistline. As well as that 289 V8, air conditioning and power steering were also on the options list.

By now, the Falcon had been slowly transformed from McNamara's new Model A into a luxury compact, though it has to be said that the basic car was still available, and most customers still opted for six cylinders rather than eight. But as far as the Mustang story is concerned, the Falcon had already done its job; as a source of cheap components it had made the Mustang possible.

The Corvair

Take three men and three very different cars. Lee Iacocca is inextricably linked with the Ford Mustang, a car which reflected his background. Lee started off in engineering, but soon moved to sales and marketing, having a flair for knowing what people wanted and what would sell. So the Mustang arose out of a marketing perspective: it was a salesman's car.

As already seen, although it had donated many components to the Mustang, the Ford Falcon was a very different beast: sensible,

straightforward and cheap to run. And it was the brainchild of Robert McNamara, a financier who regarded cars as basic transportation, no more, no less.

Now look at the Chevrolet Corvair: this was an engineer's car, aimed at the same compact car market as the Falcon but with a healthy dose of lateral thinking thrown in. And the man behind it? There are no surprises here: Chevrolet vice president Ed Cole was an engineer first and foremost, and it showed in the car he masterminded into production.

The relevance of all this to the Mustang story is simple. Although it was aimed at the Falcon as basic transportation, the Corvair was rapidly transformed into an enthusiast's car. Moreover, its success as a sporty compact, especially as the good-looking Monza coupé, more than convinced Lee Iacocca that Ford needed something similar. In the end, the Mustang won out comprehensively, partly because of a more conventional layout, partly because of a bigger range of engines and options, and partly because the Corvair had been condemned as dangerous in safety campaigner Ralph Nader's book, *Unsafe At Any Speed*.

All that was still in the future when the Corvair was announced to the world in late 1959. It made a huge impact, chiefly because it was quite unlike anything produced by the U.S. motor industry then or since. The Corvair turned the idea of a traditional American sedan on its head. Not only was the engine an air-cooled, aluminium flat six, it was also mounted in the rear, together with

a transaxle transmission and independent rear suspension. The result was a car that was long, low and wide. But although the Corvair was revolutionary by U.S. standards, its concept wasn't new at all. It was no more nor less than a VW Beetle writ large and heavily adapted for U.S. conditions. (The VW, of course, was the leading import at the time, and this was Chevrolet's response.)

There was no way that Chevrolet would attempt to meet the Beetle head-on. Instead, the Corvair was conceived as a U.S.-sized compact, designed to seat six adults in comfort, which it did very well due partly to the almost flat floor (the rear engine and transaxle meant that there was no intrusive transmission hump). Despite the advanced specification, it was no faster than a Falcon, according to *Road & Track*, which managed a pre-launch drive at General Motors's Milford proving ground. With a three-speed manual gearbox, it accelerated to 60mph (97km/h) in 19.5 seconds, hampered partly by a huge ratio gap between second and the long-striding top. Chevrolet quoted a top speed of 88mph (142km/h), which pointed to more efficient aerodynamics than a Falcon, which needed 90hp against the 80 from General Motors's 140-ci (2.3-litre) flat six. It was economical too, at 25–30mpg (8.8–10.6km/litre). So far so good.

If the Corvair had a flaw, it lay in its handling. There had already been murmurings to this effect when *R&T* published its early road test, though the magazine dismissed what it called 'the gossip about this car's dangerous handling'. Like all rear-engined cars, the Corvair was tail-heavy

(62 per cent of its weight lay on the rear wheels), so there was a tendency for the rear to swing out if the driver decelerated while driving at the limits of adhesion. This was exacerbated by the swing-axle rear suspension (actually only semi-independent), which varied wheel camber with movement. Unsafe or not, there is no doubt that the early Corvair was a very different driving experience from any other American car, and something which most of its owners would not have experienced before. But much of the motoring press refused to accept that there was a problem. *R&T* referred to the oversteer as 'the usual and expected result' of a rear-engined car. Usual and expected for an experienced, enthusiastic driver may be, but the vast majority of Corvair owners hardly fitted this category. *Sports Car Illustrated* praised the car's 'live nerves and quick reflexes that are worth more than all the seat belts and crash pads in the world'. Driving a later supercharged Corvair, *Car and Driver* decided that all that was needed to correct that sudden movement into oversteer 'was a flick of the wood-rimmed steering wheel and a steady hard foot on the accelerator'.

In other words, the Corvair was fun to drive and responded well to an experienced hand. But this was not what most of the buying public wanted. They wanted a car that (to paraphrase Ralph Nader) was safe at any speed. In late 1963, *Motor Sports Illustrated* reported that the Corvair was heading the statistics in one-car accidents, indicating that if the Corvair was to be a mass-market competitor for the no-frills Falcon, it was going the wrong way about it. Early Corvair

sales failed to match those of the compact Ford, but at 1.25 million in the first three years they were far from negligible.

Meanwhile, the Corvair was rapidly making a name for itself as an enthusiast's car. Two things make this plain: the speed with which Chevrolet came up with performance enhancements, and the number of aftermarket tuning parts available. Take the good-looking Monza coupé, the car that made Lee Iacocca sit up and take notice. As well as the sportier two-door coupé bodywork, the flat-six engine was boosted to 98bhp, a 23 per cent increase.

Better still for keen drivers, the old three-speed gearbox was replaced by a new four-speed manual; the former had so hampered performance that the Powerglide automatic was actually quicker. With the four closer ratios and 98bhp to play with, the Monza coupé could reach 60mph (97km/h) in 13.5 seconds and just break the 90mph (145km/h) barrier. As well as the added kudos of 'four on the floor', the Monza had front bucket seats and (according to Jerry Titus in *Sports Car Graphic*) 'has all the appearance of a Gran Turismo machine'. He did add that handling was 'still in the forget-it category', but that one couldn't have everything.

The standard Monza certainly looked the part, even though 98bhp wasn't enough for many drivers. The trouble was, it was no simple matter to tune Chevrolet's flat six; in America, there were generations of know-how when it came to hopped-up water-cooled V8s, but this air-cooled unit was something new. In fact, the quickest way to

boost power was to bolt on a supercharger, which is eventually what tuner Andy Granatelli did. He used a McCulloch blower and replaced the two single-barrel carburettors with a single twin-barrel. And to cope with the 7,000rpm the engine could now achieve, he also fitted heavy-duty valve springs and a Sheiffer flywheel, clutch disc and pressure plate. The result was a Monza that could sprint to 60mph in just 7.8 seconds, to 100mph (161km/h) in 21.8 and which topped out at 142mph (229km/h).

That was in June 1961, a full three years before the Mustang went on sale. Until then, the Corvair Monza became something of a cult car for those looking for a sporty-looking U.S.-made coupé with four seats. Chevrolet responded by offering its own powered-up version of the flat six later that year, the Monza now packing 102bhp from a higher-compression version of what many referred to as the 'pancake' engine. Meanwhile, tuner John Fitch began to sell what he called the Monza Sprint, a standard coupé with Paxton supercharger providing 130hp, different rear springs and shocks, in an attempt to tame the rear end, a black vinyl roof and many detail parts such as a tachometer and wood-rimmed steering wheel. It wasn't as quick as the Granatelli car, but the John Fitch Sprint did the business. In fact, Fitch became something of a Corvair specialist, selling his Sprint for quite a while, though he was to ditch the blower in favour of a four-barrel carburettor.

Then there was the California-based EMPI, which offered a package of suspension and engine modifications. Its solution to the problem of the wayward tail was a front anti-roll bar and a transverse single-leaf spring linking the rear wheels together, something later tried by Chevrolet itself. The Induction Engineering Company (IECO) offered a package of engine parts, including a megaphone-extractor exhaust and a patented four-barrel carburettor ram intake system, the result being 106hp at the rear wheels and better acceleration than Chevrolet's own turbocharged Monza up to 85mph (137km/h). Metallic brake linings, quick-steering arms and new shock absorbers were also on offer. But prophetically, the number of tuning parts available for Corvairs was starting to drop off by 1965; many specialists were turning their attention to the Mustang, which was selling in far greater numbers.

But Chevrolet hadn't been twiddling its thumbs all this time. From 1962 it offered optional suspension kits to improve the Corvair's handling, though these brought problems of their own, including heavy tyre wear, and were an unsatisfactory, temporary solution. Meanwhile, Chevrolet boss Ed Cole left the company, to be replaced by Semon Knudsen, 'Bunkie' to his friends.

Now Bunkie came straight out of the performance school of auto makers, along with men like Lee Iacocca and John DeLorean. At Ford, later in the 1960s, he was to mastermind a series of three hot Mustangs: the Boss 302, Boss 429 and Mach 1. One of his first actions at Chevrolet, however, was to order a speed-up of the open-top high-performance Corvair, then under development, which appeared in 1962

as the Monza Spyder, a good-looking four-seater convertible. With full instrumentation set in a brushed-aluminium dashboard, also bucket seats, it came over as a genuine performance car.

But the real innovation was in the engine compartment, where Chevrolet engineers used a turbocharger to bump the flat six up to 150hp at 4,400rpm, with over 200lb ft available between 3,200 and 3,400rpm. *Car and Driver* tested one, making the point that with the conventional Chevy II now in production to rival Ford's Falcon, the way was clear for the Corvair to become Chevy's enthusiast car, pure and simple. With the Monza now the best-selling model in the range, the Corvair's transformation was almost complete. To underline the fact, Chevrolet whipped the wraps off a concept car, the two-seater Corvair Monza GT, with standard underpinnings but Italian mid-engine looks.

As if to admit that the handling still needed sorting out, a transverse leaf spring was added to the rear suspension in 1964, though this was ditched the following year in favour of an all-new fully-independent set-up. At last, the Corvair's handling problems were finally at an end; the new Corsa top model, complete with a hot 180-hp turbo version of the flat six, no longer swung out its tail or displayed other nasty habits. It was also stable in a straight line at high speed, so another Corvair weakness had been overcome.

Ironically, just as the Corvair had been rectified, Ralph Nader's book was published. In it, the Corvair was castigated for its unsafe

handling, and although Nader made it plain that only 1960–64 models were at fault, the public somehow tarred them all with the same brush, with the result that sales took a tumble. In the first three years, Chevrolet had sold 1.25-million Corvairs, but in the next six, less than half found buyers. It was only a matter of time before Chevrolet dropped the car altogether, which in 1969 is exactly what happened. It was a great pity, as by then the Corvair was a good-looking sporty car, a fitting rival for all but the high-powered Mustangs. It also introduced a welcome change from Detroit's domination by the V8. But as far as the Mustang story is concerned, the Corvair had done its job helping to convince Lee Iacocca that Ford needed a sporty four-seater too.

Lee Iacocca

One man's name above all others is associated with the Mustang, even more so than those of stylists Gene Bordinat, Joe Oros and Dave Ash, who were responsible for its classic shape. Other Ford men also played their part in its birth – Don Frey, Hal Sperlich, Donald Petersen and Henry Ford II himself, but the first name that springs to mind is that of Lee Iacocca.

When the huge impact made by Mustang turned it into a media phenomenon, it was Iacocca's now-familiar face which appeared on magazine covers and ensured his place in history as 'father of the Mustang'. From then on, he was a national figure, and remained so throughout his Ford years – even more so when he managed to turn Chrysler around in the 1980s. At one point, a public survey gave

Ford was proud of its racing links and the Mustang benefited from them. Here Benson Ford (left), Jim Clark (centre) and Lee Iacocca (right) pose with Ford's dohc Indy V8.

him a recognition factor of over 90 per cent, greater than many politicians; not for nothing was there talk of him running for president in 1992.

Ebullient, seemingly super-confident and brash, Iacocca was a born salesman, a person who could sell anything to anybody. Yet there was another side to his character. Even though he had climbed the greasy pole to success at Ford, a certain shyness and insecurity lay behind the public façade. Lee Iacocca's story was that of the classic self-made man.

His parents were Italian, first-generation immigrants to America in 1921. The young couple settled in Allentown, Pennsylvania, and Lee was born three years later. His father was an entrepreneur of sorts, always involved in one scheme or another: car hire, hot dogs, real estate, Nicolà Iacocca did the lot. This energy and determination was communicated to his son, whom he was forever pushing hard, seemingly never satisfied. When Lee graduated 12th out of over 900, papa Nick's response was, 'Why didn't you come first?' It was therefore this constant need for

success that drove Iacocca on and instilled a never-to-be-satisfied conviction that the only position worth fighting for was at the top.

Fortunately, Lee was also a fighter by nature. He managed to overcome crippling shyness to become a high-school debater, and survived both prejudice at school, because of his Italian origins, and the Depression, when even Nick found it hard to bring food to the table.

The young Iacocca also survived rheumatic fever in his teens, which was a potential killer in the 1940s, and was

Ford breakthrough products of the sixties included the 1960 Falcon (left) and the 1965 Mustang, shown here with Ford executives Don Frey and Lee Iacocca. The Falcon achieved one million sales in just 26 months, at that time a record equalled only by Ford's venerable Model A.

consequently pronounced unfit for military service. But he was absolutely clear where his ambitions lay: he wanted to work in the motor industry, he wanted to work for Ford, and he wanted to be vice president of the company by the time he was 35, a goal he fell short of by only 18 days.

In August 1946, Iacocca joined the company as a student engineer, doing the rounds of the various departments so that he could learn the business. But he was swiftly disenchanted. His first job had been to design a clutch spring, which left him wondering if this was really what he wanted to do. Typically, he wasted no time, applied for a low-level sales job in Chester, Pennsylvania, and got it.

At first, Iacocca's innate shyness was something of a stumbling block. But he succeeded in mastering the sales jargon, and after those first uncomfortable cold calls became something of a rising star. His boss, Charlie Beacham, was a hard taskmaster, described by Iacocca half-jokingly as 'my mentor and tormentor'. Maybe Beacham reminded him of his father, but Iacocca seemed to thrive in the high-pressure atmosphere.

By 1953, Iacocca had worked his way up to assistant sales manager, but what really made his name was his '56 for 56' campaign. Ford was having a bad year, and Iacocca devised a scheme that enabled customers to buy a new Ford for just $56 a month. It was a huge success and promotion followed, just as Iacocca finally married Mary, a Ford receptionist he had courted for eight years. Then in November

1960 he was called to the august presence of Henry Ford.

It was, he later wrote in his autobiography, 'like being summoned to see God' since, despite having worked for Ford for 14 years, he had barely spoken to the big boss. This time Iacocca learned that he was to be general manager of the Ford Division, and would be able to realize his ideas for a new, smaller, sportier Ford, a car that in 1964 was launched as the Mustang

The Mustang's phenomenal success secured Iacocca's future as an important part of the Ford empire, and ensured his eventual promotion to the top job, even though he and Henry Ford really didn't get along. The two men had similar volatile temperaments, and were men of decision, even though their backgrounds were as different as chalk and cheese. Lee had worked his way up from the bottom, while Henry had always been heir-apparent of the Ford dynasty. It was acknowledged that Ford could be difficult: he drank heavily and was inclined to be impulsive. He was also wary of Iacocca, suspecting that he had designs on the company himself, and Lee's flamboyant behaviour did nothing to allay his suspicions: Iacocca surrounded himself with supporters, and was fond of booking the company's 727 for personal use, like flying his parents up to Detroit. He certainly worked hard, was usually out of the house by 7.15 am and rarely left the office before 8 in the evening; but he also loved the trappings of a top executive lifestyle, not to mention a salary to match, which by now was close to $1 million. Meanwhile, Henry

Ford was forced to grin and bear it for, by now, Iacocca had made the company a lot of money.

Things came to a head when Henry brought in 'Bunkie' Knudsen, promoting him over Iacocca's head. According to Iacocca it was Bunkie who ruined the original Mustang concept by making the car fatter and heavier. By now, Iacocca had such support within the company that after just 18 months at Ford Bunkie was fired, and in 1970 Lee finally became president of the entire company; such political manoeuvrings wouldn't have been out of place in an medieval Italian court.

Now Lee was just a rung below Henry himself, which did nothing to improve their relationship; the two hardly ever met socially, and Ford's suspicions were now at fever pitch, leading him to mount an in-house investigation of Iacocca. No evidence of wrong-doing was discovered, however, and in the meantime Iacocca launched Mustang II, his lightweight back-to-basics revenge for the obese Bunkie Mustang.

The Mark III Mustang had just been launched when Lee Iacocca, after 22 years with Ford, was finally fired. Typically, he wasn't out of work for long. Iacocca accepted the top job at Chrysler and actually succeeded in turning around what many thought was a doomed company. Millions of people remember Lee Iacocca for that, while millions more remember his as the father of the Mustang.

OPPOSITE
Lee Iacocca and Don Frey, pictured with an early Mustang. These two men did much to encourage the Ford racing programme of the 1960s.

1960–63:
DESIGN AND DEVELOPMENT

Mustang designers, hard at work on a clay model in 1962.

Reading Lee Iacocca's autobiography, and trusting its veracity, one is left in no doubt that he was indeed the father of the Mustang. But as with anything that is successful (the Mustang set a new Detroit record for first-year sales), many others have also claimed paternity over the years. 'So many people have claimed to be father of the Mustang,' Iacocca later wrote, 'that I wouldn't want to be seen in public with the mother!' The reality is that many talented people were involved in the creation of Mustang, but Iacocca really was the driving force. He also took the crucial decision to make the Mustang a four-seater, which is what transformed it into a mass-market car.

Already general manager of the Ford Division, and a vice president, Iacocca was the company's fastest-rising star. He was just 37, and had gathered about him a group of other Young Turks from different departments. It was 1960, the first Kennedy administration was soon to be in place, and it seemed as though anything was possible. 'We were young and cocky,' he later recalled, 'We saw ourselves as artists, about to produce the finest masterpieces the world had ever known.'

They would all meet for dinner in the Fairlane Inn, just a mile up the road from Ford headquarters. Iacocca, of course, was the boss, but the others were of importance in most major departments of the company. Don Frey was chief engineer; Hal Sperlich was a product man, and would work with Iacocca again many years later at Chrysler; Frank Zimmerman represented marketing – he had joined Ford at the same time as Iacocca and had been his best friend in their training-programme days; Walter Murphy, another friend, was from public relations; and Sid Olsen was a brilliant advertising copywriter. It is noticeable that there were no accountants in the 'Fairlane Committee', as they called themselves, perhaps because Iacocca contemptuously regarded money

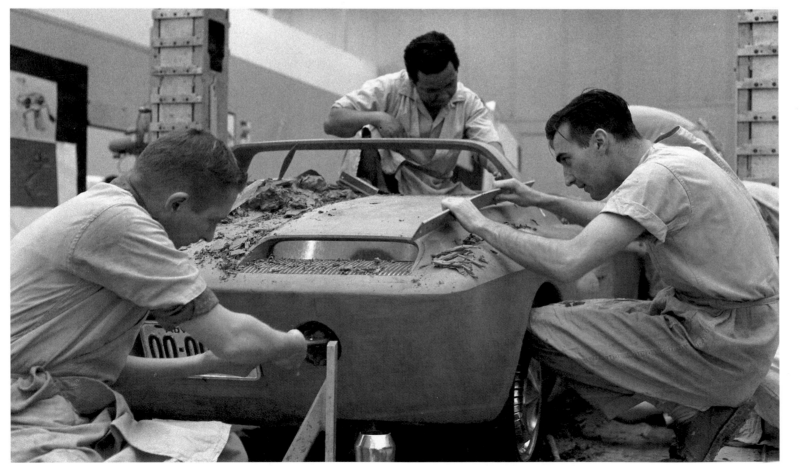

men as unimaginative 'bean counters'. Not that there needed to be an accountant on the committee; all the members were Ford men through and through, which meant that cost was nearly always uppermost in their minds.

Was Henry Ford II aware of these cosy dinners? Maybe, maybe not, but there's little doubt that Iacocca and his group were able to talk more freely at the Fairlane. At first, meetings were purely social, but they

gradually evolved into serious brainstorming sessions. By the time the Mustang concept had become a serious issue, the Fairlane group had taken to meeting for breakfast on Saturday mornings

Chevrolet's sporty Corvair provided part of the inspiration for the Mustang.

1962 Mustang Roadster concept car.

(still at the hotel, of course) with a 7 am start.

The topic that occupied them most was what to do about the Chevrolet Corvair in general and the sporty Monza in particular. General Motors had transformed the economy Corvair into a sporty compact, simply by adding bucket seats, stickshift and a few other flashy bits and pieces. Mechanically, it was identical to the sensible four-door sedan, and even the basic body shape was unchanged. But it was selling like hot cakes, and Ford was offering no competition. Iacocca quickly tried the same trick on the Falcon, adding bucket seats and a sporty trim to make the Futura two-door, and added a fastback to the big Galaxie. But these were stopgap measures. What Ford needed was a genuinely new, sporty car.

The American public seemed particularly receptive, and Iacocca thought he knew why. The baby-boomers were coming of age, and in the 1960s most of them were buying cars; moreover, the 20–24 age group was set to grow by 50 per cent. A huge increase in car sales was predicted for the new decade, with 18–34-year-olds accounting for at least half of the increase. They were more likely to be college-educated than previous generations, which meant a higher income and the greater likelihood of buying a new car. Not only that, but Ford's market research was suggesting that older buyers were also changing: they may have had a sensible, economical Falcon in 1960, but now they were ready to be a little more frivolous where cars were concerned. Everything pointed to a massive new market

for something small, youthful and sporty. 'Here was a market in search of a car', recalled Iacocca. It all fitted. When Robert McNamara headed Ford, he had taken the company out of racing and had produced an economy car. Now Iacocca, the brash salesman who loved cars, reversed the situation, and started work on the Mustang.

It sounds like a triumph of market research, but not everyone remembers it like that. Don Frey had his doubts. 'The market research stuff was done after the fact,' he told an interviewer much later. 'They made it all up afterwards – somebody did – in order to sanctify the whole thing … The market research that you read is a bunch of bull.' Indeed, Iacocca himself had little time for market researchers; to him they were in the

26

same category as bean counters. '[People] don't know what they want,' he said, 'Ya gotta have an idea and then ya gotta push it down their throats.'

But Iacocca, the instinctive salesman and marketeer, could see that buyers loved the Monza and had a gut feeling that youth was a new force to be reckoned with in the 1960s. Of course, kids had been building and street-racing hot rods for years, but now they could afford to buy new cars from their local Ford dealer. All Ford needed was the right car to draw them in.

Small and Sporty

The first thoughts were of a two-seater, a true sports car to rival the MGs and Porsches. And the styling studio came up with just the thing, a small car with a big air scoop. Here again, there are conflicting views as to who thought of it first. Some say the two-seater rose directly out of the Fairlane meetings, and that Don Frey made the first sketch; others maintain it originated in Gene Bordinat's design department. After he retired, Bordinat remarked, 'That car was developed seven months before he [Iacocca] saw it. That car would have made it to the marketplace without Lee.'

Whoever thought of it first, the two-seater reached the clay mock-up stage, and Iacocca was certainly involved by then, inviting a group of racing drivers and enthusiasts to come and take a look. They loved it. These were the people who'd been clamouring for Ford to bring back the two-seater Thunderbird, but as a proper sports car this was their dream come true. A show car

was built to test public reaction in 1962, and it certainly wowed the crowds. With a mid-mounted Ford Taunus V4 and all-independent suspension, it seemed just the thing to inject a new shot of adrenalin into the tired old Detroit product line.

But it wasn't to be. Even as they were raving over the little two-seater, Iacocca was having second thoughts. 'I looked at the guys saying it – the offbeat crowd, the real buffs – I said, "That's for sure not the car we want to build, because it can't be a volume car." ' This was confirmed by Ford's finance department: horrified, it predicted that the sports car would sell only 35,000 a year, which simply wasn't enough for a mass-market producer like Ford. Iacocca and his team made a few changes. All right, maybe 50,000, said the bean counters – but it was still not good enough.

Then Lee Iacocca had his big idea, one that would transform his fortunes, that of the Mustang and the entire Ford Motor Company. His concept was for something he called 'small-sporty' – not a sports car like a spartan two-seater MG, notice, but sporty all the same. He ordered the design team to lengthen their sports car and add two rear seats. This was the masterstroke which instantly transformed an uncompromising sports car into a sporting yet adaptable family car. It was the moment that made the Mustang and the rest soon followed. If it couldn't be a 100 per cent sports car, the new model had to be lightweight and cheap: it was decided to aim at 2,500lb (1134kg) and $2,500. It had to be simple and easy to drive, with a decent-sized trunk, 'a car you could

drive to the country club on Friday night, to the drag strip on Saturday and to church on Sunday'.

Even the finance guys had to admit that this was more like it. OK, perhaps 100,000, they said. Iacocca was contemptuous of this estimate, countering that it would sell 200,000 at least, and they thought he was probably mad. Bill Bourke, Ford's number three, certainly did when he was shown the prototype, but the events of 1964 would show that even Iacocca's sales estimate was

Ford Mustang badge with the horse motif.

way too low. Bourke later admitted he had been wrong about Iacocca and his new wonder car. 'The guy's a genius! He gets a gut feeling from a piece of clay.'

But it wasn't only Bourke who had to be convinced, but also a whole phalanx of senior executives, not to mention Henry Ford himself. Iacocca and Co. had the advantage of price on their side; because great use would be made of existing components, the Mustang would cost £75 million to put into production. This was a relatively modest sum, as an all-new Mustang, with its own engines, transmissions and other parts, would usually have cost Ford closer to £300 million. But Iacocca still had a tough selling job to do: many top Ford men were terrified of producing another Edsel (the famous Ford flop that had been launched a few years earlier), and were understandably wary when it came to producing a new model as radical as this. In any case, the company was planning to retool its line-up for 1965, and this in itself would cost a lot of dollars.

From the start, Henry Ford had been rather lukewarm about the Mustang. At a meeting, in the middle of one of Iacocca's sales pitches, Ford had abruptly stood up and walked out. For a moment Lee thought that the game was up; but it turned out that the boss was simply feeling unwell (he had mononucleosis) and he returned in a more positive mood. Iacocca's patient work of planting positive spin in other parts of the company and even in the rumour-hungry motoring press, seemed to be taking effect at last. In the end, Ford came down to the studio to look the prototype over. He climbed

in the back: 'It's a little tight in the back seat. Add another inch for legroom.' Later he came down for another look, a moment pictured in *The Reckoning* by David Halberstam.

Ford: 'I'm tired of hearing about this goddam car. Can you sell the goddam thing?'

Iacocca assured him on that point.

Ford: 'Well, you damn well better.'

Grudging and petulant this may have seemed, but it was as close to a 'yes' as they were ever going to get. The Mustang was finally a reality.

Choosing a Name

By the summer of 1962, the project was in urgent need of another decision. It was still to be agreed what the car would actually look like. Although the Mustang would borrow most of its running gear from the Falcon and other Ford sedans, there was unanimous agreement that it would have to have its own distinctive body, rather than that of a fastback Falcon. Of course, this was what Plymouth had been doing, turning the Valiant into the classy fastback Barracuda, which would make its debut just a couple of weeks before the Mustang. The Barracuda was nice enough, but it was nothing special – the Mustang had to be.

Time was at a premium, with only 21 months to the projected launch. Earlier that year, the styling department had built seven different clay models, but none of them seemed quite right. So it was decided to make a concentrated effort by holding a competition. Styling chief Gene Bordinat called in his top men and gave them two

weeks to prepare full-sized clay mock-ups for a management viewing, the best of which would go into production. When the top brass gathered in the courtyard outside the styling department one day in August, the winner was clear. It was a design by Dave Ash, though his boss and Ford studio head Joe Oros often got the credit in press reports. It had the classic long hood, short trunk that would become a Mustang trademark – even the mock-up looked as if it were in motion. Ash and Oros named it the 'Cougar'. On the one hand, the Cougar had a Falconesque side to its basic shape, but on the other hand was more sporting; Iacocca and his team voted for the sporty side of Cougar, and top management approved.

Another show car was built, strongly hinting at the production shape, but with a sharper front end and more radically-raked windshield. It was shown to the public at the 1963 U.S. Grand Prix at Watkins Glen, officially to test reaction, after which the project would be canned if no one liked it. By this stage, however, abandonment of the whole concept was unlikely, as everyone was committed to making Iacocca's concept of 'small-sporty' work.

Meanwhile, Don Frey, Jack Prendergast and a group of engineers were busily transforming the car from a non-running mock-up into a production-ready driveable car. It is said that most of the engineers hadn't even glimpsed the new shape until then; now they had barely 18 months to make a working product of it, ready to sell. In this process, it is the details that take time: for example, the Mustang's low hood didn't leave enough room for a conventional air cleaner, so Frey had to design a new one that nestled down around the carburettor. Similarly, the Falcon radiator was too tall to squeeze under the hood, so it had to be redesigned with a recessed filler cap. Another difficulty was that the shapely Mustang body used extensive roll-under to expose more of the wheels, and this required new production techniques.

Fortunately, the body was the only major new part of the Mustang. Engines, transmissions, suspension and brakes were all taken from existing Ford cars, which radically cut development time.

While all this was going on, Ford's new small-sporty was still without a name. Early on, reflecting the source of much of its hardware, it had been termed 'Special Falcon'. Henry Ford wanted to call it 'T-Bird II', but the idea was soon dropped, proof that the boss didn't always get his own way. Joe Oros and Dave Ash, of course, had come up with the evocative 'Cougar' and that became the unofficial project title. Monte Carlo, Monaco and Torino were other possibilities, until it was discovered that the first two had already been used by other companies. As for Torino, this was a front-runner, until the word came that Henry had vetoed it. Why? Well, he was in the middle of a messy divorce, and in the meantime was stepping out with an attractive Italian divorcée, which would have given rise to unfavourable comment.

Consequently, a wordsmith from Ford's advertising agency was sent to the Detroit Public Library to research animal names, and

came back with Cheetah, Bronco, Puma, Colt, Cougar (again) … and Mustang. The styling guys had been very keen on Cougar, their own idea, and even sent Iacocca a diecast cougar in a little walnut box, with the message, 'Please don't name it anything but Cougar'. But Mustang won hands down; the name had been used before but, according to the ad agency, it had 'the excitement of wide-open spaces and was as American as all hell'. Mustang it was.

In the meantime, while running prototypes were being road-tested, there were fully-finished prototypes available for viewing. This time, despite Iacocca's

professed dislike of asking customers what they wanted, 52 Detroit couples were invited in to see the Mustang. They liked it: white collar types were impressed with the styling, while others associated the car with status and prestige. But would they buy it? No, they said, they wouldn't. It seemed too small, too cramped and too expensive. Then they were told Mustang's actual price and immediately changed their minds. For $2,500, Detroiters were suddenly able to come up with a whole new set of reasons why they needed a car such as this. It was a good omen, but would the dream come true?

1964 Mustang hardtop.

1964:
THE LAUNCH

BELOW and OPPOSITE
1964 Mustang convertible.

Car and Driver called it 'easily the best thing to come out of Dearborn since the 1932 V8 Model B roadster'. *Road & Track*'s Gene Booth described the Mustang as 'a car for the enthusiast who may be a family man, but likes his transportation to be more sporting'. After all the years of talking and planning, the Mustang had finally arrived.

Not all the early press reports were quite as complimentary, but one thing was sure: when the Mustang was unveiled on 17 April 1964, the public loved it. The Ford showrooms were swamped with would-be customers and 22,000 cars were ordered on the first day. Demand was so overwhelming that Ford had to turn a second factory over to Mustang production, merely to keep up with demand, and eventually a third. In fact, it was impossible to cope with demand in those early days, and at one point

there was even a three-month waiting list.

Maybe it was the abundance of choice that dazzled those first Mustang buyers. There were just two basic models – a convertible and hardtop – but each was available with a huge range of options. These were not restricted to different-coloured carpets or fancy trim, but offered a real choice of engines and transmissions. There were four of the former, seven of the latter, not to mention three clutches, two driveshafts, four brake systems, four wheel types (three tyre sizes to suit), plus three different steering systems. There were, of course, long lists of minor elements such as whitewall tyres and the 'Rally Pac', a tachometer and clock mounted on the steering column.

It should be remembered that the Thunderbird had been described by Ford as a 'personal car' that could be tailored to the requirements of each buyer. So also was the Mustang, only this time the choice was so staggering that in spite of the 400,000 Mustangs sold in the first year, it was still possible, unlikely though it was, to have one that was completely unique. And this is what appealed to the buying public.

After years of a choice of two or four doors, or maybe a station wagon, Americans now had the chance to buy something genuinely different. And it had come along at

BELOW and OPPOSITE
Rear view and engine detail of a 1964
Mustang convertible.

precisely the right time, when interest in performance, or to be more accurate, in a sporty image, was on the increase. There were three items of equipment that every Mustang had as standard: a sporty three-spoke steering wheel, bucket seats and stickshift (whether one opted for manual or automatic transmission). To American car buyers of the late 1950s, these were hot items previously associated with exotic European sports cars, but soon destined to be part of the American muscle-car ethos.

The Mustang certainly needed these goodies, as most of the rest of the interior had been plucked straight out of a Falcon, complete with the dull strip speedometer, plus fuel and temperature gauges. The curvaceous bodywork may have led one to expect a sporting array of switches and dials,

but these were sadly absent, which was one of the reasons why the basic Mustang was so cheap. So although the bucket seats, three-spoke wheel and stickshift added a little to the price of each Mustang, they added immeasurably to its showroom appeal. And making an impression was what the Mustang was all about.

Under the Skin
So what were these people actually buying? Under the sporty skin was a straightforward, simple platform-steel frame with galvanized structural members and torque boxes. A strong propshaft tunnel, running from toeboard to rear-axle kick-up, did a lot to strengthen the platform, as did cross-ribs and reinforcements. In fact, the Mustang platform was so rigid that it could be driven without a body. However, the convertible's platform was reinforced with heavier-gauge steel to compensate for the lack of a roof. It has been said that the Mustang platform was shared with that of the Falcon; this would certainly have made sense, as the cars shared so many other components, and the dimensions were very similar, though the Mustang's wheelbase was 1.5in (3.8cm) shorter.

The body itself was welded to the platform, creating a unitary lightweight structure; throughout the design process, it had been necessary for the Ford engineers to fix their eyes on the prize of a basic weight of 2,500lb (1134kg). The front fenders were bolted on.

Body complete, it was time to turn to the front suspension, which was a straight transplant from the Falcon. This consisted of

coil springs enclosing telescopic dampers, an upper wishbone and lower control arm, plus an anti-roll bar. Coming straight from Ford's econo-car, this was a pretty soft set-up, so one of the Mustang's many options was a 'handling package', with heavy-duty springs, special shock absorbers, bigger, wider wheels (5.5 x 14in/14 x 35.6cm instead of 13in/33cm, though the tyres were still 6.50 section) and a quicker steering box.

The latter had a ratio of 16:1 instead of the standard 20:1, or 3^1/2 turns lock to lock instead of 4^1/2, but was still too slow to give sports-car responses. It was the usual story of endless compromises. A car like the Mustang would be bought by thousands of drivers who would not want, and might even be alarmed by, ultra-quick steering, so the standard steering resembled that of a sluggardly sedan. It was difficult to understand why the optional set-up wasn't made quicker, though on its first drive, *Car and Driver* judged road feel to be quite good, even with power steering.

Rear suspension also came from the Falcon, but here there were some changes, and even the promise of an all-new optional set-up designed specifically for the Mustang. Leaf springs were mounted on a live axle, as on the saloon, but the forward spring mounts were different and the bump stops were beefed up, as were the springs themselves, once the optional 289 V8 produced axle tramp and spring wind-up during development. Ford's top engineers insisted that nothing else was needed – neither torque rods nor anything else. The trouble was, these stiffer springs failed to combine happily

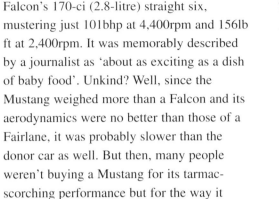

Falcon's 170-ci (2.8-litre) straight six, mustering just 101bhp at 4,400rpm and 156lb ft at 2,400rpm. It was memorably described by a journalist as 'about as exciting as a dish of baby food'. Unkind? Well, since the Mustang weighed more than a Falcon and its aerodynamics were no better than those of a Fairlane, it was probably slower than the donor car as well. But then, many people weren't buying a Mustang for its tarmac-scorching performance but for the way it looked on their driveway. And it looked just as good with a little six-cylinder hidden under the bonnet as it did with a V8.

THIS PAGE and OPPOSITE
1964 Mustang 260 coupé.

with the soft front end, barely moving over gentle bumps while the front bobbed up and down. Sharply-angled shock absorbers helped to reduce axle sway in relation to the body.

Moreover, should anyone be disappointed with this fairly basic rear end, Ford could point to the projected all-new independent rear suspension. It would be a similar system to the one used on the Mustang I show car, with four transverse semi-trailing links with narrow-diameter inclined coil springs. An advanced design, promising good wheel travel with negative camber at all times, it sounded good, but did it ever appear on a standard road-going Mustang? Well, in 1973, when the Mark 1 Mustang finally turned up its toes, it was still wearing a live axle with leaf springs at the rear.

Given its Falcon suspension, how did the

Mustang handle? *Car and Driver* was pleasantly surprised, finding that the lower centre of gravity reduced body roll, though roll it did, which they likened to the cornering behaviour of the original two-seater Thunderbird; history really was repeating itself. In fact, overall, they pronounced it well balanced and neutral at normal speeds, and fairly stable when driven hard, ultimately oversteering. Later magazine road tests would have plenty to say concerning the differences between the standard set-up and the 'handling package'.

Engines: Six or V8?
The Falcon story continued with power units. Yes, it was possible to buy a Mustang for the amazingly low price of $2,368, but that meant a three-speed manual gearbox and the

four-speed or even a new three-speed Cruise-O-Matic.

Most Mustang buyers chose to pay extra for a V8, based on the smaller Ford Fairlane unit, a lightweight cast-iron engine that had made its debut in 1958 with 221ci (3.6 litres). The 221 wasn't offered; instead the cheapest V8 Mustang came with 260ci (4.3 litres), yet another Falcon/Fairlane original. This brought 164hp at 4,400rpm and 258lb ft at 2,200rpm, so it was considerably more poky than the six. Finally, serious performance began with a 289-ci (4.7-litre) version of the same engine which, thanks to a four-barrel carburettor and higher 9.0:1 compression, offered 210hp.

For real performance freaks, there could be only one choice which, though listed as an option right from the start, wasn't actually available until two months later. This was the HiPo (for high performance) 289-ci V8, a considerably reworked version of the standard 289. There were high-compression 10.5:1 pistons, low-restriction air cleaner and 'opera-throat' four-barrel carburettor, with individual headers for the exhaust, high-tensile-strength connecting rods, chrome-plated valve stems and a high-lift camshaft with mechanical lifters. The crankcase was strengthened with cross-bolts and a new vibration damper was fitted to the crank to cope with the HiPo's higher crank speeds.

ABOVE and RIGHT
1964 Mustang 260 coupé engine and wheel detail.

OPPOSITE
1964 289 convertible automatic.

However, not many people skimped by opting for a six-cylinder Mustang, with the result that today they are rare indeed. One would have expected this to have made them more valuable than the more common V8s, but no; it seems that collectors of Mustangs, like the 1964 customers, prefer a Mustang that woofles. If Ford's three-speed transmission didn't appeal (which with its non-synchromesh first gear was quite likely), one could pay extra for the all-synchromesh

The result of all this was a claimed 271hp at 6,000rpm and 312lb ft at 3,400rpm, enough, said Ford, for the top-powered Mustang to keep up with the already legendary Pontiac GTO. It didn't quite reach the magic one horsepower per cubic inch (the actual figure was 0.95), but Ford's Fairlane V8 had been around long enough for some tuning folklore to have accumulated. Over 300hp was possible without affecting reliability.

The HiPo could only be had with the four-speed manual transmission, because Ford was under no illusion that there would be many Mustang buyers seeking the ultimate performance car. So the C4 Cruise-O-Matic automatic transmission was a popular option; it was actually a new unit, having been introduced on the Fairlane and Mercury Comet earlier in the year. Left to itself, the auto box changed up at 40 and 70mph (64 and 113km/h), but could still be held in low until 50mph (80km/h), which cut the acceleration times a little.

Rearwards of the gearbox, six-cylinder Mustangs had a shortened Falcon propshaft and final drive, while the V8s used adapted Fairlane parts. Donor brakes worked out in exactly the same way, with low-powered Mustangs using the Falcon's 9-in (23-cm) drums, while the V8s benefited from bigger 10-inch (25-cm) ones, with discs an option. At launch, Ford promised that a limited slip differential would eventually be available with any of the power unit/transmission combinations. There were, of course, various final-drive ratio options, and larger 15-in (38-cm) wheels (in place of the standard 13-in/33-cm) with 5.5-in (14-cm) rims available with the handling package.

Making an Impact

Today, the Mustang's long hood/short trunk shape is seen as something of a design classic, combining sports-car looks with near-sedan practicality at a low price. In 1964, it won a Tiffany Gold Medal for excellence in American design. So it comes as something of a shock to find that not everyone liked it. *Car and Driver*, in particular, was unimpressed. 'We can well understand Ford management's wish to give the Mustang a distinctive or possibly unique appearance,' went the initial reaction in print, 'but the result strikes us as inexplicably amateurish.'

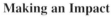

Sacrilege! Could it be referring to the Mustang? Sadly, yes. The anonymous writer went on to criticize the 'clumsy' front grille and the fit of the hood, which reminded him (in those days, all motoring writers were male) of 'one of our mother's more experienced saucepans'. The grille's side panels were a 'scatter-brained afterthought', and it was clear that he didn't approve of the non-functional air scoops, which would become a Mustang trademark. He liked the rear bumper and tail-light treatment, but came to the caustic conclusion that 'better preparation for future improvement could hardly be devised'.

However, *Car and Driver*'s opinion of the Mustang's styling seemed to matter not one jot to the American public; it loved the car. Moreover, the magazine was in no doubt that the Mustang had the makings of a huge success; it predicted that sales might

even exceed Ford's projected 250,000 in the first year. They did, and how!

There were probably some sighs of relief at Dearborn, especially as the Mustang's launch and publicity had been carefully planned and had cost a great deal of money; the campaign was actually Detroit's most expensive ever for a new car. Because the Mustang was a new idea, its launch had to be innovative as well. So a full month ahead of the official unveiling, a member of the Ford family drove a black pre-production Mustang to a lunch in downtown Detroit. Result? Blurred 'spy' photos in the *Detroit Free Press* and even *Newsweek*. These supposedly 'secret' pictures served to heighten anticipation of the official launch on 17 April, which of course had been the whole idea.

The night before that launch, Mustang commercials were shown on all three commercial TV channels, reaching 29 million viewers. The following day, the car was finally unveiled at the New York World's Fair. Simultaneously, every Ford dealer in the country pulled the covers from a Mustang in their showrooms, so everyone who wanted to could get right up close. College graduates were key target customers, so the editors of college newspapers were each lent a Mustang for a few weeks. (Imagine being a 21-year-old editor, and driver of the only Mustang on campus!)

The media coverage was unprecedented, with Mustang making the cover of both *Time* and *Newsweek*. Full-page advertisements were run in 2,600 newspapers, with a simple profile of the car, that low sticker price, and the line 'The Unexpected'. TV ads favoured a Walter Mitty theme, in which antique dealers and harpsichord players were transformed into dashing sports-car drivers once they got behind the wheel of their new Mustang. The message was simple: whoever you are, whatever you do, this is a car that will make you feel special.

The public responded in kind, and Ford showrooms were inundated. A dealer in Chicago had to lock his doors when the crowd outside became frighteningly large. In Texas, another found he had 15 people desperate to buy the same car. Being a professional, he sold it to the highest bidder, a man who proceeded to spend the night in his new car while his cheque cleared, so anxious was he that no one should sneak in during the night and cap his offer. On that first day, 22,000 Mustangs were sold, and over the first weekend, four million people passed through Ford showrooms to take a peek.

Within weeks, two things became clear: the original target of 250,000 sales in the first year was a gross underestimate, and Ford's single factory would not be able to keep up with demand. So a second Ford plant, in San Jose, California, was turned over to Mustang production, and then a third, at Metuchen, New Jersey. Lee Iacocca later recalled that this had been a costly business, and may well have been a gamble, the new car having only been in production for a few months. But fresh in the minds of Ford top management was the Falcon. They had underestimated the demand for Robert McNamara's economy car and had lost sales as a result. They were determined the same thing would not happen with the Mustang.

To test the strength of the demand, marketing man Frank Zimmerman arranged an experiment with Ford dealers in Dayton, Ohio. Each was given ten Mustangs as stock, and a quick turnaround on fresh orders, a situation any other Mustang-starved dealer in the country would have died for. The result was astonishing: the Mustang alone grabbed around 10 per cent of the entire local car market, indicating how strong demand really was.

Despite the impressive sales figures, there was both good and bad news for Ford. The bad news came in October 1964, only six months after the launch, when *Car and Driver* came to the conclusion that the Mustang had failed to damage sales of its natural rivals: the Corvair Monza, GTO or Valiant. On the other hand, it had already overtaken the Falcon, and there was evidence in the sales returns that Mustang buyers would alternatively have bought a Falcon Sprint or perhaps a Fairlane. Some of those early Mustang owners were conquest sales from other makes, but many were not.

The good news was that although Ford was not making a fortune on the basic Mustang price of $2,368, and if buyers had restricted themselves to that amount the whole project could have turned into a financial flop, in fact they didn't. Almost everyone paid extra for a string of options, all of which made Ford a great deal of money. Nearly three-quarters of first-year Mustangs, for example, were ordered with a

OPPOSITE
1964 289 automatic convertible.

V8 instead of the standard six, and the HiPo 289 added $442 to the sticker price. Nearly half opted for automatic transmission (close to $200) and 20 per cent for the four-speed manual. Since the basic car didn't even come with a heater or radio, most people paid extra for these too. Ford's strategy of offering a cheap basic car with plenty of money-making options had worked a treat. The Mustang had arrived.

MUSTANG LINE-UP/PRODUCTION (1964¹/₂ MODEL YEAR)

Hardtop coupé	91,532
Convertible	28,468
TOTAL	120,000

ENGINE LINE-UP
170 Six

Type	Water-cooled cast-iron straight six, ohv
Bore x stroke	3.50 x 2.94in (90 x 75mm)
Capacity	170ci (2.8 litres)
Compression ratio	8.7:1
Fuelling	Single-barrel carburettor
Power	101bhp @ 4,400rpm

260 V8

Type	Water-cooled cast-iron V8, ohv
Bore x stroke	3.80 x 2.87in (96.5 x 73mm)
Capacity	260ci (4.3 litres)
Compression ratio	8.8:1
Fuelling	Twin-barrel carburettor
Power	164bhp @ 4,400rpm

289 V8

Type	Water-cooled cast-iron V8, ohv
Bore x stroke	4.00 x 2.87in (102 x 73mm)
Capacity	289ci (4.7 litres)
Compression ratio	9.0:1
Fuelling	Four-barrel carburettor
Power	210bhp @ 4,400rpm

289 HiPo V8

Type	Water-cooled cast-iron V8
Bore x stroke	4.00 x 2.87in
Capacity	289ci (4.7 litres)
Compression ratio	10.5:1
Fuelling	Four-barrel carburettor
Power	271bhp @ 6,000rpm

OPPOSITE and BELOW
Bucket seats, sports steering wheel, T-shifter amounted to showroom magic in a 1964 convertible.

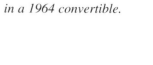

1965:
FASTBACKS & SHELBYS

Given the Mustang's huge success, one could have forgiven Ford for planning no changes for 1965 and concentrating on keeping up with demand, especially as the 1965 model-year changes came in August 1964, only four months after the original launch. But this was not the case. The 1965 Mustangs came with a whole host of new features, though some should have been available from the start, had not production delays prevented them from making an appearance.

The reason for this short gap before the new model year was simple. Lee Iacocca had been determined to launch the Mustang at the New York World's Fair in April. Not only was it great publicity, but being months away from the traditional August launch (when most manufacturers introduced their new cars) it also enabled Ford to hog the new-car limelight, whereas in August, the Mustang would be competing for attention with a plethora of other new launches. This way, it was the only brand-new car the public had seen for months. Consequently, these very early Mustangs, built and sold between April and August 1964 were neither 1964 nor '65 models, and in retrospect became known as '1964½' cars, which seemed to satisfy everyone.

The dust from that original launch had barely settled and the queues outside Ford dealers grown only a little shorter when the 1965 cars were announced. Behind the scenes, Ford knew it had to make the most of the next 18 months. It had stolen a march on General Motors and Chrysler, neither of which had a true Mustang rival. Of course, the pony car's arrival meant that Ford's competitors were already hard at work on ponies of their own, but in the meantime, Ford had the floor to itself.

The first and most obvious innovation was the new fastback body shape. It was planned that it would make its debut as part of the original range, but tooling problems held it up. Although identical to the hardtop and convertible below the window line, it was in fact quite different, with its raked rear roofline, larger rear window glass and shorter trunk. The big fresh-air vents, which had the appearance of cosmetic add-ons, were actually functional, and could be opened or closed from the inside, allowing through-flow ventilation.

Inside, the big news was the addition of

a fold-down rear seat (Ford billed the car as a 2+2 rather than a full four-seater). With a fold-down opening into the trunk, Mustang owners were able to carry bulky items such as skis inside the car, which added a new dimension of practicality; however, tall rear passengers, cramped by the rear roofline, would more likely have agreed with the 2+2 tag! Despite costing over $200 more than the hardtop (and only a few dollars less than the ragtop) the fastback proved popular, and just over 77,000 were sold in the 1965 model year. To put this into perspective: Ford sold over 400,000 hardtops.

There were engine changes for 1965 as well. Although many Mustang buyers were buying looks rather than performance (one in four opted for the basic six-cylinder motor), it soon became obvious that a mere 101hp was something of an embarrassment. Remember the 'dull as babyfood' jibe? There was a real danger that the Mustang would be dismissed as all surface appearance and no serious performance.

On the other hand, it was unwise to lose the economy six-cylinder option, as making a V8 standard would bump the basic price up by $100 or so. So a compromise was made. The Falcon-derived six was ditched in favour of the beefier 200-ci (3.3-litre) unit from the company's bigger cars. This seven-main-bearing engine was still in a fairly low state of tune, but boosted power by nearly 20 per cent over the old 170 to 120bhp at 4,400rpm. It was still no tarmac-melter, but the plan worked, and almost 200,000 Mustang sixes were sold in 1965, now making up 35 per cent of the total, to the consternation of

OPPOSITE and LEFT
The 1965 Mustang coupé. Furry dice
are a strictly personal touch!

OPPOSITE and LEFT
1965 Mustang 289 2+2 fastback.

modern-day collectors. Early six-cylinder Mustangs are still worth about 20 per cent less than the basic V8s, while a 271-hp HiPo costs around 30 per cent more.

The V8s were hopped up, and the 164-bhp 260-ci (4.3-litre) option was dropped in favour of a detuned version of the 289 with a two-barrel carb. This was beginning to seem like very good value as a performance

option, adding only $108 to the price of the basic car but boosting power right up to 200bhp. At the same time, the four-barrel V8 was boosted to 225bhp, thanks to a higher compression ratio. The 271-hp HiPo was unchanged, and of course this was the engine that attracted most attention in the motoring press. But in reality, only a tiny proportion of Mustang buyers actually opted for it (only

1.3 per cent in 1965). Cost had something to do with it, as the hottest V8 came with a mandatory handling package and wider 6.95- x 14-in (17.6- x 35.6-cm) tyres, so the total bill for this option was $442. Opt for the still-lively 225-hp V8, and there would be enough change to specify air conditioning as well, or maybe front disc brakes, the handling package and four-speed transmission.

The handling package, incidentally, brought stiffer springs, bigger shocks, a quicker steering ratio and thicker front anti-roll bar. Indeed, an enthusiastic driver trying the standard softly-sprung Mustang would have expected nothing else.

This is partly why early HiPos command such a premium today – they are very rare. The other thing that restricted early HiPo sales was the driving experience. They were undoubtedly fast and exciting, but the Mustang's basic leaf-sprung rear end wasn't really up to that much power, and axle tramp was a serious problem under hard acceleration. As if to underline the point, only 2 per cent of buyers paid extra for a limited slip differential, and less than 4 per cent for the dual exhaust. Comfort, convenience and appearance items, such as air conditioning, whitewall tyres and windshield washers were far more popular.

The new GT package did find favour, however, and combined the handling package with front disc brakes, dual exhaust, five-dial instrument pack, front fog lights and various GT badges and stripes; one could have the GT pack without the stripes, if one wished to

ABOVE and OPPOSITE
Early Shelby GT fastback.

1965: the first Shelby Mustang GT350.

avoid too much attention. The instrument pack did a lot for a Mustang, which in standard form kept the Falcon's strip speedometer, though it still didn't offer a rev counter. This remained part of the Rally Pac, a combined rev counter and clock which was mounted on top of the steering column.

So that was the sporty-optioned Mustang, but from April 1965 one could opt for a luxury feel as well. Available on any hardtop, convertible or fastback, this was affectionately known as the 'pony interior', due to the galloping horses embossed onto the back of each seat. The five-dial instruments made another appearance, this

time with wood/vinyl trim, while the three-spoke steering wheel had a simulated walnut trim. There were integral armrests and door courtesy lights, plus pistol-grip door handles.

Meanwhile, Mustangs were already being raced. The majority of Mustang owners may have preferred pistol-grip door handles to serious performance, but they still appreciated the reflected glory of race wins. One of the first (it predated even Carroll Shelby's racer) was from the Comstock Racing Team of Canada. Canadian sedan-class racing had liberal rules, so the Comstock car was powered by a 384-hp Cobra-specification version of the 289 V8. It could pull 6,800rpm in top gear (equating to 142mph/228km/h) and rocket through the standing quarter at 12.3seconds/109mph/175km/h. In fact, around the Mosport race track, it was only two seconds a lap slower than a genuine AC Cobra.

It was helped along the way by a serious weight-reduction programme, when the complete interior was stripped out and weight was removed from both hood and trunk-lid. Kelsey-Hayes front disc brakes were fitted, and there were many suspension modifications to tame the Mustang's underpinnings, whose waywardness under horsepower pressure was already legendary. There were stiffer springs, of course (up from 270lb/in at the front, to 440lb/in), plus Armstrong adjustable shocks. To prevent spring wind-up and axle tramp at the rear, Gabriel shocks were fitted vertically, with stiffer springs and an extra half-leaf running from the forward pivot and wrapping once around the rear axle. One test driver reported

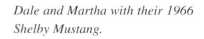

Dale and Martha with their 1966 Shelby Mustang.

RIGHT and OPPOSITE
1965 Mustang 289-ci GT fastbacks.

OPPOSITE
1965 Mustang GT fastback.

LEFT
1965 Mustang 289 coupé.

that it completely eliminated the Mustang's hop and tramp. Consequently, when built to race specification, the Mustang really could handle.

Meanwhile, in California, a retired Texan racing driver was about to turn the Mustang into a serious performance machine. His name was Carroll Shelby and he was an ex-chicken farmer, driver and race-car tuner,

who had won at Le Mans, and was perfectly placed for the job. He had already become Ford's public face of racing, ever since the company agreed to sell him its 260-ci (4.3-litre) V8. Shelby fitted these to the lightweight English-made AC to make the Cobra. Wild, featherweight and fast, the Cobra swiftly became a legend in its own lifetime, beating all comers on the race track

and proving to be the hairiest road car it was possible to buy.

By the time the Mustang appeared, Shelby was therefore on good terms with Ford, and had his own limited-production facility in California. Who better to build a race-ready Mustang to take up where the Cobra had left off? 'I was called into Lee Iacocca's office,' he later recalled. 'He asked

OPPOSITE
1965 Mustang hardtop with vinyl roof.

BELOW
1965 Mustang hardtop with rostyle wheels.

me what we had to do to race the Mustang. "Build a hundred of them," I told him … and that's how the GT350 happened.' The HiPo 289 may have been hot, but it was still no race-winner. What Ford needed was an image-building Mustang that could win races and fulfil the ancient adage which Iacocca firmly believed: win on Sunday, sell on Monday.

The GT350, the first Shelby Mustang, was no cosmetic race car. The modifications were extensive, one reason why the complete package cost over $4,400. A full-specification HiPo could cost $3,500 (a Pontiac GTO was $3,800), so one had to be totally committed to pay nearly $1,000 extra for the Shelby version. Incidentally, the GT350 tag came not from a radically upsized engine but from the fact that Carroll Shelby had asked how many feet there were between the main assembly line and the engine department. It therefore had nothing to do with the car – but it sounded right.

So Ford shipped 110 Wimbledon White Fastbacks over to California, and work began. There had to be at least 100 in that first batch to qualify the car for production-class racing by the Sports Car Club of America. Legend has it that they weren't ready when the SCCA inspectors came to call, but Shelby simply moved them all over to the 'finished' parking lot; they were all converted soon enough anyway.

The conversion, as already mentioned, was comprehensive. The hood was removed and replaced with a lighter fibreglass version, the rear seat was stripped out (also to save weight), and the stock exhaust was ditched in favour of a side muffler. This being a Mustang, there was plenty of suspension work, which went far beyond the quick-fix of stiffer springs and shocks: there was a thicker front anti-roll bar, longer idler and Pitman arms, lowered upper-control arms, override traction bars and Koni adjustable shocks. Big 11-in (28-cm) disc brakes were bolted to the front, while the rear drums gained larger sintered metal linings. To prevent the body from pulling out of shape, a 'Monte Carlo' bar was used – simply a strong piece of steel braced between the two front shock towers.

Given all these changes, the engine modifications were relatively minor, though Shelby did claim 306bhp from the hopped-up 289. It had an aluminium high-rise intake manifold, 751-cfm Holley carburettor, cast-aluminium sump and valve covers, 'Tri-Y' exhaust headers and low-restriction mufflers. The standard four-speed gearbox was swapped for an aluminium-cased Borg-Warner T-10 four-speeder, and there were 5.5-in (14-cm) wide steel wheels straight off Ford's big station wagon. If they seemed too plain, it was possible to pay extra for American Racing wheels.

In white, with the optional blue racing stripes and the GT350 stripes along the sills, the Shelby Mustang was certainly the image of a road-going racer, which included performance. Once it had been approved by the SCCA, the GT350 went on to dominate production racing, where Jaguar XKEs and Chevrolet Corvettes had had things their own way for a long time. If the truth be known, a GT350 couldn't actually be raced competitively, straight off Shelby's production line. There were S (street) and R (race) versions, and over 500 of the former were built, with up to 36 of the latter.

There is no doubt that even in S form the GT350 resembled a genuine race car that happened to find itself on the road. It rattled and roared, bucked and bronco'd. Water and exhaust fumes found their way in through holes cut for the new torque arms. It was fast and noisy and rude, the brakes and steering needed a hefty shove, and the whole thing could blast to 60mph (97km/h) in just 6.5 seconds. Crude it may have been, but in the right hands a GT350 was highly effective.

MODEL LINE-UP	PRODUCTION
Hardtop	409,260
Fastback	77,079
Convertible	73,112
GT350	562
TOTAL	560,013

ENGINE LINE-UP
200 six

Type	Water-cooled cast-iron straight-six, ohv
Bore x stroke	3.68 x 3.13in (93.5 x 79.5mm)
Capacity	200ci (3.3 litres)
Compression ratio	9.2:1
Fuelling	Single-barrel carburettor
Power	120bhp @ 4,400rpm

289 2bbl V8

Type	Water-cooled cast-iron V8, ohv

OPPOSITE
1965 Mustang 289-ci fastback 2+2.

PAGES 62 and 63
The Mustang fastback 2+2 arrived in the car's second year

PAGES 64 and 65
A 1965 2+2 Mustang fastback early model.

Bore x stroke   4.00 x 2.87in (102 x
                  73mm)
Capacity   289ci (4.7 litres)
Compression
  ratio   9.3:1
Fuelling   Two-barrel carburettor
Power   200bhp @ 4,400rpm

289 4bbl V8

Type   Water-cooled cast-iron V8,
                  ohv
Bore x stroke   4.00 x 2.87in
Capacity   289ci (4.7 litres)
Compression
  ratio   10.0:1
Fuelling   Four-barrel carburettor
Power   225bhp @ 4,400rpm

289 HiPo V8

Type   Water-cooled cast-iron V8
Bore x stroke   4.00 x 2.87in
Capacity   289ci (4.7 litres)
Compression
  ratio   10.5:1
Fuelling   Four-barrel carburettor
Power   271bhp @ 6,000rpm

GT350

Type   Water-cooled cast-iron V8
Bore x stroke   4.00 x 2.87in
Capacity   289ci (4.7 litres)
Compression
  ratio   10.5:1
Fuelling   Four-barrel carburettor
Power   306bhp

OPPOSITE
1965 Mustang limited-edition fastback 2+2.

LEFT
1965 Mustang hardtop with non-standard wheels.

LEFT
1965 Mustang four-speed fastback.

RIGHT and OPPOSITE
1965 Mustang 289 four-speed fastback.

1966:
MUSTANG'S FIRST MILLION

In 1966 Ford made the extraordinary claim that it had built the three fastest-selling cars of all time. And it was true. The Model A, the Falcon and the Mustang had all set records in their own time, though it has to be said that the Mustang only beat Falcon's first-year record by a thousand or two. Not surprisingly, Ford wasn't slow to hype up the Mustang's continuing success in advertisements. 'What do you do after you build a million Mustangs?' went one. 'Build the second million!' There was even a 'Millionth Mustang Sale' promotion in 1966, when anyone buying a Mustang received a personalized nameplate – quite appropriate for what was still billed as the 'personal car'.

Unlike the 1965 models, 1966 Mustangs saw few changes, yet 1966 remained the car's most successful year ever, with over 600,000 rolling off the lines. This was all the more impressive when one considers two

other factors: in late 1966 the Chevrolet Camaro and Pontiac Firebird appeared as the first serious challengers to the Mustang's leadership of the pony-car sector, though strictly speaking these were 1967 model-year cars. (As it happened, the Mustang remained the best-selling pony car right into the 1970s). The year 1966 saw the end of the early 1960s car-sales boom, as the economic effects of the Vietnam War made themselves felt, with interest rates rising and purchasing power on the decline. Car sales fell drastically in the second half of the year.

Ford reacted swiftly. Instead of the glamorous V8s, it pushed the more sensible six-cylinder Mustangs as the right sort of car for more austere times. At least one advertisement was aimed at women ('Six and the single girl'), while another highlighted the six's superior fuel economy. 'Now don't

*OPPOSITE, LEFT and BELOW
1966 Mustang 289 coupé.*

forget to wave when you pass your gas station!' There was a special-edition Mustang Sprint too, with the six-cylinder power unit, stripes, wheel covers, chrome air cleaner and a centre console.

The plan worked. Six-cylinder Mustangs made up 42 per cent of the total for 1966 and Mustang sales as a whole were higher than ever before. The few changes included Silent-Flo ventilation for the fastback, and several now mandatory safety features. All Fords were now fitted as standard with front and rear seat belts, a padded instrument panel, hazard flashers, electric windshield wipers and washers. Most exciting for Mustang fanciers was the fact that the five-dial instrument pack was made standard as

the car began to distance itself from its budget Falcon roots. However, one still had to pay extra for the steering-column-mounted tachometer.

While Ford may not have been making great changes to the Mustang for 1966, other people were. Barney Clark, Bob Cumberford and Jim Licata built themselves a Mustang station wagon, based on a 1964 hardtop with a 289-ci V8. One might say built, but in

reality young Cumberford converted a Mustang and all three paid for it to be shipped over to Intermeccanica of Turin for the work to be done.

There was plenty of work involved, as Cumberford's sleek adaptation required that the complete roof and rear deck be removed and new roof, tailgate, rear windows, cargo floor and folding rear seat be built up. They had intended to redesign the fuel tank as

well, and move the spare tyre somewhere else, thus enabling a lower load floor and more luggage space, but the money ran out. As it was, 27cu ft (0.77m³) was available with the rear seat in place, 50cu ft (1.4m³) with it folded down.

Well designed and beautifully converted, the Cumberford Mustang wagon looked terrific, and created huge interest on the road. *Car and Driver* tried it and was flagged

OPPOSITE
Engine detail of a 1966 Mustang 289 coupé.

BELOW
1966 Mustang hardtop coupé.

1966 Mustang 289 fastback with metallic glitter paint job.

down by people interested to know where it had come from. It also found that it drove very much like a standard Mustang, with the modest extra bulk of the extended rear roof hardly noticeable. It was very promising, but never went into even limited production, while officially, Ford showed no interest in the project at all. But it did give General

Motors executives a heart-stopping moment when one of them spotted it on Detroit's Southfield Expressway. Why? Because General Motors was working on an identical conversion of its Firebird/Camaro, and here was an apparently production-ready Mustang wagon. Ford had beaten them to it again! (The Camaro wagon, incidentally, fell at the

first hurdle. It got to the non-running mock-up stage before being rejected as too expensive to build.)

Meanwhile, changes were afoot on the Shelby production line. The original GT350 had done much to raise the Mustang's profile as a muscle car. It was good in magazine road tests, but not many people actually

1966 Mustang 289 coupé.

wanted to buy one. It was too expensive (nearly $1,000 more than a top-flight Galaxie), too noisy and too crude, and (a sacrilege in Mustang terms) it only had two seats.

So Ford dispatched its production planners and cost experts westwards to the Shelby factory and they soon got results.

First to go was the Detroit Lock limited slip differential, which was highly effective on the track but clunky and noisy in traffic. Then the race-ready suspension was toned down, the geometry returned to standard, and those expensive Koni shocks ditched, while the traction override bars were replaced with cheaper units. The back seat returned and

Shelby's pricey English-made wood-rimmed steering wheel was dropped in favour of one from a stock Mustang GT, albeit with a GT350 logo. The result was over $100 slashed from the price of the GT350 and a softer car that was easier to live with. Now, it even came in a range of colours, with automatic transmission and a radio as an

option. There was no doubt about it: the GT350 had gone soft.

Hertz, however, welcomed the move. Originally, Ford had approached the hire-car giant, proposing that it put 100 GT350s on its fleet. The idea of allowing a fast, hairy road car to be driven by anyone who could show a driving licence and pay the $17 a day (in New York) hire fee must have seemed like madness. Inevitably, many of the GT350Hs (as the Hertz cars were known) ended up worn out in weekend drag races, official or otherwise. It must have worked though, as Hertz ended up buying a thousand of the cars, though it later asked Ford for auto transmission only and a brake booster, as not everyone got on with the super-heavy Shelby stoppers. The end result for both Hertz and Ford was good, however, giving the former plenty of extra publicity, and putting thousands of drivers behind the wheel of a hot Mustang. Some of them went on to buy one as a result, having in effect paid for their own demonstration drive!

MODEL LINE-UP   PRODUCTION

Hardtop	499,751
Fastback	35,698
Convertible	72,119
GT350 fastback	2,374
GT350 convertible	4
TOTAL	609,946

ENGINE LINE-UP
200 six

Type	Water-cooled cast-iron straight-six, ohv
Bore x stroke	3.68 x 3.13in (93.5 x 79.5mm)
Capacity	200ci (3.3 litres)
Compression ratio	9.2:1
Fuelling	Single-barrel carburettor
Power	120bhp @ 4,400rpm

289 2bbl V8

Type	Water-cooled cast-iron V8, ohv
Bore x stroke	4.00 x 2.87in (102 x 73mm)
Capacity	289ci (4.7 litres)
Compression ratio	9.3:1
Fuelling	Two-barrel carburettor
Power	200bhp @ 4,400rpm

289 4bbl V8

Type	Water-cooled cast-iron V8, ohv
Bore x stroke	4.00 x 2.87in
Capacity	289ci (4.7 litres)
Compression ratio	10.0:1
Fuelling	Four-barrel carburettor
Power	225bhp @ 4,400rpm

289 HiPo V8

Type	Water-cooled cast-iron V8
Bore x stroke	4.00 x 2.87in
Capacity	289ci (4.7 litres)
Compression ratio	10.5:1
Fuelling	Four-barrel carburettor
Power	271bhp @ 6,000rpm

GT350

Type	Water-cooled cast-iron V8
Bore x stroke	4.00 x 2.87in
Capacity	289ci (4.7 litres)
Compression ratio	10.5:1
Fuelling	Four-barrel carburettor
Power	306bhp

RIGHT and OPPOSITE
1966 Shelby Mustang GT350s.

OPPOSITE, LEFT, PAGES 90 and 91 *1966 Mustang GT350 Hertz rental model.*

OPPOSITE
1966 Mustang notchback.

LEFT
1966 Mustang hardtop coupé in Amber Glow.

LEFT
1966 Mustang coupé.

RIGHT, OPPOSITE, PAGES 96 and 97
1966 Mustang GT convertible.

1967:
'FAT PIG'

BELOW and OPPOSITE
1967 Mustang GT fastback with Weber
carburettor-fed 289 V8; the massive
hood bulge is there to make room for it!

Lee Iacocca didn't approve. 'No longer a sleek horse,' he wrote in his autobiography, 'it was more like a fat pig.' He was referring to the 1967 Mustang, which for that year gained weight, size and power. Looking at the 1966 and '67 Mustangs now, it's hard to see what all the fuss was about.

But there's no denying that the pony car had strayed far from its origins as a simple, sporty compact. It was going upmarket.

But there were good reasons for this, not least of which were the Chevrolet Camaro and Pontiac Firebird. General Motors was determined that its new pony car should offer

more power, space and comfort than a Mustang, which it did, partly due to big-block V8s that produced well over 300bhp, making the HiPo Mustang seem a little feeble by comparison. Plymouth had a new Barracuda to rival the Mustang, and Ford itself had in-house competition in the form of Mercury's Cougar, an upmarket, luxury version of the Mustang itself. Hal Sperlich was in no doubt as to what was needed: make the Mustang big enough to accept Ford's big-block 390 FE series.

The upshot was that it was made nearly 3-in (7.6-cm) wider than the old car, with an extra couple of inches on both front and rear tracks, plus more room in the engine bay. The wheelbase was unchanged, but the 1967 model was 2 inches longer as well. Not surprisingly, it was also heavier, with 130lb (59kg) added to the all-in weight. On the other hand, it did get that much-needed injection of cubic inches; moreover, the 390 option cost just $264, which was something of a bargain.

There were other changes too. For the first time, the Mustang received a proper sporty car instrument pack that included same-sized speedo and rev counter. To ease entry, the steering wheel tilted to one side, while the heater/air conditioner was built in, and the SelectShift automatic could be shifted manually.

Ford urged potential customers to take the 'Mustang Pledge' – that is, not to brag about their new car too much or charge eager passengers for rides. They were tempted with the Sports Sprint package in the spring of 1967, a cosmetic special that offered sporty hood vents, whitewall tyres (and full wheel covers), recessed indicators, bright rocker panel mouldings and a chrome air cleaner. Buyers were also given a good deal on the SelectAire air conditioning (Ford was pushing air conditioning on the Mustang that year, and 16 per cent of buyers opted for it).

But what everyone wanted to know about wasn't the Mustang Pledge or even the new hood vents, but the new 390 V8 option. This was really the Mark II Mustang's reason for being, so how did it work in practice? *Car and Driver* started off cautiously, pointing out that the 390GT carried 400lb (181kg) more weight over the front wheels than the 271-hp HiPo: the weight distribution was 60.3/39.7 per cent. In theory, it should have suffered terminal understeer, but the *C/D* testers were

OPPOSITE
1967 Mustang GT fastback with teardrop hood.

BELOW
1967 Mustang coupé.

impressed. It had, they wrote, '... balance and handling ... Initial understeer is there, but oversteer can be induced by a flick of the wheel here, a poke of the throttle there ... it's very hard to throw it off balance.' As for the

straight-line stuff, they considered it the fastest pony car yet, faster even than a big-block Camaro or Firebird, with a 15.2-second quarter for the automatic tested, and an estimated 14 seconds for the four-speed manual.

Eric Dahlquist tested a GTA 390 for *Hot Rod* and echoed every word, down to surprise that such a nose-heavy car could handle so well. He also liked the new automatic ('the best of both worlds'), the ride and the steering,

ABOVE and OPPOSITE
1967 Shelby Mustang GT350.

BELOW
1967 Mustang GTA convertible.

OPPOSITE
1967 Shelby Mustang GT500 427 four-speed.

though according to *Hot Rod*'s figures, a Camaro 350 (let alone a 396) was a whole half-second quicker over the quarter-mile. And that was after the road-test team had gone to the trouble of removing the belts powering the air pump, power steering and air conditioning

to give the latest Mustang its best shot.

By and large, however, he liked it. Martyn L. Schorr (*Cars* magazine) agreed, after driving a 390 fastback for 5,000 miles (8000km). Not as fast as a GTO, perhaps, but it '... handles, performs and looks like a

well-designed foreign machine ... the original is still the greatest!' Ford must have been even more pleased when *Car and Driver* readers voted the 390 the best sports sedan over 300ci (4.9 litres) for that year.

Before long, however, cracks were

beginning to show. What really mattered in muscle cars like these was performance, pure and simple, and despite *C/D*'s optimistic assertion that the 390 was the fastest pony car on offer, it clearly was not. The truth emerged late in 1967, when Tasca Ford manager, Dean Gregson (Tasca was a prominent Ford dealer), spilt the beans to Eric Dahlquist : 'We sold a

lot of 390 Mustangs last fall and into the winter,' he said, 'but by March they dropped off to practically nothing. That's when the snow melted off the asphalt. We found the car so non-competitive we began to feel we were cheating the customer.' It was Tasca, of course, which offered its own 427-engined Mustangs, prompting Ford to do the same.

If anyone doubted that the Mustang was falling behind, they need only have read *Car and Driver*'s six-car test in early 1968, which comprised Mustang 390 versus Javelin SST, Camaro 396, Cougar XR-7, Barracuda Formula S and Firebird 400. On points, the Mustang came last (73 points against the winning Firebird's 118). It scored bottom, or

close to it, on starting, servicing, steering effort, handling predictability, brake fade resistance, ease of entry/exit, rear-seat comfort, driver controls, heater/demister, trunk space, rear fender protection and visibility.

It understeered, the fastback shape restricted passengers, and the 390 engine

OPPOSITE
1967 Mustang coupé.

BELOW
1967 Mustang GTA fastback with 390-ci (6.4-litre) engine.

OPPOSITE
1967 Shelby Mustang GT500.

LEFT
1967 Mustang 289 convertible automatic.

BELOW LEFT
1967 Mustang GT390 V8 hardtop.

was a disappointment in almost every respect. 'Ford has been content to rest on its laurels,' concluded *C/D*, 'while the rest of the industry has gone all out to win a piece of the Mustang market.' Despite all this, none of the testers thought it the worst car of the group. The Mustang may have had its flaws, but it evidently had its charm too.

Back in California, the Shelby Mustangs continued to distance themselves from the original hardcore GT350s. As a result, they were cheaper, and Ford sold more of them. They were still available only as fastbacks, but the emphasis was now on visual appeal rather than rock-hard suspension and a stripped-out interior. A new fibreglass hood had twin air scoops and racing-style locking pins, while there were air scoops on the C-

OPPOSITE and BELOW
1967 Mustang 351 convertible.

RIGHT
1967 Mustang X-code.

OPPOSITE
1967 Mustang 289 with three-speed automatic transmission and convertible top.

PAGE 116
1967 Shelby Mustang GT350.

PAGE 117
This 1967 Mustang 289 convertible doesn't look fat or pig-like from this angle.

BELOW and OPPOSITE
1967 Mustang fastback.

pillar and in front of each rear wheel. That is, there were air scoops if Shelby could get any from his supplier; the specifications weren't exactly written in stone, but depended on parts available that week. There was a spoiler on the fibreglass trunk lid, and every Shelby had two large high-beam

lights, side by side in the centre of the grille. These were later moved apart after there were objections in certain states.

The 1967 GT350s and new GT500 had a serious-looking roll cage and inertia-reel seatbelts, but the Shelby (at least the 350) had really become a cosmetic upgrade on the

stock Mustang GT. The de-luxe interior was standard, as was a tachometer, fold-down rear seat, power steering and power brakes. The handling package was standard, however (still an option, even on Mustang GTs), as were adjustable Gabriel shock absorbers. Officially, the HiPo 289 V8 still

RIGHT
*A much modified 1967 Mustang 351
hardtop.*

OPPOSITE
*1967 special-edition Mustang High
Country.*

BELOW and OPPOSITE
1967 Mustang fastback GT.

produced 306bhp, though the tubular headers had been dropped in favour of Ford's own high-performance cast-iron manifold.

Proof that cosmetic add-ons cost less than performance hardware, the price was again slashed, now to £3,995 for the GT350, and Shelby dealers sold 1,175 of them that year. It wasn't all cosmetic, however, as Shelby had levered in Ford's 428-ci (7.0-litre) 'Police Interceptor' under the hood to create the GT500 with around 360hp. At $200 more than the 350, and little more than a HiPo 289, it

was good value, and helped to maintain some Shelby credibility as the real performance variant of the standard Mustang. Even this had an automatic transmission option, however (a C6 in place of the GT350's C4), underlining the fact that the Shelby's days as a hairy, uncompromising sports car were fading fast.

MODEL LINE-UP	PRODUCTION
Hardtop	356,271
Fastback	71,042
Convertible	44,808
GT350	
fastback	1,175
GT500	
fastback	2,048
TOTAL	475,344

ENGINE LINE-UP
200 six

Type	Water-cooled cast-iron straight-six, ohv

Bore x stroke	3.68 x 3.13in (93.5 x 79.5mm)
Capacity	200ci (3.3 litres)
Compression ratio	9.2:1
Fuelling	Single-barrel carburettor
Power	120bhp @ 4,400rpm

289 2bbl V8

Type	Water-cooled cast-iron V8 ohv
Bore x stroke	4.00 x 2.87in (102 x 73mm)
Capacity	289ci (4.7 litres)
Compression ratio	9.3:1
Fuelling	Two-barrel carburettor
Power	200bhp @ 4,400rpm

289 4bbl V8

Type	Water-cooled cast-iron V8, ohv
Bore x stroke	4.00 x 2.87in
Capacity	289ci (4.7 litres)
Compression ratio	10.0:1
Fuelling	Four-barrel carburettor
Power	225bhp @ 4,800rpm

289 HiPo V8

Type	Water-cooled cast-iron V8
Bore x stroke	4.00 x 2.87in
Capacity	289ci (4.7 litres)
Compression ratio	10.5:1
Fuelling	Four-barrel carburettor
Power	271bhp @ 6,000rpm

390 V8

Type	Water-cooled cast-iron V8
Bore x stroke	4.05 x 3.78in (103 x 96mm)
Capacity	390ci (6.4 litres)
Compression ratio	10.5:1
Fuelling	Four-barrel carburettor
Power	320bhp @ 4,600rpm

GT350

Type	Water-cooled cast-iron V8
Bore x stroke	4.00 x 2.87in
Capacity	289ci (4.7 litres)

Compression ratio	10.5:1
Fuelling	Four-barrel carburettor
Power	306bhp

GT500

Type	Water-cooled cast-iron V8
Bore x stroke	4.13 x 3.98in (105 x 101mm)
Capacity	428ci (7.0 litres)
Compression ratio	10.7:1
Fuelling	Twin four-barrel carburettors
Power	355bhp

1968:
MUSCLE-BOUND

1968 Shelby Mustang GT500.

With a screech of burnt rubber and ever more horsepower, the muscle-car boom went crazy in late-1967/early-'68. Chevrolet's Z28 Camaro had served notice as a race car for the road, while full-sized muscle cars like the Hemi-powered Chryslers and the Chevy Impala offered buyers over

400 horsepower that could be driven out of the showroom and onto the street. And Ford? Well, Ford had the 320-hp 390 Mustang. It was not enough. Ford had to do something to beef up the Mustang, and fast.

So there were a number of holding operations for the 1968 model year before

the new breed of Boss Mustangs appeared for 1969. So far, the 428 Cobra Jet had been the factory car with the most cubes, while Shelby was already offering the GT500 and had now come up with a tuned GT350, not to mention the option of a supercharger.

But it wasn't all about performance. The

ABOVE and LEFT
1968 Mustang special-edition
California.

basic Mustang was still rolling off the line with that 200-ci (3.3-litre) straight six, actually derated for 1968 to 115hp, which didn't sound much when compared with the opposition; but as *Motor Trend* pointed out, the cheapest Mustang wasn't such a slug as one might think. Unlike the Camaro or Barracuda sixes, it used smaller brakes and lighter running gear than the V8-equipped cars, and consequently weighed about 300lb (136kg) less. That made it at least as quick as the Chevy and Plymouth, and it was more

economical to boot. The price had crept up since 1964, but at $2,602 for the hardtop, the basic Mustang was still good value.

One option which didn't place performance to the forefront was the limited-edition California Special; this too came with the 200-ci six. Inspired by the Shelby look, this was a hardtop with Shelby-style rear spoiler, blacked-out front grille, special badges and GT-style wheels. Only 5,000 were built, and only West Coast dealers got to sell them; however, a smaller number of similar High Country Specials was offered in Colorado.

Meanwhile, the sixes went on selling, but it wasn't these sensible Mustangs that grabbed the headlines, it was the V8s. Thanks to the efforts of Rhode Island dealer Tasca Ford, the company realized that the

ABOVE, LEFT and OPPOSITE
1968 429 Shelby Mustang GT500
police vehicle.

OPPOSITE and LEFT
1968 Mustang GT428.

OPPOSITE
1968 Shelby Mustang GT500
convertible.

LEFT
1968 Mustang 289 coupé.

PAGES 132 and 133
1968 Shelby Mustang GT350.

stock 390 wasn't quick enough, and that the big-block 428 would slot straight in. It did just that, fitting the same 428 Police Interceptor V8 that had been used by Tasca.

Ford claimed just 335hp (only 15hp more than the 390), but judging by the car's enthusiastic reception, that was a conservative estimate.

'Ford fans rejoice!' wrote John Raffat at *Car Craft*. 'Get away from that bridge, throw away your razor blades and dump out the strychnine!' At *Hot Rod*, Eric Dahlquist

OPPOSITE, LEFT, PAGES 136 and 137
1968 Mustang GT390 fastback four-speed.

predicted that the Cobra Jet '... will be the utter delight of every Ford lover and the bane of all the rest because, quite frankly, it is probably the fastest regular production sedan ever built'. In terms of straight-line acceleration, he was probably right: one pre-production CJ did the standing quarter in 13.56 seconds, and if that wasn't fast enough, there were various states of tune for cars heading exclusively for the drag strip. Drag racer Don Nicholson made a whole series of radical modifications and his CJ whipped through the lights at 11.62 seconds and 119.7mph (192.6km/h). There was no doubt about it: the Mustang was back in the performance business.

Carroll Shelby, of course, had beaten Ford to it, and by a large margin. As soon as the 1967 Mustang appeared, with its wider

engine bay to take the big-block V8, it was clear that Ford's biggest, the 428-ci (7.0-litre) unit would slip in there quite nicely. The GT500 was the result, a 428 Mustang on sale long before anything from Ford.

Or was it? Things had changed at Shelby since the early GT350s were hand-built in southern California. The GT500 was actually built by Ford – even the engine was fitted at its San Jose plant. Admittedly, it came with a 6,000-rpm camshaft, hydraulic lifters and dual Holley four-barrel carbs on an aluminium manifold, all of which Shelby supplied. But all Shelby employees did engine-wise was to bolt on the finned aluminium valve covers and an air filter. They also did the show-off parts, the spoilers, scoops and extra lights, plus a roll bar, and that was it.

The Shelby Mustang had changed its spots. Now, it was a Mustang fresh from the Ford production line, with some minor changes to justify the use of the Shelby name. Even the 428 motor wasn't unique once Ford came up with its own Cobra Jet.

But there were advantages in all of this: the latest GT500 may have been less hairy than the original 350, but it was more civilized too, quieter and less demanding. Power steering and power brakes were standard, with automatic transmission on the options list. Yet with a claimed 355hp at 5,400rpm, and 420lb ft at 3,200, this was serious performance in a velvet glove.

Car and Driver recorded 6.5 seconds to 60mph (97km/h) from a standing start, and exactly 15 seconds over the standing quarter. According to *C/D*, 'the viciousness has gone

OPPOSITE and BELOW
1968 Mustang special-edition California coupé.

out of the car, without any lessening of its animal vitality'. Better still, the mass-production techniques resulted in the GT500 costing little more than a plain 390 loaded with extras, the basic price being $4,400. In early 1968, moreover, there was the GT500 KR (King of the Road) option, with the official Cobra Jet 335-hp (for which Shelby claimed 400bhp), while all the Shelby Mustangs could be had as either convertibles or fastbacks.

Of course, if viciousness was required, Shelby was happy to oblige. The GT350 may have been toned down a little since its early days (no noisy limited slip differential now, nor rock-hard suspension), but it still ran with the rev-happy, vocal small-block V8, now upsized to 302ci (4.9 litres) for 1968, and if that wasn't quick enough, there was the option of a Paxton supercharger. This claimed 335hp (ostensibly the same as Ford's 428 Cobra Jet). That sounded wild enough, but Carroll Shelby was an ex-racer, so he naturally built a prototype 428 with supercharger as well. *Car and Driver* had a quick blast in the car, and found that it would squeal its rear tyres at 80mph (129km/h), and had plenty of acceleration on tap from one hundred. It never went on sale.

Anyone disappointed that this most powerful Shelby Mustang failed to make an appearance could take solace from the tune-up kit available for 1968 GT350s. The standard 350 now offered 250hp, which was 56 down on the old 289-powered 350, and no match for the Camaro Z28; but for just under $700, customers could specify a whole raft of tuning parts. There were special cylinder heads with

larger valves (1.875-in/4.762-cm inlets, 1.600-in/4.064-cm exhausts); an 11.0:1 compression ratio; high-rise aluminium intake manifold; 715-cfm Holley four-barrel carb; and longer-duration cam timing, for which Shelby claimed 315hp. The limited slip differential made a return too, as did stiffer rear springs with supplementary anti-wind-up leaves added. In other words, it seemed like a return to the original, animalistic 350 of 1965 – a racer for the road.

Road & Track judged it to be 'a close match for the Z28'. The hotter 302 could rev up to 6,000, with valve float at 6,400, and actually got off the line more quickly, whereas the Camaro could only overhaul it as it passed the quarter-mile mark, going on to a higher top speed of 132mph (212km/h, thanks to its 7,100-rpm rev limit. However, *R&T* thought that the Mustang's power steering and brakes let it down, these being unchanged, and as feedback-free as on any other Mustang, while driving fast on winding roads was 'tricky'. The hot 350, it concluded, simply accentuated the Mustang's faults: too heavy, too compromised. And in any case, a Z28 handled better, and was cheaper into the bargain.

As ever, cars like this were aimed at a limited market. Far more relevant to many more was the Cougar. Mercury had long since been the luxury marque at Ford, turning out upmarket versions of the standard Detroit sedans; in fact, the Cougar was no more nor less than a luxurious Mustang. It came with soft suspension and a cosseting interior – 'all very British'– according to *Car and Driver*, 'with lots of switches and peculiar numbering and funny-shaped needles on the gauges'. In

early tests, it quite liked the Cougar but, pitted against five pony-car rivals, it seemed soft, floppy and outperformed. Nevertheless, the luxury Mustang had its place, probably alongside leafy suburbs and white picket fences, but it wasn't a sporty pony car.

MODEL LINE-UP	PRODUCTION
Hardtop	249,447
Fastback	42,325
Convertible	25,376
GT350 fastback	1,227
GT350 convertible	404
GT500 fastback	1,046
GT500 convertible	402
GT500KR fastback	1,053
GT500KR convertible	518
TOTAL	321,798

ENGINE LINE-UP
200 six

Type	Water-cooled cast-iron straight-six, ohv
Bore x stroke	3.68 x 3.13in (93.5 x 79.5mm)
Capacity	200ci (3.3 litres)
Compression ratio	8.8:1
Fuelling	Single-barrel carburettor
Power	115bhp @ 3,800rpm

289 2bbl V8

Type	Water-cooled cast-iron V8, ohv
Bore x stroke	4.00 x 2.87in (102 x 73mm)
Capacity	289ci (4.7 litres)
Compression ratio	8.7:1

OPPOSITE
1968 Mustang special-edition California coupé.

PAGE 142
1968 Mustang fastback 2+2.

PAGE 143
1968 Mustang 289 coupé.

RIGHT, OPPOSITE, PAGES 146 and 147
1968 Mustang hardtop GT302 with automatic transmission.

Fuelling	Two-barrel carburettor	Fuelling	Two-barrel	Fuelling	Four-barrel carburettor
Power	195bhp @ 4,600rpm	Power	220bhp @ 4,800rpm	Power	230bhp @ 4,800rpm

302 2bbl V8   **302 4bbl V8**   **390 V8**

Type	Water-cooled cast-iron V8, ohv	Type	Water-cooled cast-iron V8	Type	Water-cooled cast-iron V8
Bore x stroke	4.00 x 3.00in (102 x 76.2mm)	Bore x stroke	4.00 x 3.00in	Bore x stroke	4.05 x 3.78in (103 x 96mm)
Capacity	302ci (4.9 litres)	Capacity	302ci (4.9 litres)	Capacity	390ci (6.4 litres)
		Compression ratio	10.0:1		

ABOVE
1968 GT Mustang fastback with 428 Cobra Jet four-speed.

OPPOSITE
1968 Mustang GT500 KR.

PAGE 152
1968 Mustang hardtop with white vinyl roof.

PAGE 153
1968 GT500 KR convertible.

Compression ratio	10.5:1
Fuelling	Four-barrel carburettor
Power	325bhp @ 4,800rpm

428 Cobra Jet V8

Type	Water-cooled cast-iron V8
Bore x stroke	4.13 x 3.98in (105 x 101mm)
Capacity	428ci (7.0 litres)
Compression ratio	10.7:1
Fuelling	Four-barrel carburettor
Power	335bhp @ 6,000rpm

GT350

Type	Water-cooled cast-iron V8
Bore x stroke	4.00 x 3.00in (102 x 76.2mm)
Capacity	302ci (4.9 litres)
Compression ratio	10.5:1
Fuelling	Four-barrel carburettor
Power	250bhp

GT500

Type	Water-cooled cast-iron V8
Bore x stroke	4.13 x 3.98in

Capacity	428ci (7.0 litres)
Compression ratio	10.5:1
Fuelling	Four-barrel carburettor
Power	360bhp

OPPOSITE, LEFT, PAGES 160 and 161

1968 Mustang fastback J-code 302.

OPPOSITE and LEFT
A rare 1968 X-code convertible – one
of only nine ever made.

OPPOSITE, LEFT, PAGES 166 and 167
1968 Shelby Mustang GT500 KR 428 Cobra Jet.

1969:
LOOK OUT, IT'S THE BOSS!

Lee Iacocca described the 1967 Mustang as 'a fat pig', so what he thought of the 1969 can only be imagined. The car was again bulked up, gaining nearly 4in (10cm) in length. It also gained a bewildering variety of engine options (no less than nine V8s alone,

including the 375-bhp Boss 429). Its origins as a compact sporty car were becoming more and more remote.

To make matters worse, the man responsible for all this (at least in part) was 'Bunkie' Knudsen. Iacocca had been sure that

he was in line for the presidency, being a Ford career man with a good track record. Instead, Henry Ford II took the unprecedented step of recruiting Semon E. Knudsen from General Motors. This caused something of a sensation in Detroit, as most potential managers joined Ford, GM or Chrysler from college and stayed there till the golf links beckoned.

So Bunkie's arrival at Ford in February 1968 caused something of a stir and not a little resentment. There was even talk that he would be bringing his young protégé, John Z. Delorean, with him, to put Iacocca in his place. But this never happened, and Bunkie's Ford career lasted a mere 18 months before he was fired. An argument over long-term business strategy? Not according to Iacocca. Bunkie had the habit of walking into Ford's office without knocking, which amounted to the eighth deadly sin; when Knudsen left, there was rejoicing throughout the company. The original Henry Ford had famously said that history is bunk. 'Today,' said a wit in the PR department, 'Bunkie is history.'

Bunkie nevertheless bequeathed a legacy to the Mustang. In 1969, the range was wider than ever, in the General Motors's way of covering every conceivable gap in the market, and included the luxurious Grande, sporty Mach 1 and the race-ready Boss Mustangs, the 302 and 429. There was a new six-cylinder option, a 155-bhp 250-ci (4.0-litre), which

OPPOSITE, LEFT and OVERLEAF
A 1969 Mach 1 modified to Cobra Jet
specification.

slotted in between the 200-ci (3.3-litre) and the V8s, while sixes still made up one in five Mustang sales. The base V8 was a two-barrel 302 (220-bhp), with a 290-bhp four-barrel version to power the Boss 302. The mid-range cooking Mustangs used the 351-ci (5.7-litre) Windsor or Cleveland V8s (in 250- or 290-bhp forms), while the faithful 390 was in its final year. The 428-ci (7.0-litre) Cobra Jet was still on offer, now in standard 335-bhp or Super 360-bhp form, with the 375-bhp Boss 429 topping off the range.

All of these motors sat in the bigger 1969 bodyshell, longer and with more windshield rake, though the wheelbase stuck at the original 108in (274cm). There were quad round headlights (only for this year) and the fastback became a 'SportsRoof', with

a lower roofline than before and a small rear window behind the door glass. This fatter Mustang had probably been planned before Bunkie Knudsen arrived, but there's no doubt that he was the man behind the two Boss Mustangs.

The rationale for these was simple. Ford needed to qualify its small-block 302 V8 for Trans Am racing and the big-block 429 for NASCAR, and the two Boss Mustangs would do the job. In concept, however, they were quite different from one another.

The 302 was a high-revving screamer, with a supension package aimed at twisty circuit racing. It was lowered with heavy-duty suspension, 7-in (17.8-cm) wide wheels and fat tyres. *Hot Rod* described it as 'the best handling car Ford has ever built'. The crankshaft was balanced both statically and dynamically, and there was a high-lift camshaft and big 780-cfm Holley carburettor. And it could rev: owners reported that it kept on producing power right up to 8,000 (that was if the factory's 5,800-rpm rev limiter was bypassed). Ford had just one car in the 302's sights, the Camaro Z28, another high-revving Trans Am racer for the road. *Car and Driver* tested the two side by side, publishing the results in the summer of 1968. The Mustang, it found, was slightly lighter than the Camaro, couldn't quite stay with it on straight-line acceleration (there was 0.2 seconds between them over the standing quarter), but was nearly half a second quicker around Lime Rock race track, so *Hot Rod* was right about the handling. *C/D* loved it.

The Boss 429 was different again. Ford didn't want to qualify the Mustang for

NASCAR racing (this being the preserve of larger cars with better aerodynamics), just the engine. It was necessary to build 500 429 hemi-head V8s to qualify the engine for NASCAR, which it did, and slipped them into Mustangs. The result was the most powerful Mustang ever: Ford claimed 375bhp, but it was sandbagging and *Car Life* thought 400 horsepower was nearer the mark. Whatever it produced, the engine was a special: aluminium hemi heads, O-ring head gaskets and huge valves (2.3-in/5.8-cm inlet and 1.9-in/4.8-cm exhaust). To squeeze this into a Mustang, Ford had to move the entire front suspension outboard by an inch; there was no doubt about it, the Boss 429 was a homologation special rather than a production-line car. *Car Life* recorded a 14.09-second quarter-mile (many 429s were destined for the drag strip), but maintained that it was even better mannered than the street-only Mach 1 and credited it with race-car handling.

The Boss Mustangs created reams of press coverage. They boosted the Mustang's image and became muscle-car legends. But they were not big sellers. The new mainstream sporty Mustang, the kind of car that most people would buy, having read about and drooled over the Boss twins, was the Mach 1. Now this was a very different beast, basically the new SportsRoof body with the two-barrel 351-ci (5.75-litre) Windsor V8, with a four-barrel 351 and the 390 and 428 Cobra Jet as options.

It certainly looked the part of a sporty Mustang, with its matt-black hood with big scoop, spoilers, stripes and chrome wheels,

colour-keyed racing mirrors and a luxury-look interior. It also had what Ford called 'competition supension' (or what used to be known as plain 'heavy-duty'.) But was it any good? Well, it depends whom you believe. *Car Life* loved it, describing the 428 Mach 1 it tested as 'the first great Mustang … with handling to send imported car fans home mumbling to themselves'. In fact, it was the fastest-accelerating four-seater it had ever tested.

Car and Driver was less complimentary. 'Look at the Mustang Mach 1 and you expect miracles,' it said. 'Drive it and they are not forthcoming.' It was quick enough (14.3 seconds was recorded over the quarter) and it liked the C6 automatic. But with over 59 per cent of its weight over the front wheels the Mach 1 understeered drastically, 'the front tires howl and smoke and absolutely refuse to go in the direction they're pointed'. *Car Life* agreed about the understeer on the limit, but maintained that at 'seven-tenths' driving, Ford engineers have exempted the Mach 1 from the laws of momentum and inertia'. All this conjecture didn't seem to bother the customers, however, as over 70,000 of them bought Mach 1s that year.

Another 22,000 or so opted for the new Grande hardtop, which was a pony of a very different colour. The Boss twins were aimed at serious racers (or street-based wannabes), the Mach 1 at everyday enthusiasts, but the Grande was a new type of Mustang, a luxury hardtop which had strayed into Mercury Cougar territory, with no spoilers, no NASCAR-style hood pins or scoops, no performance pretensions whatsoever.

Instead, it had thick carpeting, vinyl/wood trim on the dashboard and a centre console. The seats came with hopsack (cloth) trim and there was a whole 55lb (25kg) of extra sound insulation. The suspension was in stock soft-sprung form with the addition of voided rubber bushes in the front eyes of the rear leaf springs. This allowed the axle to move back a little over bumps, which was bad news for racing starts but good for comfort, while full wheel covers rounded things off.

Did a luxury Mustang really make sense? *Car Life* seemed to think so, finding the Grande quiet, comfortable and well-mannered. And with the standard 351-ci (5.75-litre) four-barrel it actually seemed better balanced than the nose-heavy 428

OPPOSITE
1969 Shelby Mustang GT500.

BELOW
1969 Mustang Mach 1 Cobra Jet.

RIGHT and BELOW
1969 Grande hardtop: the new 'luxury'
Mustang was a big hit.

OPPOSITE
1969 Mustang Mach 1 390 in a rare
colour.

Mustangs. It wasn't exactly fast, but the magazine remarked that with a standing quarter of 15.6 seconds, it was still quicker than some recent performance cars, not to mention any 1969 luxury sedan. 'Brisk, nimble, quiet and stable', the Grande came along at just the right time, when buying habits were beginning to change.

This may have been why the 1969 model year was the end of the Shelby era. By now, the Shelby Mustangs only came as body-kit cars, spruced up with fibreglass panels and scoops, but mechanically identical to their mass-produced cousins. It was Carroll Shelby who persuaded Ford to end the series; he could see that the steadily tightening emissions and safety legislation

OPPOSITE and THIS PAGE
1969 Shelby Mustang GT500 428
Cobra Jet.

would make an old-school Shelby Mustang impossible to build, so for 1969 (and with a few hundred leftover cars sold in the 1970 season) the GT350s and 500s made their last appearance. It was a sign of the times.

MODEL LINE-UP	PRODUCTION
Hardtop	127,954
Hardtop Grande	22,182
SportsRoof	61,980
SportsRoof Mach 1	72,458
Convertible	14,746
GT350 fastback	935
GT350H fastback	152
GT350 convertible	194
GT500 fastback	1,534

RIGHT and BELOW
1969 Shelby Mach 1 390 automatic.

1969 Mustang 351 coupé.

OPPOSITE and LEFT
1969 Mustang 351 coupé; the V8 was
one of the Windsor series.

OPPOSITE, LEFT and OVERLEAF
1969 Mustang Boss 429 with Hemi V8.

PAGE 189
1969 Mustang fastback automatic.

GT500 convertible	335
TOTAL	302,470

ENGINE LINE-UP

200 six

Type	Water-cooled cast-iron straight-six, ohv
Bore x stroke	3.68 x 3.13in (93.5 x 79.5mm)
Capacity	200ci (3.3 litres0
Compression ratio	8.8:1
Fuelling	Single-barrel carburettor
Power	115bhp @ 3,800rpm

250 six

Type	Water-cooled cast-iron straight-six, ohv

OPPOSITE and THIS PAGE
1969 Shelby Mustang GT500 with four-speed Cobra Jet.

Bore x stroke   3.68 x 3.91in (93.5 x
                       99.3mm)
Capacity   250ci (4.0 litres)
Compression ratio   9.0:1
Fuelling   Single-barrel carburettor
Power   155bhp @ 4,400rpm

302 2bbl V8

Type   Water-cooled cast-
                       iron V8, ohv
Bore x stroke   4.00 x 3.00in (102 x
                       76.2mm)
Capacity   302ci (4.9 litres)
Fuelling   Two-barrel
                       carburettor
Power   220bhp @ 4,800rpm

302 4bbl Boss V8

Type   Water-cooled cast-
                       iron V8
Bore x stroke   4.00 x 3.00in
Capacity   302ci (4.9 litres)
Compression ratio   10.5:1
Fuelling   Four-barrel carburettor
Power   290bhp @ 5,000rpm

351 2bbl V8

Type   Water-cooled cast-
                       iron V8, ohv
Bore x stroke   4.00 x 3.50in (102 x
                       90mm)
Capacity   351ci (5.75 litres)
Compression ratio   9.5:1
Fuelling   Two-barrel carburettor
Power   250bhp @ 4,600rpm

351 4bbl V8

Type   Water-cooled cast-iron
                       V8, ohv
Bore x stroke   4.00 x 3.50in

Capacity   351ci (5.75 litres)
Compression ratio   10.7:1
Fuelling   Four-barrel carburettor
Power   290bhp @ 4,600rpm

390 V8

Type   Water-cooled cast-
                       iron V8
Bore x stroke   4.05 x 3.78in (103 x
                       96mm)
Capacity   390ci (6.4 litres)

Compression ratio   10.5:1
Fuelling   Four-barrel
                       carburettor
Power   320bhp @ 4,800rpm

428 Cobra Jet V8

Type   Water-cooled cast-
                       iron V8
Bore x stroke   4.13 x 3.98in (105 x
                       101mm)
Capacity   428ci (7.0 litres)

ABOVE and OPPOSITE
1969 Shelby Mustang GT350.

Compression ratio   10.6:1

Fuelling   Four-barrel carburettor

Power   335bhp @ 5,200rpm

428 Super Cobra Jet V8

Type   Water-cooled cast-iron V8

Bore x stroke   4.13 x 3.98in

Capacity   428ci (7.0 litres)

Compression ratio   10.5:1

Fuelling   Four-barrel carburettor

Power   360bhp @ 5,400rpm

429 Boss V8

Type   Water-cooled cast-iron V8

Bore x stroke   4.36 x 3.59in (111 x 91.2mm)

Capacity   429ci (7.0 litres)

Compression ratio   11.3:1

Fuelling   Four-barrel carburettor

Power   375bhp @ 5,600rpm

GT350

Type   Water-cooled cast-iron V8

Bore x stroke   4.00 x 3.50in (102 x 89mm)

Capacity   351ci (5.75 litres)

Compression ratio   10.7:1

Fuelling   Four-barrel carburettor

Power   290bhp

GT500

Type   Water-cooled cast-iron V8

Bore x stroke   4.13 x 3.98in

Capacity   428ci (7.0 litres)

Compression ratio   10.6:1

Fuelling   Four-barrel carburettor

Power   335bhp

OPPOSITE and BELOW
1969 Shelby Mustang GT350.

RIGHT and OPPOSITE
1969 Mustang Mach 1, with rear
louvres, spoilers and hood scoop.

1970:
HAVE WE GOT TROUBLE!

Nineteen-seventy was an unadventurous year for the Mustang, with dealers, parts countermen, journalists, perhaps even customers too, breathing a sigh of relief after the avalanche of new models for 1969. There was a mild restyle, front and rear. The car lost its quad headlight set-up in favour of just two, set in a full-width black grille, while the air intakes either side of it looked cool but were in fact fakes. However, the fake intakes behind the doors, a Mustang trademark since 1964, were now banished, and the rear lights were slightly restyled, and that was it. Engine options were unchanged, though the choice of V8s was trimmed back to a mere seven, from 220-hp 302-ci/4.9-litre to 375-bhp 429. The two sixes were also unchanged.

But something was wrong. Despite the huge choice on offer, Mustang sales had been steadily declining since the mid-1960s. The car was still king of the pony cars, and would remain top-seller into the early 1970s; but since the peak of 1966, when over 600,000 cars were built, the downhill slide had been inexorable. The year 1967 had seen 472,000 Mustangs leave the line, but there were only 317,000 in 1968 and just under 300,000 the year after. In 1970, the figure was 190,000. In other words, Mustang sales had more than halved in three years.

There were two good reasons for this. As

the 1960s ended and the 1970s began, the golden era of the muscle car was already on the wane. It wasn't only the ever-tougher safety and emissions legislation that was beginning to bite – customers' wallets were also hurting too. The horsepower war had had the effect of introducing young, inexperienced drivers to 300-horsepower cars. Inevitably, they ran off the road and

into other cars and people were killed. Consequently, insurance premiums went through the roof and high-performance was no longer an option. Even in 1969, only 16 per cent of Mach 1 buyers opted for the full-house 428-ci (7.0-litre) fire-breather; the most popular choice (nearly half of all Mach 1s sold) was the mild two-barrel 351and this trend could only continue. Inside Ford, there

had also been a change of heart. Bunkie Knudsen had been a hot-car enthusiast, but he was no longer there; in these less hedonistic times, Ford decided to pull out of racing and rejig its production schedules.

The second reason for the decline in the Mustang's fortunes was the ever-encroaching competition. The Camaro and Firebird were now into their second phase, the Barracuda

had been transformed from a clumsy coupé into a true mini-muscle car, and Dodge had its Challenger. The happy days when Ford had the pony-car market to itself were long since gone.

So how did the Mustang stack up in these more troubled times? Two press reports underline how American-oriented the Mustang had become. Lee Iacocca's personal car had always been aimed at the American market, pure and simple, and had never been exported in large numbers. So what did the Australians make of it? *Motor Manual* tested a 351 convertible in early 1970, and the results were not good reading for anyone at Ford.

In those pre-politically correct days, few would have objected when *Motor Manual*

OPPOSITE
1970 Mustang fastback.

ABOVE and LEFT
1970 Mustang Mach 1.

BELOW
1970 Mustang Boss 302.

OPPOSITE
1970 Mustang fastback 302.

concluded that the Mustang was a terrific 'fluff-catcher' – or in plain English, that it attracted the opposite sex. Unfortunately, that was the only good thing the writers could find to say about it. 'A fine example of precise engineering it is not. In fact, compared to a Falcon GT [Ford Australia's hot saloon] it handles and performs in a manner reminiscent of a soft-top truck.'

Actually, it did like the powered soft-top part of the equation. It powered up and down in seconds and proved completely impervious to Australian downpours. But it was impossible for a six-foot driver to get comfortable behind the Mustang's wheel, and with the seat right back there was almost zero legroom for the rear passengers. One passenger, incidentally, considered the four-track stereo to be the car's best feature. As for driving, it didn't like the pitching and tail-wander on less than perfect surfaces, and reckoned that the Falcon GT (also 351 V8-powered) would leave the Mustang for dead. Moreover, the American Ford cost

10,000 Australian dollars, twice the price of a home-grown Falcon after it had been shipped across the Pacific. The Aussies were not impressed.

For the American view, it is necessary to consult *Motorcade*'s test of a Boss 302, just three months later. Of course, the Boss 302 (now in its second of just two years on the market) was a very different machine from the softer convertible, but *Motorcade*'s report still highlights the different expectations of American magazines. The

ABOVE and OPPOSITE
1970 Mustang 302-ci fastback.

PAGE 210
1970 Mustang Boss 302.

PAGE 211
1970 Mustang coupé.

Boss 302 (it wrote) 'is without a doubt the closest thing to a sports car, in the traditional sense of that term, that Ford has ever built in this country'. It revelled in its uncompromising feel, in the obvious priority of a precise four-speed manual gearchange over rear-seat comfort. It loved the handling ('body lean is minimal'), brakes and stability. Remember the Mustang's original launch, and how an optional independent rear suspension system had been promised? Well, six years on, the Boss 302 was still using the old leaf-sprung live rear axle, albeit with Ford's staggered rear shocks in an attempt to control axle tramp, though even *Motorcade* thought the system was about as far as it could go. And the independent set-up? Tests apparently showed that the leaf-sprung rear end was actually quicker on race tracks, so it never saw the production line.

The only thing *Motorcade* didn't like about the Boss was the new option of rear-window louvres and a rear spoiler, which together cost $150. These were fashionable at the time, but there were better bargains to be had on the Mustang options list. Power steering, for example, cost just $95, and a steering wheel that tilted to allow taller people to squeeze themselves in was $45. Power front discs were well worth having at $65, though one had to be a seriously committed driver to spend $43 on a limited slip differential. The latter was useful on the drag strip, but whined and clonked its way around town. Perhaps the best bargains of all were under the hood. For just $45, it was possible to upgrade from the basic 200-ci (3.3-litre) six to the 250-bhp 351-ci (5.75-litre) V8. Make that $93, and one could have the full-house four-barrel version, with 300bhp. Then, of course, there was the small matter of insurance.

MODEL LINE-UP   **PRODUCTION**

Hardtop	82,569
Hardtop Grande	13,581
SportsRoof	45,934
SportsRoof Mach 1	40,970
Convertible	7,673
GT350/500	789 (est.)
TOTAL	191,516

ENGINE LINE-UP

200 six

Type	Water-cooled cast-iron straight-six, ohv
Bore x stroke	3.68 x 3.13in (93.5 x 79.5mm)
Capacity	200ci (3.3 litres)
Compression ratio	8.8:1
Fuelling	Single-barrel carburettor
Power	115bhp @ 3,800rpm

250 six

Type	Water-cooled cast-iron straight-six, ohv
Bore x stroke	3.68 x 3.91in (93.5 x 99.3mm)
Capacity	250ci (4.0 litres)
Compression ratio	9.0:1
Fuelling	Single-barrel carburettor
Power	155bhp @ 4,400rpm

302 2bbl V8

Type	Water-cooled cast-iron V8, ohv
Bore x stroke	4.00 x 3.00in (102 x 76.2mm)
Capacity	302ci (4.9 litres)
Fuelling	Two-barrel carburettor
Power	220bhp @ 4,800rpm

302 4bbl Boss V8

Type	Water-cooled cast-iron V8
Bore x stroke	4.00 x 3.00in
Capacity	302ci (4.9 litres)
Compression ratio	10.5:1
Fuelling	Four-barrel carburettor
Power	290bhp @ 5,000rpm

351 2bbl V8

Type	Water-cooled cast-iron V8, ohv
Bore x stroke	4.00 x 3.50in (102 x 90mm)
Capacity	351ci (5.75 litres)
Compression ratio	9.5:1
Fuelling	Two-barrel carburettor
Power	250bhp @ 4,600rpm

351 4bbl V8

Type	Water-cooled cast-iron V8, ohv
Bore x stroke	4.00 x 3.50in
Capacity	351ci (5.75 litres)
Compression ratio	11.0:1
Fuelling	Four-barrel carburettor
Power	300bhp @ 5,400rpm

428 Cobra Jet V8

Type	Water-cooled cast-iron V8
Bore x stroke	4.13 x 3.98in (105 x 101mm)
Capacity	428ci (7.0 litres)
Compression ratio	10.6:1
Fuelling	Four-barrel carburettor
Power	335bhp @ 5,400rpm

428 Super Cobra Jet V8

Type	Water-cooled cast-iron V8
Bore x stroke	4.13 x 3.98in
Capacity	428ci (7.0 litres)
Compression ratio	10.5:1
Fuelling	Four-barrel carburettor
Power	360bhp @ 5,400rpm

429 Boss V8

Type	Water-cooled cast-iron V8
Bore x stroke	4.36 x 3.59in (110.7 x 91.2mm)
Capacity	429ci (7.0 litres)
Compression ratio	11.3:1
Fuelling	Four-barrel carburettor
Power	375bhp @ 5,600rpm

OPPOSITE
1970 Mustang Boss 302.

1971:
WRONG CAR, WRONG TIME

BELOW and OPPOSITE
1971 Mustang Mach 1.

History does not record what Lee Iacocca thought of the 1971 Mustang, but it certainly wouldn't have been favourable. After all, here was the man who described the 1967 car as a fat pig because it was a bigger, heavier version of his original. In Iacocca's view, the original Mustang concept (his concept, of course) of a small, compact personal car was now in tatters. So what must he have thought of the 1971, nearly 7-in (18-cm) wider and 8-in longer than the slimmer, more svelte model of 1964? From sleek horse to fat pig to baby rhino?

Needless to say, it was also fatter; the basic hardtop now tipped the scales at 2,937lb (1332kg); nearly 250lb (114kg) more than the 1970 equivalent, 500lb (227kg) more than the 1964 original. To add salt to the wound, the bigger, fatter Mustang was still perceived as Iacocca's car. In November 1970, shortly after it was launched, he finally became president of the Ford Motor Company, a job he had coveted for years, and boss of an automotive giant. In 1970, Ford employed over 400,000 people building 2.5-million cars (that was just the United States), producing over $500 million on a turnover of nearly $15 billion. And now that Henry Ford II had at last relented, albeit reluctantly, and given Lee the top job, he could not fail to be associated with a car that was plainly out of tune with its times.

This didn't last long, of course, as Iacocca pushed through development of the compact Pinto and Maverick, but to endure three years of selling the biggest Mustang ever must have been a bitter pill to swallow.

The press certainly didn't warm to this supersized 'compact'. Take *Car and Driver*, for example: 'The new Mustang has ballooned another notch closer to an intermediate sedan. From the driver's seat it seems enormous: you can hardly see the surrounding earth.' Nor did it like Ford's attempt to combine the Mustang's traditional long hood with the elongated rear of the Le

Mans-winning MkIV: 'The Dearborn stylists came to a fork in the path and tried to follow two different trails … In the Mach 1 you get the bread-van rear of the racing car grafted to the traditional Mustang nose, and the combination wallows in indecisiveness.'

The hardtop and convertible had more of the Mustang family feel to them, with similar proportions to the old car, but for many commentators this latest fastback, with its near-horizontal rear deck (and consequently near-useless rear window), was a restyle too far. But in making this Mustang bigger than any other, Ford was doing what had seemed the right thing at the time. First, it had been born of the Bunkie Knudsen era; the ex-General Motors's man had only been Ford president for a short time, but he had certainly left his mark. He loved performance and hot cars, and was the driving force behind the Boss 302 and 429 Mustangs, which sold in tiny numbers but did much for Ford's image, as did the racing programme which he enthusiastically endorsed.

Second, the 1971 Mustang had been planned, designed and developed in 1968/69, when the horsepower war was in full swing and there was little sign of it letting up. At the time, buyers of muscle cars appeared to be interested in two things – cubic inches and horsepower – and anything falling short in these areas lost sales. The signs of change may already have been there for anyone who had eyes to see: increasing insurance rates on hot cars, the first Californian emissions legislation, and a growing concern for safety. On the other hand, Ford had been caught out before, in that the previous Mustang hadn't been available with a big-block 428 until enterprising dealer Tasca Ford had stepped in and done the job. The company had no intention of being embarrassed again, so the fourth-generation Mustang was designed from the start to accept any big-block V8 from its own inventory. To make room in the engine bay, it had to be both longer and (especially) wider.

At the time, all this probably made sense, but the 1971 Mustang emerged into a different world, where insurance premiums were heading for the moon and tighter emissions and safety legislation were coming into effect right across the country.

To underline just how far the Mustang had strayed from its origins, compare its dimensions with those of the car which provided some of its inspiration, the Shelby AC Cobra. The Cobra, of course, had always been a very different car from the Mustang, a little open two-seater against the Ford's four-seat interior. But Iacocca's dream had been to

provide a more practical four-seat alternative to just that sort of sports car. The Cobra was 151.2-in (384-cm) long, the 1971 Mustang 189.5. It was 61-in (155-cm) wide (Mustang 74.1) and just 49-in (125-cm) high (Mustang 50). And it weighed 2,322-lb (1053-kg), 1,000lb (454kg) less than the 1971 Mach 1 Mustang.

Apart from size, what else had changed? The three body choices were still there, hardtop, convertible and SportsRoof, with the same Grande and Mach 1 options for the hardtop and SportsRoof respectively. The Boss 302 and 429, the cars of the Knudsen

era, were dropped, to be replaced by a 351. This Cleveland motor was actually a derivative of the 302, but with a longer stroke and aluminium pistons. A big four-barrel carburettor could cope with 750cfm and had twin bore sizes, 1.56-in (4-cm) primaries to ensure good fuel/air mixing at low throttle openings, with 1.96-in (5-cm) secondaries for full-blooded wheelspin starts.

The 351 turned out to be a good performer, far more powerful than the Boss 302, with 330hp at 5,400rpm, plus 370lb ft at 4,000rpm. That was enough for a standing quarter of 13.8 seconds at 104mph (167km/h), according to *Motor Trend*. It came at a cost of 9.2mpg (3.24km/litre), but in 1971 one couldn't have everything. The testers also liked the handling, apart from some wheel hop when accelerating out of corners, as the latest Boss had the optional harder suspension as standard. What they didn't like was the Hurst shifter ('darn near impossible to downshift at any speed') and the wheel hop. Moreover, despite the 1971 Mustang's extra length, it was still lacking space for rear-seat passengers, which was partly due to the SportsRoof, raked at just 14 degrees from horizontal.

As before, the Mach 1 constituted a less committed, more comfortable alternative to the Boss Mustang, and was loaded with visual sports-car cues. There was a colour-keyed front spoiler/fender, dual racing mirrors (also in body colour), sport lamp grille, competition suspension, wheel trims, quick-release gas cap, E70-14 whitewall tyres, plus various stripes and scoops; but it lacked the Boss's lower rear axle with

Traction-Lok, low-profile tyres and black hood. Base engine was the 302 V8, but serious performance addicts could order the big-block 429. This came in 370-hp Cobra Jet form (with or without Ram Air, the quoted power was the same) or as a Super Cobra Jet with Dual Ram Air and a claimed 375hp.

Choose the 370-hp 429 with Ram Air, and it was necessary to pay an extra $436 for the privilege, though this 429 brought with it competition suspension, heavy-duty battery and alternator, extra cooling package, dual exhaust, 3.25:1 rear end, bright engine dress-up kit (to impress bystanders at the gas station), hydraulic lifters and four-bolt main caps. If the top-powered Dual Ram motor was specified, one had to have the Drag Pak option and 3.91:1 or 4.11:1 rear axle – good for tyre-smoking starts, but making for a thirsty, noisy, high-revving motor on the freeway. It seemed like serious stuff, but in practice the non-Drag Pak 429 was barely faster than the much cheaper 351. *Sports Car Graphic* tested both, and found the 429 to be only 0.3 seconds quicker to 60mph (97km/h), and just 0.1 faster over the quarter.

So unless nothing but the biggest-engined Mustang would do, a 302 or 351 were far better buys. In any case, this 429 was not the same engine as the Boss 429's semi-hemi racing unit. It was far more mundane, being a destroked version of the 460-ci (7.5-litre) V8 Ford offered in Thunderbirds and Lincolns. Buyers must have had their suspicions, however, because only 1,250 of them paid extra for a 429 in 1971, making up less than 1 per cent of

Mustang sales that year; the 429 option was actually withdrawn before the 1971 model year was out. This was the last big-block Mustang offered by the factory, and there would never be another.

More relevant to most buyers was the base 302-ci (4.9-litre) V8, which even with its two-barrel carburettor still gave a respectable 210hp and 300lb ft. According to *Motor Trend* it was the 'let's go to market' car, suitable for taking the kids to school and economical enough for family motoring. At 17mpg (6km/litre), the base Mustang V8 was laughably inefficient by modern standards, but nearly twice as economical as the Boss 351, let alone the 429. It could also turn in a standing quarter of 17.5 seconds, so it wasn't exactly slow either.

If that was insufficient, $45 bought a detuned, lower-compression two-barrel version of the 351, with 240hp at 4,600rpm, or a 285-hp four-barrel, the latter with a higher 10.7:1 compression. However, there was still a six-cylinder Mustang, though bearing in mind the latest car's Sumo wrestler proportions, the faithful 200-ci six, which had powered Mustangs almost since day one, was dropped. The 250-ci (4-litre) single-barrel six now became the base engine, though with ten horsepower less than the previous year, at 155hp. In fact, buyers had to go out of their way to specify this economy option, as the 302 V8 was now the standard motor.

According to *Motor Trend*, the 302 was the classic Mustang motor in that it was nearer to the original concept of a sporty-looking yet relatively economical car. As already mentioned, the 1971 Mustang, especially in its hotter guises, was the wrong car at the wrong time, none more so than the Boss 351, which had never been intended as a pure road car. Like its 302 and 429 predecessors, its function was simply to qualify the Mustang for Trans Am racing.

Trans Am had been good for Ford. Parnelli Jones won the championship in 1970 with a Boss 302 (albeit just one point ahead of Mark Donahue's Javelin) and *Road & Track* lived up to its name by track-testing team mate George Follmer's Boss. To say that it was impressed by this state-of-the-art 460-hp Trans Am missile would be an understatement. The Follmer Mustang did the standing quarter in 12.9 seconds, reached 60mph (97km/h) in 5.5 seconds and 100 in 11.4. It suffered no brake fade whatsoever and R&T testers were in no doubt that Ford engineers' claim of a 1.1g cornering force was true.

Ford had won the championship with a thoroughly developed, highly-effective racer, and looked like having a worthy successor in the Boss 351. But the climate had changed: for 1971, Ford decided it was no longer good for publicity to spend money on racing, perhaps even counter-productive, with the result that there would be no official Ford Trans Am racers for years. That left the Boss 351 high and dry, and with no Trans Am involvement one is tempted to ask what it was for. In an economy, safety and emissions-conscious 1971, maybe the question could have been asked of the entire Mustang range.

MODEL LINE-UP / PRODUCTION

Model	Production
Hardtop	65,696
Hardtop Grande	17,406
SportsRoof	23,956
SportsRoof Mach 1	36,449
Convertible	6,121
TOTAL	149,628

ENGINE LINE-UP

250 six
Type	Water-cooled cast-iron straight-six, ohv
Bore x stroke	3.68 x 3.91in (93.5 x 99.3mm)
Capacity	250ci (4.0 litres)
Compression ratio	9.0:1
Fuelling	Single-barrel carburettor
Power	145bhp @ 4,000rpm

302 2bbl V8
Type	Water-cooled cast-iron V8, ohv
Bore x stroke	4.00 x 3.00in (102 x 76.2mm)
Capacity	302ci (4.9 litres)
Fuelling	Two-barrel carburettor
Power	210bhp @ 4,800rpm

351 2bbl V8
Type	Water-cooled cast-iron V8, ohv
Bore x stroke	4.00 x 3.50in (102 x 89mm)
Capacity	351ci (5.75 litres)
Compression ratio	9.0:1
Fuelling	Two-barrel carburettor
Power	240bhp @ 4,600rpm

351 4bbl V8
Type	Water-cooled cast-iron V8, ohv
Bore x stroke	4.00 x 3.50in
Capacity	351ci (5.75 litres)
Compression ratio	10.7:1
Fuelling	Four-barrel carburettor
Power	285bhp @ 5,400rpm

351 Boss V8
Type	Water-cooled cast-iron V8, ohv
Bore x stroke	4.00 x 3.50in
Capacity	351ci (5.75 litres)
Compression ratio	11.1:1
Fuelling	Four-barrel carburettor
Power	330bhp @ 5,400rpm

429 Cobra Jet V8
Type	Water-cooled cast-iron V8
Bore x stroke	4.36 x 3.59in (110.7 x 91.2mm)
Capacity	429ci (7.0 litres)
Compression ratio	11.3:1
Fuelling	Four-barrel carburettor
Power	370bhp @ 5,400rpm

429 Super Cobra Jet V8
Type	Water-cooled cast-iron V8
Bore x stroke	4.36 x 3.59in
Capacity	429ci (7.0 litres)
Compression ratio	11.5:1
Fuelling	Four-barrel carburettor
Power	375bhp @ 5,600rpm

1972:
RETREAT, RETREAT

1972 Mustang 351 Ram Air.

If the 1971 Mustang had been a brave attempt to extend the golden age of the muscle car, its 1972 successor brought it down to earth with a bump. Gone was the big-block 429, gone the Boss 351; until a high-performance 351 returned halfway through the model year, the most powerful Mustang offered 200hp, down from 375hp in 1971. Actually, that wasn't quite the disaster it seemed for hot-car aficionados. Part of the drop was due to measurement of horsepower in SAE net figures rather than gross.

So there were fewer Mustang models and fewer engine choices, reduced now to just five; four V8s (of which three were 351s) and the solitary six. This was a far cry from 1970, when buyers had the choice of two six-cylinder engines and no less than

seven V8s! There was a good reason for this retrenchment, however: Mustang sales had been slipping for several years, even though it managed to hang on to its market leadership ahead of the Camaro. Almost 300,000 were sold in 1969, 191,000 in 1970 and less than 150,000 the following year. In 1972 they fell again, to just 125,000 (110,000, according to another source).

It was a low point in Mustang production. Remember those glory days of the mid-1960s when Ford had to turn over a second factory to Mustangs, then a third, just to keep up with demand? Now the reverse was true. In 1971, the San Jose, California, plant built its last Mustang, while the following year Ford's Metuchen factory in New Jersey began to make Pintos instead. For 1972 and '73, Dearborn was the only Ford plant that was building Mustangs.

But it was not only Ford which was suffering – the entire pony-car sector was also on a slide. At its peak, sales of pony cars made up 10 per cent of the entire U.S. market – by 1972, this had slumped to 4.5 per cent. In mid-1972, General Motors actually announced that the Camaro (a good seller in pony-car terms) was to be dropped, as the cost of re-engineering it to meet new fender legislation could not be justified; but General Motors's engineers found a way around the problem and the Camaro was saved in the nick of time.

It is odd that sales of these sporty compacts were not booming in the early 1970s, when customers were demanding smaller, more economical cars. The trouble may have been that the pony cars were no

longer compact, and had become too sporty for their own good. All of them, like the Mustang, had grown bigger and fatter over the years to accommodate bulkier engines and more goodies. True compacts, like Ford's own Pinto, represented the real growth area, and the company was busy designing an all-new Mustang to accommodate this brave new world.

In the meantime, the old heavyweight was forced to soldier on, and the Mustang saw very few changes for 1972. The three body styles remained, as did the three transmissions, still 3- and 4-speed manuals, plus an automatic, as had always been the case. There were some changes to certain option packages, such as the Protection Package and the exterior Décor Group (now even basic Mustangs could be had with Mach 1 racing mirrors). But more revealing were the new safety and emissions features, reflecting both new legislation and the public's awareness of these issues. Take the front seat belt reminder system. In the event of the front occupants failing to clip on, a warning light would flash onto the instrument panel and a buzzer sound when the car was put into forward or reverse, a sensor on the passenger side having detected that the seat was occupied. All seat belts, front and rear, now had retractors.

As for emissions, the Mustang received an evaporative emissions control system for 1972 to prevent gasoline fumes from escaping from fuel tank or carburettor into the atmosphere. In the fuel tank, this consisted of a liquid/vapour separator, which sent vapour through to a carbon canister in

the engine bay. The canister was able to store vapour while the engine was not running, releasing it into the air cleaner when the engine was started. To clean up the Mustang's act still further, all engine options for 1972 were detuned, with lower compression ratios to allow the use of regular gasoline. That was the other reason for those lower power figures – it wasn't all down to the stricter SAE measurement system. According to these, the 250-ci (4.0-litre) six now offered 98bhp at 3,400rpm, and the 302-ci (4.9-litre) V8 140bhp at 4,000. As for the 351-ci (5.75-litre) V8s, these initially came in 168-bhp two-barrel and 200-bhp four-barrel form.

With so much effort going into cutting emissions, there weren't many man-hours left for major changes to the 1972 Mustang, although the car had had a major restyle the previous year. It could be made to look different, however, if one opted for the Sprint Décor package, basically a patriotic red, white and blue colour scheme available on SportsRoofs and hardtops. White racing mirrors were part of the package, along with colour-keyed seats and carpets, hubcaps and trim rings. F60-15 tyres, competition suspension and mag wheels came with an alternative Sprint Décor.

But it wasn't all stripes and whitewalls. In early 1972, though close to halfway through the model year, Ford belatedly reintroduced a performance Mustang. The 351 HO was really last year's Boss, but with drastic engine changes to get it through the emissions laws. Compression dropped from 11.2:1 (Boss) to 8.8:1 (HO). Milder cam

to cover the standing quarter-mile than the Boss (15.1 seconds) and 5mph (8km/h) slower. It could reach 60mph (97km/h) in 6.6 seconds and 100 in 16.4. That still didn't make the HO slow, and in practice it felt, sounded and drove like any other hot Mustang.

Tick the HO option box, and one also got wide tyres (F60-15s) on 7-inch (18-cm) wheels, competition suspension, disc brakes, plus heavy-duty battery and radiator. What one didn't get was the look-at-me stripes of a Boss or Mach 1; Ford's marketeers seem to have realized that it was no longer cool to shout 'performance' on the street. So clean was the HO (by 1972 standards) that it could even be sold in California, something that Chevrolet's muscle-bound 454s were unable to manage. In any case, keen owners could quite easily substitute a wilder camshaft,

OPPOSITE and THIS PAGE
1972 Mustang Boss 351 Ram Air.

timing reduced unburnt fuel ('the engine's bad breath', as a journalist described it) from finding its way out of the pipe. The carburettor and spark advance curve were also changed, though the Cleveland heads retained their big ports and valves, and the motor even kept its strong forged pistons and special alloy rod bolts – shades of this 351's origins as a Trans Am motor. The big-capacity exhaust survived the changes too, as did the lightweight aluminium intake manifold.

The end result was 275bhp at 6,000rpm, not such a drastic fall from the 1971 Boss's 330hp, especially given the SAE measurement. Still, less power there certainly was, with the 351 HO taking a second longer

increase the compression and even add a high-capacity inlet manifold and carburettor. The result? A 1972 Boss Mustang.

Even though it was no longer cool to look hot, the showy Mach 1 remained the best-selling Mustang model, with over 27,000 sold in 1972. The runner-up slot was occupied by the ever-popular Grande hardtop, just over 18,000 of which found homes that year. The concept of a luxury Mustang had succeeded, appealing to many buyers for whom a Mach 1 was too loud and the base Mustang too austere. An interesting perspective on the Grande came when Britain's *Autocar* magazine tested one in late 1972. American cars sold in Britain only in tiny numbers, being too big, too thirsty and too flashy for most British drivers, but one could order a Mustang hardtop, SportsRoof or convertible, Mach 1 or Grande through Ford Personal Import Export Limited of Regent Street, London.

To suit European tastes, even the luxury Grande was equipped with E70 tyres, competition suspension and front disc brakes; consequently *Autocar* praised the handling but found the ride a little firm. It was also thought that there was insufficient space in the back, even in this biggest Mustang of all (compared with most European cars, the Mustang was remarkably space-inefficient). The testers seemed mildly surprised by the Mustang's good points, and certainly approved of its understated appeal: 'There will always be a demand from those who like the impressiveness of a Detroit product. This the Mustang provides without stooping to the vulgarity of some of its predecessors.'

MODEL LINE-UP	PRODUCTION
Hardtop	57,350
Hardtop Grande	18,045
SportsRoof	15,622
SportsRoof Mach 1	27,675
Convertible	6,401
TOTAL	125,093

ENGINE LINE-UP
250 six

Type	Water-cooled cast-iron straight-six, ohv
Bore x stroke	3.68 x 3.91in (93.5 x 99.3mm)
Capacity	250ci (4.0 litres)
Compression ratio	8.0:1
Fuelling	Single-barrel carburettor
Power	98bhp @ 3,400rpm

302 2bbl V8

Type	Water-cooled cast-iron V8, ohv
Bore x stroke	4.00 x 3.00in (102 x 76.2mm)
Capacity	302ci (4.9 litres)
Compression ratio	8.5:1
Fuelling	Two-barrel carburettor
Power	140bhp @ 4,000rpm

351 2bbl V8

Type	Water-cooled cast-iron V8, ohv
Bore x stroke	4.00 x 3.50in (102 x 89mm)
Capacity	351ci (5.75 litres)

Compression ratio	8.6:1
Fuelling	Two-barrel carburettor
Power	168bhp

351 4bbl Cobra Jet V8

Type	Water-cooled cast-iron V8, ohv
Bore x stroke	4.00 x 3.50in
Capacity	351ci (5.75 litres)
Compression ratio	8.6:1
Fuelling	Four-barrel carburettor
Power	200bhp

351 HO V8

Type	Water-cooled cast-iron V8, ohv
Bore x stroke	4.00 x 3.50in
Capacity	351ci (5.75 litres)
Compression ratio	8.6:1
Fuelling	Four-barrel carburettor
Power	275bhp

OPPOSITE
The 1972 Mustang Boss 351 Ram Air 'fastback' had almost become 'flatback'.

1973:
THE END OF AN ERA

BELOW and OPPOSITE
1973 Mustang Mach 1.

Everyone knew the big, traditional Mustang was living on borrowed time. It was an open secret that Ford was developing a new, radically-downsized Mustang for 1974, though it was still thought that the new pony car would stay big and feature a new body on the existing Torino chassis and running gear.

Whatever the case, the long-nosed pony car was in its final year; in the final test of a 351 Mach 1, *Road Test* magazine went overboard on the pony analogy: 'Corralled by squatters on its own range and saddled by too much weight, the Mustang as we know it will disappear, and a final round-up shows why.' This was interesting. The motoring press didn't seem too sorry to see the back of the old Mustang, but today, it's often regarded as a sad day. As John F. Katz wrote in *Road & Track* in 1988: 'The Mustang we thought we had loved was gone, martyred by the environmentalists, the insurance companies, the OPEC cartel.'

But in 1973 there was no such misplaced nostalgia. 'It is a good thing to get back to basics,' wrote Chuck Koch of the forthcoming smaller, simpler Mustang, 'and

BELOW and OPPOSITE
1973 Mustang Mach 1.

Ford and the Mustang will be doing just that.' The media seemed to agree with Lee Iacocca that the 1970s Mustang had strayed too far from its original concept.

For 1973, however, it grew even more. A bigger impact-resistant front fender was needed to meet new federal safety legislation. Made of polyurethane, it was based on a steel backing with supplementary rubber shock absorbers for extra protection. The idea was

that it would return to its original shape following low-speed impacts, and Ford claimed that the plastic facing was cheaper to repair than rebending and rechroming a traditional fender. It added an extra 4in (10cm) to the Mustang's length (now almost 194in/493cm from nose to stern), though in colour-keyed form it didn't actually seem too intrusive. Compare the 1973 Mustang to little MGs of the same period, dwarfed by their

big black body protectors, and see how unattractive federal fenders could be. The Mustang's rear fender wasn't quite as elaborate, the old steel one being mounted on a collapsible aluminium carrier that gave extra protection to the bodywork, but which wouldn't rebound upon impact. What with other changes, the final big Mustang weighed up to 900-lb (408-kg) more than its 1964 ancestor.

One of the selling points of that original had been that it was quite easy to drive and manoeuvre, despite its sporty styling, just one of the features that made it generally popular and not only to the youth market, being flashy but unintimidating. But the 1973 version was big enough to deter nervous drivers, which was especially true of the SportsRoof, the near-horizontal fastback intended to evoke images of NASCAR racers and Ford's Le Mans winner. This it did, but the 14-degree rear slope effectively reduced the big rear window to a tiny arrow-slit, creating blind spots behind the small side windows and making entering a freeway or backing into a parking space a nerve-wracking experience; maybe those impact-absorbing fenders weren't such a bad idea after all. Another factor was that in all Mustangs the hood stretched forwards and sideways into invisibility, making parking even more of a challenge. To add insult to injury, it was necessary to pay extra for a passenger side-door mirror. It would seem, therefore, that some of the original Mustang's key attractions – its compact dimensions and ease of use – were gone.

However, the last big Mustang did have

an advantage in that it was still possible to buy it as a convertible. These were becoming rare beasts, and in fact the open-top Mustang was now the only Ford convertible available. Convertible sales in general had been falling, perhaps because of safety concerns, and Ford sold only 6,401 open Mustangs in 1972, when in 1965 more than ten times

that number had left the showrooms.

In Detroit's world of mass-production, figures like these were not economically viable, and early in the year Ford announced that the final Mustang convertible would be built in 1973. It seemed likely that it would survive only until existing stocks and contracts for soft tops and linkages ran out.

Ironically, this public announcement stimulated a rush of orders as buyers flocked to Ford showrooms for what they believed would be the last Mustang convertible (perhaps even the last Ford convertible) of all time; more than 11,000 were sold in that final year. But it was not the last, and the Mustang convertible was to return with a

vengeance, though not for another ten years. But in the gloomy climate of 1973, no one could have predicted that 30 years later it would again be possible to choose between a Mustang coupé and a convertible.

The Mustang's engine options were similar to those of 1972, except that the 351 options were rejigged to just two. The HO, which had arrived late the previous year and which had seemed like a beacon of light to performance freaks, was dropped. Basic Mustangs were still powered by the 250-ci/4.0-litre six (98bhp) or 302-ci (4.9-litre) two-barrel V8 (140bhp), while the 351-ci (5.75-litre) choices now consisted of a 177-bhp two-barrel and 248-bhp Cobra Jet four-barrel. Both 351s included front disc brakes as part of the package, though it was possible to pay extra for these on the 250 and 302.

Rear-axle options were cut right back where Mustang buyers had traditionally been offered a plethora of rear-axle ratios for each engine, from ultra-low gearing for the street and drag racers to relaxed high ratios for the freeway cruisers. But now every combination of engine and axle had to pass emissions legislation, which entailed running two of each over 50,000 miles (8050km). This made a choice of half a dozen or more axles prohibitively expensive, so Mustang buyers now had the choice of just two, one of them with mandatory air conditioning.

Not that there was a dearth of options. There were still 49 separate extras, ranging from $6 for door-edge guards to $368 for SelectAire air conditioning. The popular SelectShift Cruise-O-Matic auto transmission came in at $204, and over 90 per cent of

Mustang buyers opted for it. But only 2.9 per cent paid extra for the four-speed manual with Hurst shifter (a three-speed was still standard), leaving no doubt that the Mustang was an American performance car rather than a European sports car. Most customers wanted power steering as well (again, over 90 per cent) and nearly 78 per cent chose power brakes. Again, these convenience features underlined the Mustang's size; customers still wanted a car that was easy to drive, but they now needed power brakes, steering and an auto transmission to achieve it.

So what did all this add up to? What was the final big Mustang like to live with? *Road Test* magazine tried a Mach 1 and quoted the top-powered 351 V8 as producing 266bhp at 5,400rpm and 301lb ft at 3,600rpm. Although derived from last year's HO motor, both power and performance were down, due to emissions equipment and the car's extra weight. *Road Test* was quite polite, remarking that there was 'adequate power for most of today's motoring needs … sufficiently fast to provide safe entrance to high-speed freeways'. In other words, the most powerful Mustang money could buy was fast enough to be safe and convenient – just. But it wasn't a muscle car.

Handling, from the independent front suspension and live rear axle, was thought to be 'quite controllable and very docile'; the long-nosed Mustang never did get that independent rear end that Ford had promised at the 1964 launch. The official explanation was that the live axle gave near-identical lap times to the independent prototype. In the

OPPOSITE and LEFT
The Mustang 351 convertible for 1973
was the last year for the big Mustangs.

real world, of course, not many roads are surfaced like race tracks. *Road Test* reported that when pressing on, the Mach 1's understeer would build up until the car was ploughing towards the outside of the corner, at which point even full lock was incapable of getting it pointing in the right direction, which made backing off the only means of escape. Some things, it seemed, had not changed; the Mustang was still sacrificing ultimate handling to a comfortable ride.

It was 'an amiable vehicle on a highway', according to *Road Test*, and it also considered the front disc brakes a great advance on the old drums; as ever, the Cruise-O-Matic transmission got top marks. But despite all that extra length and width, two adults would still find a Mustang too cramped in the back; moreover, the front bucket seats had uncomfortably upright backs to make a little more room. But the magazine's most telling criticism came at the end. At $4,446.86, the Mach 1 was getting on for twice the price of an original basic Mustang, and in this, writer Chuck Koch echoed the words of many others: that the Mustang could no longer claim to be a low-priced car and was no longer true to its original concept. Ford, however, had an answer.

MODEL LINE-UP	PRODUCTION
Hardtop	51,340
Hardtop Grande	25,274
SportsRoof	10,820
SportsRoof Mach 1	35,440
Convertible	11,853
TOTAL	134,817

ABOVE, LEFT and OPPOSITE
1973 Mustang 351 convertible.

ENGINE LINE-UP

250 six

Type	Water-cooled cast-iron straight-six, ohv
Bore x stroke	3.68 x 3.91in (93.5 x 99.3mm)
Capacity	250ci (4.0 litres)
Compression ratio	8.0:1
Fuelling	Single-barrel carburettor
Power	98bhp @ 3,400rpm

302 2bbl V8

Type	Water-cooled cast-iron V8, ohv
Bore x stroke	4.00 x 3.00in (102 x 76.2mm)
Capacity	302ci (4.9 litres)
Compression ratio	8.5:1
Fuelling	Two-barrel carburettor
Power	140bhp @ 4,000rpm

351 2bbl V8

Type	Water-cooled cast-iron V8, ohv
Bore x stroke	4.00 x 3.50in (102 x 89mm)
Capacity	351ci (5.75 litres)
Compression ratio	8.6:1
Fuelling	Two-barrel carburettor
Power	177bhp @ 3,800rpm

351 4bbl Cobra Jet V8

Type	Water-cooled cast-iron V8, ohv
Bore x stroke	4.00 x 3.50in
Capacity	351ci (5.75 litres)
Compression ratio	8.6:1
Fuelling	Four-barrel carburettor
Power	248bhp @ 5,400rpm

1974:
MUSTANG II – BACK TO BASICS

How they would have laughed back in 1968! Just think of it: a Ford Mustang, a front-running, fire-breathing, tyre-spinning muscle car with just four cylinders, the top motor a mere 172-ci (2.8-litre) V6 (made in Germany, not Detroit!), mustering a whole 105bhp. This new 'Mustang' is smaller, not only than the car it replaces, but also than the 1965 original. Moreover, there is no convertible. Seated at the wheel of his 428-ci (7.0-litre), 335-hp V8 'Stang, the Steve McQueen tough cop character in the famous movie, Frank Bullitt, would have permitted his craggy features to crack into a rare smile at the very thought.

But in 1974, the world had changed from the time when Frank four-wheel-drifted his Mustang through the streets of San Francisco. We have already seen how the Mustang had outgrown its simple origins to become a fat, heavy and fast performance car. That was fine in 1968, but by 1971 it was clearly the wrong sort of car to cope with high insurance and gas prices, safety concerns, emissions legislation and a new breed of Japanese imports that offered sporty motoring and good mileage at a low price. To survive, it was necessary for the Mustang to change.

No one knew this better than Lee Iacocca, the man behind the original Mustang. From the sidelines, he had been appalled to see his baby grow into a 'big fat

pig'. 'Late in 1969 we began planning the Mustang II,' he later wrote in his autobiography, 'a return to the small car that had been so successful. A lot of people in Detroit could hardly believe we were doing this, because it violated an unwritten rule that an established car could only be made bigger – never smaller. To put out a smaller Mustang was tantamount to admitting we had made a mistake. Of course we had.'

When it was launched in the fall of 1973, Mustang II, as it was named, certainly was smaller than its predecessor. It was 17-in (43-cm) shorter, to be precise, and 4-in (10-cm) narrower, and almost a foot had been lopped off the wheelbase. It weighed over 360lb (163kg) less (comparing base models) and there was no V8 option.

But although it marked a massive downsizing from the 1973 Mustang, the new pony car wasn't as radically different as it seemed; in fact, it was returning to its origins, and in more ways than one. For a start, the new car was very similar in size to the first Mustang, just 2-in (5-cm) wider and $4^1/2$-in (11.5-cm) shorter. It weighed nearly 200lb (91kg) more, which could have been due to a higher level of standard equipment, plus the extra safety and emissions gear that a 1974 car was obliged to carry. But the concept was the same: that of a small, relatively simple and sporty-looking car – cheap to buy and

easy to drive. The idea was to make full use of existing components, to keep the cost down, and to concentrate on showroom appeal to attract buyers, while offering a long list of options so that they could personalize it themselves. In short, this was the same sort of good-value 'personal' car that the original Mustang had been, or so Ford hoped.

There was good reason why the new-generation Mustang was so similar in concept to the first: many of the same people, as then, were still involved. With Bunkie Knudsen gone, Lee Iacocca was in charge of the project, remembering that from November 1970 he was president of the entire Ford empire, which made him the ultimate boss apart from Henry Ford II himself. Hal Sperlich was there too, a loyal Iacocca man for a decade, and one who was part of the Fairlane committee that had come up with the original Mustang concept in the early 1960s, while Gene Bordinat, who had overseen the appearance of that first Mustang, was still there to do the same job ten years later.

However, the new Mustang wasn't entirely an in-house effort, not a Dearborn one, anyway. Iacocca knew that time was of the essence and ordered Ford's new subsidiary, the Italian design studio Ghia, to come up with a proposal. 'Hal and I flew over to visit the Ghia studios in Italy,' Iacocca later recalled, 'where we met with Alejandro de

Tomaso, the studio head, Within two months, De Tomaso's prototype arrived in Dearborn, and we had ourselves a terrific design.'

Although Ghia had produced a driveable prototype in double-quick time, that was just the start of the process, and input from Ford's own stylists (Gene Bordinat, Al Mueller, David Ash and Dick Nesbitt) over the following months was to produce the final shape. Significantly, it retained the long hood, short deck shape that had been such a hit in the original Mustang, so there would be at least some family resemblance between the two. A large oval grille was flanked by single round headlamps, and to give the side some attitude there was a body crease below the door handle that gave just a hint of an air intake. This was again reminiscent of the original Mustang, though that had had fake intakes as well.

The question was whether or not to offer more than one body style. Convertibles seemed to be on the way out, both in terms of likely legislation and what people actually wanted to buy. A targa-top show car, the Sportiva II, did do the rounds, but a full convertible never seems to have been on the cards for Mustang II.

But the argument still raged over whether the new car should be a fastback or a notchback. Eventually, the fastback camp won through, when right up to just 16 months before the official launch a three-door hatchback was intended to be the only Mustang II on offer. Then a customer clinic in San Francisco came down firmly in favour of the notchback and Ford made the decision to

LEFT AND BELOW
Mustang Ghia coupé, one of the new downsized Mustangs for 1974.

produce both. It was the right decision, as the new-generation Mustang was a good enough seller to justify two body styles, though in the event the notchback sold better throughout. One theory was that the hatchback Mustang resembled the Pinto a little too much for its own good.

A Modest Start

The compact Ford Falcon formed the basis of the original Mustang, and the compact Pinto did the same for Mustang II; in fact the hatchback's resemblance to Ford's first 1970s compact was undeniable. But although it sold well at first (400,000 in the first year), the Pinto represented a shameful aspect of Ford's long history. The rear-mounted fuel tank was very vulnerable to rear-end collisions and 900 Pinto occupants were killed or seriously injured before the car was finally recalled in 1978.

Thankfully, even though it used many Pinto parts, the Mustang II had no such safety problems. In fact, cynics would say that the one thing the new Mustang could not be accused of was an excess of power. The basic engine, which all Mustang IIs had as standard, unless otherwise specified, was Ford's 140-ci (2.3-litre) four-cylinder unit from its Lima production plant in Ohio. With a single overhead cam, two-barrel carburettor and low 8.4:1 compression ratio, it produced 88bhp at 5,000rpm and 116lb ft of torque. This didn't sound much, but SAE figures actually put the base Mustang close to the 200-ci (3.3-litre) six utilized by its predecessor. The 2.3 was designed to be a no-frills, low-maintenance engine, and all the

necessary emissions equipment was designed in from the start, rather than added on as an afterthought.

If the 2.3 wasn't quick enough, one could pay an extra $299 for a 170-ci (2.8-litre) V6. Supplied by Ford of Germany, it was derived from the European Capri's 2.6-litre unit, though it was substantially new; only the cam, valve-train, con-rods and distributor were carried over. This oversquare engine boosted power to 105bhp and 140lb ft (though *Road & Track* recorded 119bhp and 147lb ft), which didn't seem too bad in a car the weight of the new Mustang; however, the V6 would brings problems of its own, notably the valves, piston rings and cooling system. But should the hottest factory Mustang be required, then this, for the moment, was it. In an uncanny echo of the 1964 original, more power would come later.

Inside, Mustang II was a more luxurious beast than the original. Like the latter, it relied on certain cues to establish its sporty credentials, notably bucket seats, a floor shifter (with four-speed as standard) and a tachometer. But there was also a simulated walnut dash and Euro-style armrests. Ford had gone to great pains to make the new Mustang quiet and comfortable, melting rubber sheets into the floorpan, adding a large, thus quieter, driveshaft and a U-shaped isolation subframe. Front disc brakes were standard, as was solid-state ignition and steel-belted tyres. Front suspension was independent, with a live rear axle on semi-elliptical leaf springs, while steering was rack and pinion, with power assistance an option.

Initially, there were four models, the

basic fastback (called a 2+2 by Ford, courtesy of a folding rear seat) and the basic notchback, this with two seats as standard. It was possible to spend a little more and opt for the Ghia notchback, which Ford hoped would act as a sort of mini-Mercedes SL. To the standard car, this added remote-control door mirrors, a Super Sound package, shag-pile carpeting, extra fake wood on the door trims, a digital clock, choice of seat trim and other baubles, turning it into the luxury Mustang.

The Mach I catered for keen drivers, and was a re-use of a revered Mustang name that must have had traditionalists spluttering into their lite beers. This came only as a 2+2 fastback, with the 170-ci (2.8-litre) V6 as standard, plus remote-control mirrors, wider tyres, various stripes and patches of black paint and styled steel wheels, none of which would have been enough to satisfy sporty types but was at least a start. A Rallye package included limited-slip differential, competition suspension (stiffer springs, beefier anti-roll bars and adjustable shocks), a dual-exhaust system and less functional items such as colour-keyed door mirrors and raised white lettering on the tyres.

None of this came cheap, and despite its new modesty, sensible size and Pinto origins, Mustang II actually cost more than the car it replaced. The basic notchback coupé, weedy four-cylinder engine and all, came in at $3,081, over $300 more than the equivalent 1973 six-cylinder Mustang. The 2+2 fastback demanded a $400 premium, while a Ghia coupé was $3,427 against $2,946 for the 1973 Grande (the previous luxury Mustang). As for the Mach 1, Ford was asking $3,088 for the old V8 in 1973, but over $500 more for the compact new V6.

This, of course, was before paying extra for options. In the Mustang tradition, buyers were offered a whole raft of bits and pieces to 'personalize' their cars. The Rallye pack cost $150 on the Mach 1, but rather more on lesser models, because the V6 was a compulsory part of the package. SelectShift auto transmission cost $212, or if the Ghia's luxury trim was required could be had on any other Mustang for an extra $100. There was a host of other things, everything from pinstripes ($14) to power brakes ($45) to a leather-wrapped steering wheel ($30). There may not have been a convertible Mustang II, but it was still possible to enjoy fresh air from the factory-fitted sunroof ($149). Tick enough boxes, and a Mach 1, optioned to the eyebrows, could cost a cool $4,500. Ford would argue that the higher basic prices merely reflected the new car's superior level of equipment, but it was the important area in which the new Mustang differed from the original – it did not have a low sticker price.

Not that that seemed to bother buyers. In fact, the Mustang II was a huge success, maybe not the phenomenon of 1964, but a success nonetheless. Like the original, its first-year figures were boosted by an 18-month selling season, but at the end of it 385,993 of them found buyers. That was nearly three times as many as the old 1973 Mustang, and not far removed from the glory days of the mid-1960s. Mustang II made up 4.75 per cent of the U.S. auto industry's entire output in 1974, a feat the old car hadn't managed since 1967. It seemed

scarcely believable: Lee Iacocca had broken the Detroit rule by producing a smaller car. Not only was the new Mustang smaller than the first, it also married the hallowed name with a little four-cylinder engine and the American public flocked to buy it.

Ford's advertising described Mustang II as 'the right car at the right time', which is exactly what it was. The 2.3-litre four with manual transmission promised around 23mpg (8km/litre) months after the OPEC oil embargo had begun to bite. Over the previous months, customer clinics had confirmed that U.S. buyers were ready for smaller cars with smaller engines, and the Mustang II gave them what they wanted. Most of them were canny enough to avoid the expensive Ghia and Mach 1, however, and two-thirds of those first-year sales were of the basic fastback and coupé.

In fact, when the press first tested Mustang II in late 1973, it actually seemed to prefer the no-frills four-cylinder model. 'The most welcome discovery of all was the base Mustang,' wrote Jim Brokaw in *Motor Trend*, 'Here lies the real revelation and the answer to the new Mustang's potential success ... The base interior is more than adequate, the dash is the same as the high buck layout, the base suspension gets the job done, and best of all, the 2.3-litre I-4 engine is much stronger than last year's 2.0-litre and considerably quieter. Since you're not looking for power in this car, the little overhead cammer comes on as a surprise … It handles very well, rides better than anything in its class and gives the owner a distinct sense of luxury.' So much so, that

Jim considered the four-pot Mustang 'a bargain and then some'.

Ironically, the V6 Mustangs, which one would have expected to have been less of a culture shock to V8-accustomed America, got a more equivocal reception. In that same article, Jim Brokaw, writing about the V6 Mach 1 and Ghia thought that 'the 2.8-litre V6 simply does not have the hustle to go with the image'. The Mach 1 accelerated from 0–60mph (97km/h) in 14.2 seconds, which hardly matched its sporty accoutrements, while the 1973 Mach 1, even in its final detoxed, detuned form, made that in 8.5 seconds. As for passing times, 40–60mph/64–97km/h (6.2 seconds) and 50–70mph/84–113km/h (8.1) were simply considered slow. To maximize performance, the automatic had its gear change-up points set at a frenetic 5,600rpm to wring every last ounce of go out of that hard-working V6.

Use it that hard, and the V6 auto guzzled fuel at the rate of 16–17mpg (5.6–6 km/litre). It was no way near as thirsty as the old V8, but neither was it the sort of fuel consumption expected of a post-oil crisis car. At steadier speeds, the Mach 1 four-speed manual managed **19**.5mpg (6.9km/litre) and the auto Ghia 20.7mpg (7.3km/litre), which was more like it. These were still not European- or Japanese-style figures, but represented real progress for an American-made car.

There is an interesting comparison to be made between the Ghia V6 (which British magazine *Autocar* tested in early 1974) and the Ford Capri 3000GXL. The latter was basically the European Mustang (see page

Mustangs Compared						
Model	Length	Width	Height	Wheelbase	Base weight	Base price
1964 Mustang	181.6in	68.2in	51in	108in	2449lb	$2368
1973 Mustang	194in	74in	50in	109in	2984lb	$2760
1974 Mustang II	177in	70in	52in	98in	2620lb	$3081

282), now very similar in size to Mustang II, but in this case powered by Ford U.K.'s torquey 183-ci (3.0-litre) V6. According to *Autocar* figures, the two 'Mustangs' used almost the same amount of fuel, but the Capri rocketed to 60mph (97km/h) in 8.3 seconds, topping out at 122mph (196km/h) and cost only two-thirds as much. Not surprisingly, Ford did not sell many Mustang IIs in Britain.

Road & Track, of course, that pillar of the American motoring press, would have liked Mustang II to have been more akin to a European Capri. The latest Mustang, they said, was simply too big – 'too heavy, too Detroit'. But even *R&T* admitted that Ford had made it that way for a very good reason: most American customers were ready to buy smaller cars, but not European-style smaller cars. So the Mustang II gave the impression of being bigger than it really was, especially to the driver. Unlike the Pinto, here was a compact car that still felt distinctly American, and judging by the sales figures it was

exactly what many buyers wanted.

Which didn't stop *R&T* from criticizing the V6's performance, noting that 'the Mach 1 owner is going to find himself looking at the tail lights of certain four-cylinder sedans'. Its test car gave only 16.2mpg (5.7km/litre), had little room for rear passengers and there was a lack of rear suspension travel; however, it found the handling reasonably good as long as extra was paid for the competition suspension and the adjustable shocks were turned up hard. And overall? 'It's solid, well-built, quiet and plush ... as for us, we prefer the Capri.'

PRODUCTION

Coupé	177,671
Fastback 2+2	74,799
Ghia coupé	89,477
Mach 1 fastback	44,046
TOTAL	385,993

ENGINE LINE-UP
2.3-litre four

Type	Water-cooled cast-iron, ohc
Bore x stroke	3.78 x 3.13in (96 x 79.5mm)
Capacity	2.3 litres (140ci)
Compression ratio	8.4:1
Fuelling	Two-barrel carburettor
Power	83bhp @ 5,000rpm
Torque	116lb ft @ 2,600rpm

2.8-litre V6

Type	Water-cooled cast-iron, ohv
Bore x stroke	3.66 x 2.70in (93 x 68.6mm)
Capacity	2.8 litres (171ci)
Fuelling	Two-barrel carburettor
Power	105bhp @ 4,600rpm
Torque	140lb ft @ 3,200rpm

1975:
THE RETURN OF THE V8

It had to happen. Lee Iacocca's brand-new Mustang, downsized and sensible with its economical four-cylinder engine, was the right car at the right time, according to the advertisements. But for the American market, a Mustang without a V8 seemed strangely incomplete, so only a year after the launch, one appeared.

In fact, it happened so quickly that it is tempting to speculate that it had been planned all along. While the climate wasn't right for a V8 pony car in 1974, having one ready for 1975 did make sense. By then, all talk of the OPEC oil crisis would have settled down (or so optimistic Ford planners may have hoped), and a new engine would be just the thing to rekindle interest in what would then be last year's model. Certainly no major surgery was involved in squeezing the 302-ci (4.9-litre) V8 under the Mustang II's hood; all that was needed was a new cross-member, the movement of a few items further forward, and that was it, nothing like the major rebuild needed to shoehorn a big-block V8 into the 1967 Mustang.

But this may be conjecture: the advent of the V8 Mustang may simply have been a natural reaction to customer demand, a realization that the standard V6 wasn't fast enough, together with the knowledge that General Motors had a Chevy Vega V8 on the way. (The Vega of course was Chevrolet's

Pinto, and its Mustang turned out to be the classy, fastback Monza.)

Whatever the truth, there's no doubt that ways were being sought to hop-up the Mustang II. In early 1974, John Christy of

Motor Trend wrote a piece about tuning the 2.8-litre V6, with a lead-in picture of a Mustang II blasting impressively away from the line in clouds of tyre smoke. Actually, there were no performance figures, but the

1975 Mustang Cobra.

tuned 2.8 was put on a rolling road and was found to make significantly more power than the standard motor right through the range. The advantage (at the rear wheels) was 5bhp at 2,000rpm and a whopping 14bhp at 4,500. Out on the road, the hot V6 felt more responsive, needed full throttle less often and even used slightly less fuel than the standard car. And all *Motor Trend* had done was to replace the secondary spring in the distributor, fit cooler running plugs and rejet the carburettor.

But for most customers, a tuned V6 was no substitute for the real thing – a V8. The odd thing was that while all this was going on, Ford was making and selling factory V8 Mustangs right through 1974. The only snag was that they were being built in Mexico, which was the only place where one could be bought. Not many customers in the States knew about this (which probably suited Ford just fine) until early summer, when *Hot Rod* magazine managed to scoop everyone else by crossing the border and actually driving one.

The official explanation for this premature V8 had much to do with Mexico's local content laws, which ruled that any U.S. car built in Mexico must have 60 per cent Mexican-made parts rather than those taken from an imported kit. From a Mexican point of view, this made a lot of sense – otherwise, foreign car manufacturers were apt to turn their factories into simple screwdriver operations, keeping complex work, skilled jobs (and the real profits) out of Mexico. The upshot was that Ford was making no suitable four-cylinder or V6 south of the border, so the Mexican Mustang had to be sold there

with a locally-made V8 or not at all.

The engine in question was the 302-ci (4.9-litre) V8 used in the Maverick and Comet, with a GPD Ford two-barrel carburettor, 8.2:1 compression ratio and dual/single-exhaust system. It made 205bhp and 295lb ft, which sounds impressive but was a gross figure (without any accessories connected), so could not be compared with the net power figures now used in the U.S.A. A big 11-inch (28-cm) clutch and four-speed manual transmission backed up the V8, plus a high 3.07:1 rear axle. Brakes and tyres were uprated to cope with the extra power.

Hot Rod was given a silver 2+2 fastback to drive and loved it. 'The car is an absolute ball to drive. Just incredible … The radials squealed on takeoff, the engine lagged a bit, then took off to the 5,500rpm redline, where we shifted up.' Some impromptu acceleration, run on an empty road, produced a best of 9.5 seconds 0–62mph (100km/h) and the Mexican speedometer touched 122mph (196km/h) flat out. Despite the extra front-end weight of the V8, writer Jim McCraw thought it handled pretty well too, thanks to stiff suspension and radial tyres. And Mexico? 'Just beautiful people, beautiful places and zesty little cars you can't buy here.'

By then, the fact that Ford was planning a U.S.-built Mustang V8 was common knowledge, with Jim predicting that it would be out in September, as long as it passed the 50,000-mile (80465-km) smog certification. Sure enough, the September issue of *Road & Track* carried driving impressions of just such a car, which it was permitted to try out in Ford's Dearborn proving ground.

But converting the U.S. Mustang to V8 power was rather more involved than the Mexican had been. More attention had to be paid to cooling it, thanks to the emissions equipment, and the Mexican Mustang made no provision for air conditioning, which was a must for comfort-conscious Americans. The radiator was moved forward and the side rails strengthened, while the grille was moved forward as well. To cope with the heavier motor, the suspension was uprated with stronger spindles, lower control arms and compression struts, while the spring rates were increased at both ends. Power brakes and steering were standard, and there were wider tyres (195/70 13 radials) plus harder brake linings.

What it didn't have was a manual transmission, much to the disappointment of enthusiasts, though the reason for this depends on the version one believes. According to *R&T*, Ford had told it that the four-speed wouldn't fit the existing transmission tunnel, and it decided not to spend the extra money and time to make it do so. Mexican Mustangs, apparently, had a different tunnel, so the four-speed slipped straight in. *Motor Trend*, on the other hand (which also claimed the explanation came straight from Ford), said that a manual Mustang V8 would have needed recertification, whereas the auto did not. In either case, Ford assured the journalists that a manual was on the way, so keen types were able to relax and save their pennies for 1976 or maybe '77.

Automatic or not, the V8 proved a sprightly performer. The initial figures from the Dearborn test drives indicated that the 'official' V8 Mustang wasn't quite as quick as the Mexican one, with a 0–60 time of around 10.5 seconds. That was hardly surprising, given the 302's low state of tune (compression was down to 8.0:1, with a two-barrel carburettor) and 122bhp at 4,000rpm. *R&T* couldn't help but compare it to the European-made Capri V6, which weighed 750lb (340kg) less and felt so much sharper than the 1974 Mustang.

Like Jim McGraw in Mexico, the testers found that despite the extra weight of the V8, which gave the Mustang a weight distribution of 60 per cent front/40 per cent rear, the hottest and latest Mustang II handled very well. As well as the stiffer springs and bigger anti-roll bars, the shocks had been revalved to reduce front-end float over dips or during braking. As on other Mustangs, competition suspension was an option (naturally, this was fitted to the press car) and with the adjustable shocks turned to hard there was mild understeer at high speed, with enough power to bring the tail out. The steering had been improved too, with more feel (something of benefit to all Mustangs). But the magazine had to conclude that even in V8 form the Mustang II was no performance machine; it was still a mild-mannered Clark Kent to the old-school Superman muscle cars, 'a good highway car – quiet, nice ride, comfortable – but one that is also fun to drive'. Mustangs without the benefit of the competition suspension were a different matter, however. Another journalist at the Dearborn test noted that 'a stock V6 or V8 without a suspension package leans considerably'.

Autocar tested a Ghia V8 in early 1975. Scrub the competition suspension and swap a sunny, dry Dearborn for rainy London streets and the Mustang was 'a real handful, especially for inexperienced drivers', as wheelspin resulted from 'very slight provocation'. The front suspension was considered too soft and under-damped for British tastes, with the car a 'determined understeerer'. Like everyone else, it praised the Mustang's comfort, quietness and level of equipment. It was, said *Autocar*, a good freeway car.

But while the eyes of the world were on the new V8, what of the other Mustangs? To make space for the new flagship, the 2.8 V6 was detuned slightly to give 98bhp at 4,400rpm, though it now came in manual form only. The 2.3 I-4 could be manual or auto while the V8 was auto only. A new option was the Ghia Silver Luxury group, a cosmetic package that brought silver metallic paint, silver half-vinyl roof, a hood ornament, and Cranberry interior with matching headlining, centre console and sun visors, which added $151 to the overall bill. As for the four, this too suffered a power loss (now 83bhp), but economy-conscious customers could opt for an MPG package, which added a high 3.18:1 rear axle. This depressed the 2.3's performance even more but promised over 30mpg (10.6km/litre).

As for sales, Ford sold 188,575 Mustang IIs in the 1975 model year, which seemed like a big drop over 1974 but was over 12 months instead of 18. In any case, the little Mustang II was selling better than the old Mustang had for years.

PRODUCTION

Coupé	85,155
Fastback 2+2	30,038
Ghia coupé	52,320
Mach 1 fastback	21,062
TOTAL	188,575

ENGINE LINE-UP
2.3-litre four

Type	Water-cooled cast-iron, ohc
Bore x stroke	3.78 x 3.13in (96 x 79.5mm)
Capacity	140ci (2.3 litres)
Compression ratio	8.4:1
Fuelling	Two-barrel carburettor
Power	83bhp

2.8-litre V6

Type	Water-cooled cast-iron, ohv
Bore x stroke	3.66 x 2.70in (93 x 68.6mm)
Capacity	171ci (2.8 litres)
Fuelling	Two-barrel carburettor
Power	97bhp @ 4,400rpm

302 V8

Type	Water-cooled cast-iron, ohv
Bore x stroke	4.00 x 3.00in (102 x 76.2mm)
Capacity	5.0 litres (302ci)
Compression ratio	8.0:1
Fuelling	Two-barrel carburettor
Power	122bhp @ 4,000rpm

1976:
LOOK AT ME!

It was a marketing man's dream. Ten years on from the Shelby GT350 came a new performance Mustang to inherit the legend: the same racing stripes, the same macho muscle looks and head-turning presence. Except that the Cobra II wasn't that at all. It was a sham, a sheep in wolf's clothing, seeking to bask in the Shelby's reflected glory. It may have looked the part, but beneath the hood the hottest engine option was the mild-mannered 302 V8 – as long as one paid extra – otherwise, the Cobra II's standard power unit was none other than the super-sensible 2.3-litre four with just 92bhp.

It is hardly surprising that there were sceptics. Some reviled the Cobra II as a fake of the worst kind, an insult to the memory of a real muscle car. Others thought it a bad joke, while author John Gunnell (*Standard Guide to American Muscle Cars*) considered that it 'probably did more to anger purists than attract serious performance buyers'. Inevitably, there were comparisons with the original Shelby, which found the Cobra II slower, more convenient and more comfortable.

But the critics didn't matter as far as Ford was concerned, because the Cobra II was a huge success. In an uncanny echo of the Shelby situation, the Cobra started out as an aftermarket special, with Jim Wangers, a key figure behind the original Pontiac GTO, making the conversion at his little

Motortown factory close to Dearborn. Ford sent him standard Mustang IIs – Jim converted them into Cobras.

Ford calculated that it would sell maybe 5,000 Cobra IIs in the 1976 model year. The Cobra's purpose hadn't been to add a chunk to Mustang sales, but to act as an image builder, to attract people into Ford showrooms where they would probably end up buying a standard Mustang or maybe even another kind of Ford; the Shelby had performed the same trick. However, by August 1976 the Cobra option was heading for year-end sales of 20,000. In the event, 35,000 Mustang buyers paid extra for the Cobra II, which far outsold the standard Mach I, which made less than 10,000 that year. Ford brought the Cobra II in-house, making it a factory-fitted option for 1977.

So what had been the cause of all this excitement? The Cobra II was a purely cosmetic package, only available on the fastback 2+2. According to the brochure, 'Cobra strikes again … Ford's Mustang II wrapped in an appearance package that does justice to the Cobra name'. For $325, buyers got front and rear fibreglass spoilers, a non-functional hood scoop and plastic louvres over the rearside windows. There were racing mirrors and a brushed aluminium instrument panel, white-letter tyres and styled steel wheels, plus, of course, that flamboyant paint job, either white with twin

blue racing stripes (which echoed the original GT350 exactly) or the reverse. Alternatively, there was black with gold stripes, the inspiration in this case coming from the black and gold Shelbys that were sold to Hertz as hire cars for weekend boy racers to try out.

As if that were not enough, there were big, flashy 'Cobra II' graphics on the lower side panels. The inference was clear: with the new Cobra, Ford was saying, 'this is our heritage, this is where this car is coming from'. If the message still didn't sink in, Carroll Shelby himself appeared in the brochure to give the car a street-credible stamp of approval.

The Cobra II was significant not only for Ford but also for the whole performance car climate in the U.S.A. Two years before, when the Mustang II had been launched, such an extrovert look-at-me hot car would have been unacceptable, however justified its bravado. It had been necessary for the compact Mustang to look calm, sensible and understated, even in Mach 1 form – as Ford itself said, the 'right car for the right time'. But perhaps by now the pendulum was starting to swing back the other way, however infinitesimally. The market may not have been ready for a true fire-breathing Mustang, but maybe it would be receptive to one that looked as if it were, but which still gave sensible mileage. True high

performance wasn't back in fashion yet, though it would be soon.

Since the Cobra II affected the street racer look, *Road Test* magazine borrowed one from Ford, drove it out onto the streets and put it through its paces. Late one night, it actually found an original GT350 to ride alongside, stop, and floor the throttle away from a red light. 'We were stomped. Humiliated … In a one-to-one race with the Real Thing, our resurrected cosmetic pseudo-Shelby is about as good as a '41 Dodge.'

Yet despite the fakery, *Road Test* actually liked it. The Cobra was quiet, comfortable and pleasant to drive. It managed a respectable 18.1mpg (6.4km/litre) and felt 'tight, solid and responsive'. It was no faster than a standard V8 Mustang (though all of these incidentally received a power boost to 139bhp for 1976), with 0–60 achieved in 9.9 seconds and the standing quarter in 17.7, with

a top speed of just over 100mph (161km/h). The louvred rear window restricted visibility when parking and the car understeered like any other Mustang II. But what impressed the *Road Test* team was the effect Cobra II had on passersby. It attracted far more interest than the Ferrari Dino had on test at the same time and received far more admiration from the public at large. Even though the spoilers, stripes and scoops were all for show, they looked real, as if there really was a fire-breathing V8 under the hood. This was the secret of the Cobra II's success.

Another indication of a changing climate was the return of racing as a nationwide spectator sport. Interest in the Trans Am series had previously fizzled out as the manufacturers withdrew and pony cars in general lost their shine. The 2.5 Challenge (for cars under 2.5 litres) was intended to be a successor, but it was dominated by Nissan,

Alfa Romeo and BMW, while the faithful wanted to see American cars racing and winning. Consequently, race organizers responded with the All-American GT category for IMSA races. It was an instant hit, especially when radically-modified Chevrolet Monzas began to do well against the Porsches and BMWs. No Ford enthusiast could allow Chevy to monopolize the limelight, so Charlie Kemp built an equally radical Mustang II racer with a fuel-injected 351-ci (5.75-litre) V8 and barely recognizable profile. Kemp even offered a road-going version with all the serious bodywork and suspension but with a 302 V8. As with the Cobra II, it was the first intimation that performance was on the way back.

But not to get too carried away: for all the success of the Cobra II and the media coverage it attracted, it still made up less than one in five Mustang sales in 1976. Of relevance to more buyers was the MPG package (still a popular option on Mustangs, Pintos and Mavericks) and the Stallion pack that was available on top. This consisted of yet more cosmetics, with black detailing, styled steel wheels and the choice of black, silver and bright-yellow paintwork. In fact, all four-cylinder Mustangs now came with the MPG package, which could be further enhanced by a 2.79:1 rear axle and wide-ratio transmission. So although the Cobra II may have been suggesting that performance was on the horizon, most buyers still had other priorities.

Ford's publicity reflected that, variously describing Mustang II as a 'small, sporty, personal car' or a 'small luxury car' or even 'an economy car'. Whatever its classification, the Mustang's many variations and long list of options reflected what the American industry was attempting to do with smaller U.S.-built autos. It would make smaller, more economical cars but encourage buyers to 'personalize' them with profit-making extras, and leave it to the Japanese to sell stripped-out bargain-basement little cars with low profit margins.

PRODUCTION

Coupé	78,508
Fastback 2+2	62,312
Ghia coupé	37,515
Mach 1 fastback	9,232
TOTAL	187,567

ENGINE LINE-UP

2.3-litre four

Type	Water-cooled cast-iron, ohc
Bore x stroke	3.78 x 3.13in (96 x 79.5mm)
Capacity	140ci (2.3 litres)
Compression ratio	9.0:1
Fuelling	Two-barrel carburettor
Power	92bhp @ 5,000rpm

2.8-litre V6

Type	Water-cooled cast-iron, ohv
Bore x stroke	3.66 x 2.70in (93 x 68.6mm)
Capacity	171ci (2.8 litres)
Compression ratio	8.7:1
Fuelling	Two-barrel carburettor
Power	103bhp @ 4,400rpm

302 V8

Type	Water-cooled cast-iron, ohv
Bore x stroke	4.00 x 3.00in (102 x 76.2mm)
Capacity	302ci (5.0 litres)
Compression ratio	8.0:1
Fuelling	Two-barrel carburettor
Power	139bhp @ 3,600rpm

RIGHT
1977 Mustang Ghia coupé.

1977:
PERFORMANCE EXPERIMENTS

The convertible is dead, long live the T-top! That was what the future looked like in 1977, when it seemed as though the full convertible really had died a death under the threat of new safety legislation. British manufacturer Triumph, which had sold thousands of ragtop sports cars to Americans (the TR series) certainly thought that, and its new TR7 consequently came as hardtop only. Ford evidently agreed, and never produced a convertible Mustang II.

In any case, convertibles had been falling out of public favour in the early 1970s and had dropped right off in the last couple of years, due to a combination of fears for safety, vandalism and the need for security which resulted in increased insurance.

But a T-top was a different matter. Pioneered by the Corvette and Porsche's Targa, it offered most of the fresh air of a convertible with at least some of the roll-over protection. This was applied to the Mustang, and the T-top was announced as a new option for 1977 on the Mach 1, Cobra II or 2+2 fastbacks. It was never available on the notchback, but buyers could opt for the less elaborate flip-up sunroof ($147) or a wind-back sunroof ($243). The T-top added over $600 to the price of a Mach 1, reflecting its closer approximation to the feeling of hair blowing in the wind.

As fitted to the Mustang, the T-top was

actually supplied by the American Sunroof Corporation, and consisted of two large tinted-glass roof panels which could be unclipped altogether (via a single clip on each side) and stowed in a special pouch in the luggage compartment. With the glass roof in the back and door windows wound right down, one almost got the feeling that the T-top was a proper convertible, while on cold days it was possible to drive with the roof off

and windows up, warm as toast but with little buffeting from the wind.

When in place, the tinted glass offered protection from the sun but was still transparent enough to watch overhead clouds drift past. One reason why the T-top cost so much more than a simple sunroof was the extra rigidity that had to be built into the car, most of the roof's strength having been sacrificed in the process. Consequently, the

If the Mustang's trunk wasn't large enough, an official baggage rack was available to boost capacity.

floor was beefed up, as was what remained of the steel roof itself.

Motor Trend borrowed a T-top Cobra II in early 1977 and came away impressed. The now-familiar 302 V8 and four-speed manual gearbox (Ford had brought in the four-speed/V8 combination in 1976 as promised) was found to give acceptable performance for its day, though was still slow compared with any of the original muscle cars. The 302 had been given a little extra low-end torque, thanks to smaller intake passages, though *MT* quoted power as 129bhp, 10 horsepower less than other sources. Still, in its new manual guise, the V8 Mustang could be relatively economical, the magazine recording just over 20mpg (7km/litre) on its standard test loop. But despite the great attention received by the V8, it still made up only one in four of Mustang sales, underlining the fact that most Mustang II owners were more concerned with economy than performance. The previous year, only 17.6 per cent of them had paid extra for the V8.

As ever, the test car came with the Rallye suspension package, which somehow combined a slightly stiff ride with basic understeer characteristics. However, all road tests of the time were unanimous in their praise of the Mustang's rack and pinion steering, which even in power-assisted form gave good road feel. As for the Cobra II, its option price had ballooned to $535 (up $220), even though the whole package was now fitted on the production line. Ford's economies of scale, and abandonment of Jim Wanger as the middle man, should surely have effected a price cut! But loaded with options, the Cobra

II test car now cost $6,513, which at the time was quite a large price to pay.

There were other new options for 1977 besides the T-top. The Ghia Sports group sounded promising to those wishing to combine performance with luxury in the Mustang's compact package, but it was really just another cosmetic job. For $422, it bought black or tan paintwork with a black Odense or chamois Lugano vinyl roof, body side mouldings, blacked-out grille, baggage rack, cast-aluminium wheels, centre console, leather-bound steering wheel and various colour-keyed bits and pieces.

Later in the year came the Rallye Appearance Package, which replaced the Stallion option. This offered a shortlist of functional items (racing mirrors, heavy-duty springs and cooling, adjustable shocks and rear anti-roll bar) and a long list of non-functional ones (gold stripes and highlights; black wipers, door handles, lock cylinders and antennae; black spoiler (a no-cost option), with Black and Polar White the body colour choices). Inside, the vinyl seats came in black or white with gold trim. Once again, appearance was taking precedence over performance. But there was no need to look far to see more evidence that performance was starting to make a tentative comeback among the enthusiasts. In April 1977, *Hot Rod* ran a feature on Ruggirello's very special, one-off Mustang. He had gone to Gapp & Roush, the famed Ford performance tuner, and had simply asked them to build him the ultimate street-legal Mustang II. The result was powered by a 1973 Super Cobra Jet V8, bored and stroked right up to 505ci (8.2 litres),

with 12:1 compression, big valves, special cam, lifters and con-rods, plus a suitably deep-throated 850-cfm Holley four-barrel carburettor.

At first glance, the Ruggirello Mustang appeared almost standard, but underneath the bodywork lurked Lakewood spring-bar rear suspension, adjustable shocks, a narrower front tread and massive rear slicks. *Hot Rod* did a rough and ready quarter-mile, judging it ran about 10 seconds at 140mph (225km/h).

Of course, the Ruggirello Mustang was a one-off, a $13,000 special that no one but the extremely well-heeled had a hope of owning. *Hot Rod* had other ideas concerning the Monroe Handler, a special Mustang II that the magazine had built over the summer of 1977. It was certainly radical, and would be expensive, but the idea was to build a street-legal Mustang that would give muscle-car performance but wouldn't be too difficult for the average enthusiast with a healthy bank balance to replicate.

It came in three parts. Creative Car Craft first transformed the fastback's appearance with a specially-made body kit. Fenders were removed and big spoilers added, both blending in with wheel-arch extensions, while 300 man-hours of work went into building the seven hand-made metal panels. With suitable paint and graphics, the fastback's appearance was transformed. *Hot Rod* intended the project car to mimic the look of a genuine IMSA race car, so it had to be radically lowered as well. Suspension expert, Trevor Harris, fitted low-profile Goodrich tyres (on 8-inch front and 9-inch/23-cm rear disc wheels) and custom-wound front coil springs (these alone knocked 2.5in (6.4cm) off the front ride height). At the rear, new spring shackles reduced the height by 1.5 inches, while Harris also fitted a bigger front anti-roll bar. Finally, Monroe shocks were bolted in.

At this point, the Monroe Handler still had the standard 139-bhp 302 V8 and four-speed gearbox, so it was off to Jack Roush for more radical work; this time, just about the only standard piece remaining was the 302 cylinder block. This was blueprinted and the engine bored/stroked out to a full 363ci (5.9 litres), using a modified 351 crank. Many other parts came off the shelf, underlining the principle that anyone with a Mustang II and enough cash at their disposal could do the same. With a special cam, valve train and induction, the 363 special was aiming for 400bhp at 6,500rpm and 400lb ft at 4,800. It remained to be seen how Ford's standard manual gearbox would react to all this activity.

So while Ford remained largely faithful to Mustang II's original concept as a compact personal car of limited performance, others did not; it would have been interesting to know what Lee Iacocca thought of the Monroe Handler.

PRODUCTION

Coupé	67,783
Fastback 2+2	49,161
Ghia coupé	29,510
Mach 1 fastback	6,719
TOTAL	153,173

ENGINE LINE-UP

2.3-litre four

Type	Water-cooled cast-iron, ohc
Bore x stroke	3.78 x 3.13in (96 x 79.5mm)
Capacity	140ci (2.3 litres)
Compression ratio	9.0:1
Fuelling	Two-barrel carburettor
Power	89bhp @ 4,800rpm

2.8-litre V6

Type	Water-cooled cast-iron, ohv
Bore x stroke	3.66 x 2.70in (93 x 68.6mm)
Capacity	171ci (2.8 litres)
Compression ratio	8.7:1
Fuelling	Two-barrel carburettor
Power	93bhp @ 4,200rpm

302 V8

Type	Water-cooled cast-iron, ohv
Bore x stroke	4.00 x 3.00in (102 x 76.2mm)
Capacity	302ci (5.0 litres)
Compression ratio	8.0:1
Fuelling	Two-barrel carburettor
Power	139bhp @ 3,600rpm

The 1977 Mustang Cobra in born-again Shelby colours.

1978:
GOING OUT WITH A BANG

Lee Iacocca was sacked from Ford in 1978 but was able to look back on the Mustang II as one of his better ideas. It had never achieved the massive sales of the original mid-1960s Mustangs, but had still been hugely successful, eclipsing the heavyweight early-1970s car that it had replaced. Through difficult times for the motor industry it had flown the flag for personal, distinctive cars, and had easily outsold all its rivals, consolidating Ford's domination of the pony-car market.

It had shown, too, that the American public wasn't irredeemably addicted to gas-guzzlers; even among Mustang buyers, not many had paid extra for the 302 V8, even though press coverage pushed the V8 Mustang as the desirable option. Instead, in 1978, the Mustang II's final year, over 80 per cent of buyers were still opting for the slow but economical four-cylinder or V6, and the car was selling better than ever. Over 190,000 Mustang IIs were built that year, which was its best 12-month selling season ever. It would have been even higher, but an extra 20,000 cars had to be sold off at a discount as 1977 models because they would not have met current emissions legislation. None of these 1977 or '78 models was fast, but they looked as though they were, especially when there was the option of adding sporty or luxury bits and pieces that could transform

them from stripped-out economy boxes.

Once again, however, changes were on the horizon. The Mustang II had been introduced as a back-to-basics antidote to the overkill Mustangs of the early 1970s – simpler, cheaper and less thirsty. But it was also based on early 1970s technology, and the 1980s required new standards. Quite apart from anything else, the CAFE (Corporate Average Fuel Economy) regulations had come into force in 1978, whose aim was to persuade manufacturers to build more fuel-efficient cars by setting a mandatory average fuel consumption each year. Each car range was obliged to conform to this average; if they did not, they could still be sold in the States but would be subject to a gas-guzzler tax. For 1978, the figure was 18mpg (6.3km/litre), which even the subcompact Mustang V8 had a struggle to meet, while the Cobra II averaged 17mpg (6km/litre).

Even though the end was near for Mustang II, its final year saw a few upgrades to keep it selling. Loudest and most noticeable was the King Cobra. Even more extrovert than the Cobra II, this 'Boss of the Mustang stable' (Ford's own words) came with a massive front spoiler (just 8in/20cm off the tarmac) and a smaller one to the rear. Most noticeable was the giant snake decal on the hood, covering the whole panel and echoing Pontiac's Trans Am, which had a

similar hood-dominating design. This was set off by aluminium wheels with lacy spokes in the body colour, which was bright red. The side-panel treatment was actually quite restrained, with none of the look-at-me graphics that gave the Cobra II such impact. Instead, there was some subtle pinstriping and lettering, rear quarter flares, and colour-keyed racing mirrors. Up front, the grille was blacked out (very fashionable at the time) and both bumpers were in the body colour.

Unlike the Cobra II, the King came as a 302 V8 only (highlighted by '5.0' badges on the hood scoop), so one couldn't do as some Cobra II buyers had done and order it with the mild 2.3-four or 2.8-V6 motor to make it a sheep in wolf's clothing. A four-speed manual gearbox and competition suspension was also part of the package, as were power brakes and power steering, underlining the fact that Ford was keen to promote the King Cobra as a genuine sporty small car rather than a cosmetic pretender.

This is the reason why the King Cobra package (it was an option, not a model in its own right) cost a substantial $1,253 on top of the price of a standard fastback (it wasn't available on the notchback). Meanwhile, the Cobra II option had crept up to $677–$700, depending on the Mustang to which it was applied. But tick the King Cobra option box and other desirables could be added, such as a centre console, leather-bound steering wheel, the expensive T-top, air conditioning, AM/FM stereo, tinted glass, the special light group, and some more interior extras, bringing a brand-new King closer to $7,000, an extraordinary price. Inflation, and Ford's option-heavy strategy, now indicated how far the pony car had strayed from its original value-for-money concept.

So what did the press think of the Mustang II's last hurrah? *Cars* magazine tried one in August 1978 and managed a quarter-mile time of 16.59 seconds at 82mph (132km/h) – one of the best ever for a standard V8 Mustang II. It estimated a 120-mph (193-km/h) top speed and recorded 13.4mpg (4.7km/litre) overall which, with the advent of CAFE, must have been a slight embarrassment for Ford. *Cars* liked the flat, stable handling produced by the firm competition suspension, but not the hard ride that came with it, especially on the pock-marked streets of New York. The car felt as though it was 'literally about to fly apart', wrote Don Chalkin, adding that it 'rides like an old-fashioned sports car', which seemed odd after so many magazines had praised the Mustang II's ride, even with the harder competition suspension. Once again, the lack of rear legroom was criticized (the II really was a 2+2 rather than a proper four-seater), as was the soft power steering. Moreover, Chalkin didn't like the manual gearshift either, so maybe the Mustang II, now in its fifth year on the market, was starting to show its age.

If Ford had been expecting another Cobra II success story with the King Cobra, it didn't get it. Once again, it estimated sales at a conservative 5,000, but in the event failed to sell even that many; in 1978, only 4,318 buyers paid extra for the King option, making it the rarest Mustang II of all. Meanwhile, the original Mach 1 was also languishing, with less than 8,000 finding buyers in its final year. The real Mustang II success story remained the basic fastback 2+2 (over 80,000 sold) and the notchback (nearly 70,000).

To a lesser extent, the Ghia notchback continued the modest success of the original Grande. Nearly 35,000 rolled off the production lines of Ford's Dearborn and San Jose plants in 1978 (the Mustang II had always been built in two factories), confirming that there was a small but steady market for the luxury pony car.

Ford was aiming its new Fashion Accessory Group specifically at these buyers, and at women in particular. A trifling $207 bought a four-way adjustable driver's seat, striped cloth seat inserts, illuminated entry, a driver's vanity visor mirror (also illuminated), a coin tray and door pockets, and there was a choice of nine colours. In fact, the Mustang II buyer was spoilt for choice, with 15 single colours listed (including five metallics) and 13 two-tones, indicating that appearance, marketing and image was what the Mustang II was all about. Genuine aficionados of the muscle car may have been scathing, but the Mustang had simply adapted to difficult times and had survived.

PRODUCTION

Coupé	81,304
Fastback 2+2	68,408
Ghia coupé	34,730
Mach 1 fastback	7,968
TOTAL	192,410

ENGINE LINE-UP
2.3-litre four
Type	Water-cooled cast-iron, ohc
Bore x stroke	3.78 x 3.13in (96 x 79.5mm)
Capacity	140ci (2.3 litres)
Compression ratio	9.0:1
Fuelling	Two-barrel carburettor
Power	88bhp @ 4,800rpm

2.8-litre V6
Type	Water-cooled cast-iron, ohv
Bore x stroke	3.66 x 2.70in (93 x 68.6mm)
Capacity	171ci (2.8 litres)
Compression ratio	8.7:1
Fuelling	Two-barrel carburettor
Power	90bhp @ 4,200rpm

302 V8
Type	Water-cooled cast-iron, ohv
Bore x stroke	4.00 x 3.00in (102 x 76.2mm)
Capacity	302ci (5.0 litres)
Compression ratio	8.4:1
Fuelling	Two-barrel carburettor
Power	139bhp @ 3,600rpm

1979:
FOX – THE 1980s MUSTANG

The 1979 Ford Mustang Cobra. In 1979 the Indy 500 gave pace car status to this classic Mustang, which shared its Fox platform with the Ford Fairmount, Mercury Zephyr and later the Ford Thunderbird and Mercury Cougar.

Nineteen-seventy-nine saw the beginning of a new era for the Mustang. The third-generation pony car was designed to be lightweight, aerodynamic and fuel-efficient. It offered a turbocharged four-cylinder engine to wean customers away from the thirsty V8, and for 1980 even the V8 was downsized in the aftermath of a second oil crisis.

And yet it gave rise to a muscle-car revival. Throughout the 1980s, this Mustang, in 305-ci (5.0-litre) V8 form, once again represented affordable performance, with wheelspin starts on the way to sub-9-second 0–60 times on the way back. It was also the longest-lived Mustang of all: the second-generation Pinto-based Mustang had been in production for just five years, the Falcon-based original for ten, but this latest pony stuck around for a decade and a half. Towards the end, with a no-nonsense pushrod V8 driving through the rear wheels, it came to represent the traditional muscle car, a souvenir of the 1960s as opposed to high-tech competition from Japan, Europe and the domestics.

Ironically, what came to be seen as an all-American traditionalist was actually the most Euro-influenced Mustang of them all, at least at the design stage. Lee Iacocca still had the top executive job at Ford, and the third-generation Mustang would by and large remain faithful to his original pony-car concept of the early 1960s: a relatively simple and affordable sporty small car, with a long list of options to tempt buyers to personalize it with high-profit options. As it happened, Iacocca only just saw the car into production before he was unceremoniously fired by Henry Ford II. Before the official launch, press packs had been sent out which included a picture of Lee standing proudly in front of the 1979 Mustang, the third Mustang he had masterminded for Ford. That same

The 1979 Mustang – a plain, simple, lightweight notchback.

week, he was fired; when the press came to see and drive the car shortly afterwards, it was Bill Bourke rather than Iacocca who made the presentation.

Lee Iacocca, father of three Mustangs, finally left Ford after over 30 years' service. By then, as president of the company, his design role had become more limited, compared with his involvement with the 1964 and '74 Mustangs. European influences were also filtering in under the auspices of project leader Robert B. Alexander, Ford's vice president of the Car Product Development Group, who until recently had done the same job for Ford of Europe and had brought many European engineers with him. Moreover, Jack Telnack (head of the American design department) was another recent transfer from Europe, where he had

been vice president of design. Consequently, it was hardly surprising that it was not a typical American car of the 1970s.

This was just as well. Remember the CAFE regulations that had been introduced the previous year? Even the 1978 target of 18mpg (6.3km/litre) could not be met by the subcompact Mustang V8. This target increased to 19mpg for 1979 and by 1985 was destined to be 27.5mpg (9.7km/litre), an almost unheard-of economy figure for an American-made car. If any manufacturer's car-fleet average missed that target figure (as it surely would in the short term) it was required to pay a penalty – $5 on every car for each 0.1mpg under target. In other words, the third-generation Mustang needed to be far more fuel-efficient than the second.

The CAFE regulations were a serious challenge to American car makers; General Motors, for example, built diesel versions of its existing V6s and V8s to bolster its average fleet mpg. History does not record whether Ford considered a diesel Mustang (highly unlikely), but there was the fear among enthusiasts that the 1979 Mustang would be even less of a performance car than that of 1978; there was even a rumour that the name would be relegated to an option package for a Ford sedan. This wasn't as far-fetched as it seems, and was exactly what Pontiac had done to the hallowed GTO in the 1970s.

In the event, the Mustang II's healthy sales record ensured that neither of these things happened, but the fact remained that a 1980s Mustang could not afford to be in the least bit flabby or inefficient. Consequently, when the 'Fox' project team got together in mid-1975, they kept this goal firmly in mind.

In one way, however, the new Mustang would be the same as the previous two, in that it was derived from a sedan. So where the first Mustang had leant heavily on the Falcon for many of its components and the second was Pinto-based, the third-generation car was based on the Fox platform. This was the codename for Ford's new for 1978 Fairmont (and the similar Mercury Zephyr), a thoroughly modern sedan that had been part-inspired by the German Audi Fox, an economical rear-wheel-drive with coil-spring suspension and a good balance of ride and handling.

For Mustang, the Fox platform was shortened by 5.1in (13cm), and was taken

PAGES 260 and 261
1979 Mustang Indy pace car replica.

from the unit body/chassis just ahead of the rear wheels. No casual observer would have guessed that the Mustang was based on sedan components. The body was all-new, and over 136 hours had been spent in the wind tunnel, making it the most aerodynamic Mustang ever. It had to be, to push up those crucial miles-per-gallon figures. The classic long-hood, short-deck look was still apparent, but was now based on a sharp-edged wedge-shape quite unlike any previous Mustang. The cowl was raised an inch compared with that of the Fairmont to emphasize the wedge as well as to clear the air cleaner, with the slanting grille and hood blending into the sharply-raked windshield.

Quarter-scale models were used in the wind tunnel at the University of Maryland, allowing Ford engineers to cut the drag by 11 per cent. Well-integrated fenders and an angled front cap, as well as the distinctive wedge-shape, all served to allow the new Mustang to cut the air more cleanly. The end result was a drag coefficient of 0.46 for the notchback, 0.44 for the hatchback. These are commonplace figures by 21st-century standards, but were slippery indeed for 1979. Incidentally, just four years later, the new Thunderbird had a coefficient of just 0.35, showing how fast the science of production-car aerodynamics had been advancing.

This was the first step in the efficiency war, the second being weight reduction. Mustang II was lighter than the car it replaced, but only because it was smaller (there seems to have been no serious attempt to cut out excess fat). Half-a-dozen years later, and the weight issue had become

crucial, but weight-saving technology had moved on as well.

So despite being slightly larger than Mustang II (it added 2in/5cm to both length and wheelbase), the new car weighed 200-lb (91-kg) less. Extensive use had been made of advanced plastics, of aluminium and lightweight alloy steel. Glass was thinner yet stronger, saving yet more pounds, and in fact the whole car had a greater glazed area than before, giving it an airier feel and improving visibility. The base Mustang coupé came in at 2,431lb (1103kg), actually less than the 1964 original despite an abundance of extra luxury, safety and emissions equipment.

Under this efficient lightweight shell was coil-spring suspension all round, independent up-front and four-link controlling a live axle at the rear. There was Fairmont-based rack-and-pinion steering and front disc/rear drum brakes. As with previous Mustangs, there were various suspension options to tempt keen drivers: a $33 handling package added stiffer springs and shocks, firmer rubber bushings and a rear anti-roll bar (front and rear bars were standard on all Mustangs except the non-V8 cars). On top of this, one could order the TRX package, which brought distinctive aluminium wheels, metric-sized to suit the low-profile Michelin TRX tyres that came with them, plus its own spring/shock rates and wider anti-roll bars.

So far so good: but if potential buyers were to take a closer look at the engine packages they would have found that most were simply carry-overs from Mustang II. In fact, the 1979 power units were an odd mix of old and new and most of them were old,

if not ancient. The base motor was still the faithful 2.3-litre 'Lima' four-cylinder overhead-cam unit, still in low-tune 88-bhp form but now with slightly less weight to lug around. Next up was the familiar 2.8-litre German V6, with 109bhp, though supply problems led to the motor being dropped late in 1979. To fill the gap between four-cylinder and V8, Ford hauled its venerable 200-ci straight six back into service – the very same unit that had powered base Mustangs back in 1966 was doing the same job a decade-and-a-half later. With just 85bhp at 4,000rpm, it made less power than the little four, but did offer a more relaxed, torquey alternative, especially for traditionalists unable to stomach a mere four cylinders, however efficient they may have been.

The third-generation Mustang may have been facing a brave new world of low weight, high efficiency and unheard of fuel efficiency, but it wasn't a Mustang without a V8. So Ford offered one, albeit precisely the same 302-ci (5.0-litre) unit as was fitted to the Mustang II, now with 140bhp at 3,600rpm. But as far as Ford was concerned, this wasn't the future, more a sop to the diehards for whom nothing less than a V8 would do. Little did the engineers know that, just a few years later, this same V8-powered Fox Mustang would form the basis of a muscle-car revival.

A Turbocharged Future
But in 1979 Ford envisaged that the Mustang's performance future would be provided by something very different: a

turbocharged four. It was basically the familiar 2.3-litre engine, with a Garrett AiResearch TO turbocharger and two-barrel Holley-Weber carburettor. Ford claimed almost identical performance to the V8-equipped car (it was actually quicker from a standing start to 55mph/89km/h) and superior fuel economy. It seemed to bear that out as well, with 131bhp at 5,800rpm. The 2.3-turbo also weighed 70lb (32kg) less than the V8, good news for nose-heavy handling as well as both performance and mpg. Standard transmission was a wide-ratio four-speed manual coupled to a 3.45:1 rear axle.

At first, it looked as though Ford had been right. Sixty thousand turbo Mustangs were sold in the first year, slightly outselling the V8. Sadly, the turbo's durability didn't live up to its performance. The turbocharger itself was prone to oil leakage and there were emissions problems. Ford dropped the option in 1980, though it later returned in 175-bhp form.

This being a Mustang, there was a crowd-pleasing interior as well. All models had full instrumentation, including a tachometer, fuel, oil-pressure, alternator and temperature gauges from the Fairmont. There were bucket seats, simulated woodgrain trim, and carpeted panels on the door trims. New options included cruise control, tilt-steering adjustment and even leather-trimmed seats, not to mention six different sound systems. Rake adjustment was optional for the bucket front seats, and Recaro recliners were available from mid-year.

At first, buyers could choose between base and Ghia trim, both levels being available in both the sharply-notched sedan and the three-door hatchback. Among other things, the Ghia added plenty of colour-keyed parts: dual remote-control mirrors, body side mouldings and quarter louvres, window frames and interior door panels. There were turbine-style wheel covers and BR78 x 14 radial tyres, pinstripes, low-backed bucket seats with Euro-style headrests, not to mention a choice of five interior colours for cloth and six for leather. By 1982, when the Ghia had been dropped, the package included colour-keyed seat belts, map pockets, deep-pile carpeting, courtesy lights, handholds and a vanity mirror. The Ghia had been popular, but as with Mustang II, not half as popular as the base coupé and hatchback.

But there was no Mach 1 Mustang in 1979. Sales of the old Mach 1 had dwindled in the late 1970s, its place taken by a Cobra option package. Unlike the earlier Cobra II, this was no cosmetics-only pack; part of the deal was the 2.3-litre turbocharged four (or optional V8) and the TRX set-up, with those good-looking forged-aluminium wheels, low-profile Michelin tyres and suspension to suit. There was a sports-tuned exhaust and the Cobra's appearance was set off by blacked-out window trim, side stripes, colour-keyed grille, engine-turned instrument panel, 8,000-rpm tachometer and bright tailpipe extension.

It was necessary to pay an extra $78 if loud and proud hood graphics were required. Was the subtle performance car making a comeback? Maybe after the flop of King Cobra the previous year, Ford was having second thoughts about extrovert cars.

Dispense with the graphics, and ticking the Cobra option box cost $1,173 on top of the price of a basic hatchback, though this couldn't be had on a coupé or Ghia.

Throughout the 1960s, what had been guaranteed to give a muscle car instant street credibility was to be chosen as an official pace car for the Indianapolis 500. This was a prize coveted by all U.S. car makers; not only was it an honour to have one's automobile flagging off this historic highlight of American motor racing, it was also great publicity. So Ford must have been delighted when the V8 hatchback was chosen for the 1979 race. Naturally, Ford decided to capitalize on the fact, as rivals had many times before, by building replicas.

Over 10,000 were built between April and July 1979, either V8- or 2.3-turbos. All of them were painted pewter with black trim and orange/red/black striping. 'Official Pace Car 63rd Annual Indianapolis 500' was emblazoned along each flank, in case there was any doubt, alongside a line of galloping ponies. Actually, the words were optional: they were despatched with each car in a cardboard box and could be fitted by the dealer if the customer desired. A full-length power bulge on the hood was another item unique to the pace-car replica.

Otherwise, pace-car buyers received just about every extra that Ford could think of. Of course, to go with the V8- or 2.3-turbo, there was the TRX wheel/tyre/suspension set-up. A deep front spoiler carried two foglights which, like the graphics, were separately supplied for fitting by the dealer to avoid damage during delivery.

Inside, Recaro reclining seats replaced the standard buckets, and there was an engine-turned instrument panel, tinted sun roof, centre console, de-luxe seat belts and Ghia features such as extra soundproofing, deep-pile carpeting and remote-control mirrors. A leather-bound steering wheel, centre console with digital clock, and AM/FM stereo radio with cassette or eight-track tape player completed the interior.

The pace-car replicas were much more than stripped-down performance cars, so it is little wonder that each cost $9,012 (whether one opted for the V8 or turbo), which was before delivery charges or any extra-cost options. Today, they are collector's items. Jackie Stewart drove one of the real pace cars at Indianapolis (of which there were just three) and also appeared in Ford's advertising for the Mustang. But the real pace cars and replicas did the trick, attracting plenty of extra attention to the standard Mustangs. (Ford, of course, knew that they would; the first 1964 Mustang had also been selected as a pace car, and 30 years later the 1994 Mustang would follow suit.)

Mercury, Ford's upmarket luxury marque, had long offered its own versions of the Mustang. The 1960s Cougar had been based on the first Mustang, with plusher trim and different styling, though in the 1970s, Mercury Capris were simply rebadged versions of the imported European-built Capri. For 1979, the Mercury Capri was once again American-made, a tweaked version of the new Mustang. It came in hatchback form only, with a different nose treatment (omitting the Mustang's sloping grille);

ribbed tail lights and different quarter panels were other Capri features. From 1983, the Mercury pony would have its own bubble-style rear screen in place of the Mustang's flat one, plus wraparound tail lights.

In keeping with the Mercury badge, the Capri concentrated on appearance and luxury features rather than the out-and-out sporty options, though the handling package and TRX option were still available. The Black Magic option group brought TRX, plus black or white paintwork with gold striping and detailing, non-functional hood scoop, rear spoiler, lots of blacked-out parts (window frames, door handles and locks), black seats with gold trim and a black brush-finished dash – even the TRX wheels were finished in gold.

Production figures for the Black Magic Capri are hard to come by. It was available in 1981–83, with one source quoting only 469 for the whole of 1983. In fact, Capri sales as a whole were but a fraction of the Mustang's. Mercury sold well over 90,000 of them in the 1979 debut year (a respectable one in five of total Mustang/Capri sales that year). But sales gradually slid downhill through the 1980s, bottoming out at 12,647 in 1986. Mercury dropped the car at the end of that year, but the name returned in 1991 on a rebadged front-wheel-drive two-seater sourced from Australia.

Mercury moved just over 300,000 Capris over a seven-year production run, but to put this into perspective, Ford sold more third-generation Mustangs than that in its first year alone. Like the original Mustang in 1964 and Mustang II ten years later, the

debut year of Mustang III (as logic would have named it but Ford did not) was a runaway success. At the launch, Ford announced a sales target of 330,000, which made up 16.5 per cent of its entire 1979 model-year production. Considering that Mustang II sold less than two-thirds of that figure in a very healthy previous year, this seemed ambitious, that is, until the year-end sales figures came in and Ford reported a total of 369,936. New Mustangs accounted for just over 4 per cent of all new car sales in the U.S.A. (close to the 4.75 per cent record set by the original pony car) and leapt to seventh best-selling car in the country while Mustang II had been languishing down in 22nd spot.

That six-figure total was repeated, the base models proving most popular, with over 150,000 coupés and 120,000 hatchbacks, both outselling the Ghia equivalents by around three to one. Engine choices also reflected this pattern: most popular was the 88-bhp 2.3-litre four, making up around 38 per cent of total sales: magazine writers may not always have liked it, but the buying public did. Then came the V6 (later straight six) with 31 per cent and the 2.3-turbo with 16 per cent. And what of the V8? Only 14.3 per cent of Mustang buyers paid extra for the 302 (or 5.0-litre as it was known, now that the metric scale was popular). For the moment, economy was king. This, however, was about to change.

PRODUCTION

Coupé	156,666
Hatchback	120,535
Ghia coupé	56,351
Ghia hatchback	36,384
TOTAL	369,936

ENGINE LINE-UP

2.3-litre four

Type	Water-cooled cast-iron, ohc
Bore x stroke	3.78 x 3.13in (96 x 79.5mm)
Capacity	140ci (2.3 litres)
Compression ratio	9.0:1
Fuelling	Two-barrel carburettor
Power	88bhp @ 4,800rpm

2.3-litre four turbo

Type	Water-cooled cast-iron, ohc
Bore x stroke	3.78 x 3.13in
Capacity	140ci (2.3 litres)
Compression ratio	9.0:1
Fuelling	Two-barrel carburettor
Power	131bhp @ 5,800rpm

2.8-litre V6

Type	Water-cooled cast-iron, ohv
Bore x stroke	3.66 x 2.70in (93 x 68.6mm)
Capacity	171ci (2.8 litres)
Compression ratio	8.7:1
Fuelling	Two-barrel carburettor
Power	109bhp @ 4,800rpm

3.3-litre six

Type	Water-cooled cast-iron, ohc
Bore x stroke	3.68 x 3.13in (93.5 x 79.5mm)
Capacity	200ci (3.3 litres)
Compression ratio	8.6:1
Fuelling	One-barrel carburettor
Power	85bhp @ 4,000rpm

5.0-litre V8

Type	Water-cooled cast-iron, ohv
Bore x stroke	4.00 x 3.00in (102 x 76.2mm)
Capacity	302ci (5.0 litres)
Compression ratio	8.4:1
Fuelling	Two-barrel carburettor
Power	140bhp @ 3,600rpm

1980:
IN SEARCH OF MPG

The 1980 Mustang, with smaller V8, taller gearing and more miles per gallon.

While Ford was busy churning out as many 1979 Mustangs as it possibly could, another oil crisis was brewing. Political turmoil in Iran (where the Shah had been overthrown) and failure of OPEC to agree on a worldwide tariff led to oil prices doubling that year. Result? From the point of view of American motorists it was 1973 all over again. Queues at gas stations, high prices, and suddenly fuel economy was an important consideration when buying a car.

Ford was quick to respond. For 1980, rather than receiving a power increase, the Mustang was pegged back, as had its predecessors ten years earlier. In an attempt to

increase the fleet's gas mileage (with an eye on the ever-tightening CAFE figure), the 5.0-litre V8 was downsized to 4.2 litres (255ci) by reducing the bore to 3.68in (93.5mm). Power was down to 117bhp, but the 4.2 was at least lighter and a little more economical on fuel. Like the 5.0-litre, it used a two-barrel carburettor, but could only be had with automatic transmission. Everything about the 4.2 (assembled at the same Windsor plant as the 5.0-litre) was geared towards cleanliness and economy, with integral EGR (exhaust gas recirculation) and very small valves, intake ports and intake manifold runners. To optimize economy still further, the standard rear-axle ratio was 2.26:1 (up from 2.47:1 in 1979) to allow the downsized V8 to rumble along at lower revs for a given cruising speed. Ford still made the 5.0, however, but it was not available in the Mustang that year.

That made the 2.3 turbo four the Mustang's performance flagship, now the most powerful factory engine on offer, especially as it was now quoted at 150bhp. The turbo continued for 1980 with a few minor changes such as an electric cooling fan (replacing the engine-driven one) and rerouted fuel lines. As for the non-turbo 2.3, Ford claimed a massive 23 per cent improvement in fuel economy, with the engine unchanged and the same 3.08:1 rear axle as 1979.

An indication of the climate of the times

comes from the breakdown of engine sales. With the excitement of the debut year over, Mustang sales fell to a still-respectable 271,322 in 1980; due to the oil situation, the U.S. car market itself had shrunk that year, so the Mustang's market share was unchanged. Two out of every three Mustangs were ordered with a four-cylinder engine, and nearly 30 per cent with straight sixes (still the venerable 3.3-litre/200-ci, which came with an overdrive four-speed manual gearbox). Only 2.7 per cent of buyers opted for the downsized, down-spec, really rather pointless 4.2 V8.

Not that performance was a dirty word. In spite of the downbeat climate, Ford decided to get back into motor racing in 1980, after over a decade of avoiding official involvement. There wasn't an immediate return to the glory days of Trans Am, when official factory Mustangs blustered round twisty tracks, battling against Camaros and Firebirds; but much of the new campaign did appear to centre on the Mustang.

A concept car called the Mustang IMSA did the rounds, named after the International Motor Sports Association, which organized the popular Camel GT and All-American GT series. Wide Pirelli tyres, big flares and spoilers, and the 2.3 turbo engine tweaked to produce 175bhp gave out strong hints that more was to come.

And it did. The Special Vehicle Operations group (SVO) was set up and the corporation's European competition director, Michael Kranefess, was brought over to preside. The idea was that SVO would help drivers build competitive race versions of the Mustang, and would also assemble show and concept cars like the IMSA Mustang. Finally, it would develop bolt-on parts that any Mustang owner could buy for IMSA or SCCA racing or on the road. In the long term, it would become a profit-making business in its own right, producing 'official' bolt-on parts for Ford performance freaks in general and the Mustang guys in particular.

Later in the year, the McLaren Mustang was unveiled, looking for all the world like a road-going version of the IMSA car. It had the same sort of bodykit, with massive flared wheel arches to cover the BBS alloy rims; McLaren Engines also tuned the 2.3 turbo up to 175bhp. The McLaren Mustang was strictly a limited edition, with only 250 made (which was perhaps just as well, given a price of $25,000 apiece), but it was foretaste of things to come.

Apart from downsized V8s and hopped-up fours, however, few changes were made to the standard Mustang for 1980. The Cobra got a new nose, basically that of the 1979 Pace Car, to differentiate it from the cheaper cars. There was a deep front spoiler with twin Marchal fog lights, a non-functional hood scoop, flared wheel arches, rear-window louvres, rear-deck spoiler and Recaro seats, which pushed the option price up to $1,482.

The Recaros, incidentally, with their open-mesh headrests, became a general Mustang option, as did high-backed vinyl bucket seats. Electric door windows were another new option, as was a security roller blind over the luggage area on hatchbacks; as with all such blinds it didn't actually stop anyone from breaking in but prevented them from peeking at one's shopping. The cosmetic Sport option ($168–$186, depending on model) now included a sports steering wheel as well as black rocker panels and window frames, wraparound body side mouldings and sports wheel trims. If that wasn't quite racy enough, a leather-bound wheel came in at $44–$56, depending on what it was replacing.

There was still no convertible (or even a T-top, come to that), but anyone nostalgic for open-air motoring could tick the Carriage Roof option box. This consisted of a vinyl roof covering that made the coupé look uncannily like a convertible with the ragtop in place. Aside from the options list, though it is hard to believe, some Mustang parts really did come at no extra cost; all Mustangs now had high-pressure radial tyres, aimed at improving fuel economy, while halogen headlights were also part of the basic deal, as were maintenance-free batteries and a Traveler's Advisory Band on the radio.

PRODUCTION

Coupé	128,893
Hatchback	98,497
Ghia coupé	23,647
Ghia hatchback	20,285
TOTAL	271,322

ENGINE LINE-UP
2.3-litre four

Type	Water-cooled cast-iron, ohc
Bore x stroke	3.78 x 3.13in (96 x 79.5mm)
Capacity	140ci (2.3 litres)
Compression ratio	9.0:1
Fuelling	Two-barrel carburettor
Power	88bhp @ 4,800rpm

2.3-litre four turbo

Type	Water-cooled cast-iron, ohc
Bore x stroke	3.78 x 3.13in
Capacity	140ci (2.3 litres)
Compression ratio	9.0:1
Fuelling	Two-barrel carburettor
Power	150bhp @ 5,800rpm

3.3-litre six

Type	Water-cooled cast-iron, ohc
Bore x stroke	3.68 x 3.13in
Capacity	200ci (3.3 litres)
Compression ratio	8.6:1
Fuelling	One-barrel carburettor
Power	91bhp @ 4,000rpm

4.2-litre V8

Type	Water-cooled cast-iron, ohv
Bore x stroke	4.00 x 3.00in (102 x 76.2mm)
Capacity	255ci (4.2 litres)
Compression ratio	8.8:1
Fuelling	Two-barrel carburettor
Power	117bhp @ 3,800rpm

1981:
PERFORMANCE LOW POINT

Nineteen-eighty-one was a decidedly uneventful year for the Mustang. All engine options from the previous year continued unchanged, the 4.2-litre V8 was still in its high-geared, throttled-down economy mode, while the 88-bhp 2.3-litre four remained the most popular motor of all. The turbo had not been faring well, still proving unreliable, and Ford actually dropped the option altogether at the end of the 1981 model year, though availability had already been restricted late in the season. The turbo would return for 1983 after an intensive development period finally solved its problems.

There were some changes, however, notably a five-speed manual gearbox, offered for the first time for $152. But this wasn't the performance option it seemed: the idea was to provide an extra-high overdrive fifth gear, another fuel-saving measure, rather than give a closer set of ratios. Economical cruising rather than optimum acceleration was the reason behind this first five-speed. Most initial criticism, though, had little to do with this but more to do with the eccentric change pattern that put fifth gear next to fourth. Initially, this five-speed was available on four-cylinder Mustangs only.

Meanwhile, fresh-air fiends had been frustrated by the third-generation Mustang. There was no convertible, and even the Mustang II's T-top failed to make an appearance. Ford's answer was a small conventional sunroof, which was far from satisfactory. But for 1981, the T-top was back; as before, it consisted of two tinted glass panels which could be completely removed to allow wind-in-the-hair motoring. The new T-Roof, as it was known, was an option on both coupé and hatchback, and H-shaped body reinforcements ensured that it complied with all federal regulations regarding body structure.

There were some other new options as well, such as reclining bucket seats (high- or low-back) and a convex right-hand mirror. The console option now comprised a digital display, which included a clock (including elapsed time) and warnings for low fuel, low washer level and non-working lights. It was the final year for the popular Cobra option (it would be replaced in 1982 by the GT), and introverts could now save $65 by eschewing the side stripes, bringing it closer in spirit to the subtle Mustang II Mach I which, with the front spoiler, was maybe not that subtle.

All in all, it was not a good year for the Mustang. There were substantial price increases all round and the cheapest base coupé was now listed at $6,171. Sales dropped faster than car sales in general to 182,552, with Mustang sales now making up only 2.73 per cent of the total. Once again, the overhead-cam 2.3-litre was the most popular engine; few of those were now turbos, while just 3.3 per cent of cars were sold with the V8. In terms of the Mustang performance story, this was the lowest point.

PRODUCTION

Coupé	77,458
Hatchback	77,399
Ghia coupé	13,422
Ghia hatchback	14,273
TOTAL	182,552

ENGINE LINE-UP
2.3-litre four

Type	Water-cooled cast-iron, ohc
Bore x stroke	3.78 x 3.13in (96 x 79.5mm)
Capacity	140ci (2.3 litres)
Compression ratio	9.0:1
Fuelling	Two-barrel carburettor
Power	88bhp @ 4,800rpm

2.3-litre four turbo

Type	Water-cooled cast-iron, ohc
Bore x stroke	3.78 x 3.13in
Capacity	140ci (2.3 litres)
Compression ratio	9.0:1
Fuelling	Two-barrel carburettor
Power	150bhp @ 5,800rpm

3.3–litre six

Type	Water-cooled cast-iron, ohc
Bore x stroke	3.68 x 3.13in (93.5 x 79.5mm)
Capacity	200ci (3.3 litres)
Compression ratio	8.6:1
Fuelling	One-barrel carburettor
Power	94bhp @ 4,000rpm

4.2-litre V8

Type	Water-cooled cast-iron, ohv
Bore x stroke	4.00 x 3.00in (102 x 76.2mm)
Capacity	255ci (4.2 litres)
Compression ratio	8.2:1
Fuelling	Two-barrel carburettor
Power	115bhp @ 3,400rpm

COLOUR OPTIONS

Single Colours

Tu Tone

Black

Bright Bittersweet/Black

Bright Bittersweet Red/Black

Medium Blue Glow

Bright Red/Black

Bright Yellow

IMSA racing Mustang in Miller colours.

OPPOSITE

The Miller Mustang was fielded in 1981 by the Bill Scott Racing Team with driver Klaus Ludwig.

Bright Yellow/Black
Bittersweet Glow
Bittersweet Glow/Black
Polar White
Pastel Chamois/Black
Red
Polar White/Black
Bright Red
Red/Polar White
Pastel Chamois
Light Pewter
Metallic/Black
Light Pewter Metallic
Medium Pewter Metallic/Black
Midnight Blue Metallic
Dark Cordovan Metallic/Black
Dark Brown Metallic
Medium Pewter Metallic/Light Pewter
  Metallic
Dark Cordovan Metallic
Medium Pewter Metallic

OPTION PRICES
Mechanical

3.3-litre (200-ci) six	$213
4.2-litre (255-ci) V8	$263
Sports-tuned exhaust (V8 only)	$38
Five-speed manual transmission	$152
Automatic transmission	$349
Traction-Lok differential	$63
Optional axle ratio	$20
Power brakes	$76
Power steering	$163
Handling suspension	$43
Engine-block heater	$16
Heavy-duty battery	$20
Californian emission system	$46
High-altitude emissions	$38

Option Groups

Cobra package	$1,588
Sport group	$58-$72
Interior accent group	$126–$139
Light group	$43
Appearance-protection group	$41
Power-lock group	$93–$120

Comfort/convenience

Air conditioning	$560
T-Roof	$874
Flip-up sun roof	$213–$228
Recaro high-back seats	$732
Cloth/vinyl bucket seats	$22–$48
Accent cloth/vinyl seat trim	$30
Leather low-back bucket seats	$359
Rear defroster, electric	$107
Fingertip speed control	$132
Power windows	$140
Tinted windows	$76
Leather-bound steering wheel	$49–$61
Tilt steering wheel	$80–$93
Interval wipers	$41
Rear wiper/washer	$85
Trunk light	$6
Driver's remote mirror	$20
Dual remote mirrors	$56
Cargo area cover (hatchback)	$45
Front floor mats	$18–$20
Colour-keyed seatbelts	$23

In-Car Entertainment

AM/FM radio	$51
AM/FM stereo radio	$88
+ 8 track tape player	$162
+ cassette player	$174
Premium sound system	$91
Dual rear speakers	$37
Radio flexibility option	$61
AM radio delete	$65 credit

Appearance

Carriage roof	$644
Full vinyl roof	$115
Metallic glow paint	$48
Two-tone paint	$121–$155
Lower two-tone paint	$90
Pinstriping	$34
Accent tape stripes	$54
Hood scoop	$32
Hatchback louvres	$145
Rocker panel mouldings	$30
Roof luggage rack	$90
Mud/stone deflectors	$26
Lower body side protection	$37
Console	$168
Wire wheel covers	$77–$118
Turbine wheel covers	$10–$41
TRX aluminium wheels	$340
Cast aluminium wheels	$305
Styled steel wheels	$60–$101

1982:
THE BOSS IS BACK!

In 1982, the Mustang began its long march back to high performance. As a *Hot Car* journalist remarked, '1982 was the year that launched the second golden age of muscle cars'. In fact, it wasn't really a long march at all, more a rapid turnaround. The years 1980 and '81 had been low points as far as Mustang muscle lovers were concerned – first the already detuned 5.0-litre V8 was downsized to 4.2, then the turbocharged four was dropped altogether. For over a decade, the performance Mustang had been in full retreat, tottering beneath the onslaught of new safety and emissions legislation, high gas prices and rocketing insurance premiums.

But in 1982, the tide finally turned, and how!

'The Boss is Back!' trumpeted Ford advertisements of the time, which couldn't have been more apposite. The source of the excitement was a return of a full 5.0-litre V8 to the Mustang line-up. Not only that, but it had also been tweaked to produce an extra 20 horsepower over the previous 5.0-litre, and 6 per cent more torque. With a standard four-speed manual gearbox and the new GT package (which replaced the Cobra), it was clear that this latest V8 Mustang was intended to be a muscle car for the 1980s rather than a boulevard cruiser.

The return of the muscle-bound pony car came about partly because of Ford's tentative return to racing, setting up SVO (Special Vehicle Operations) to help race drivers build extra-fast Mustangs and to develop hot parts for the street driver. The public response was enthusiastic and Ford marketeers sensed that the time was right to hazard a return to the performance-car market.

They weren't alone either. That same year, General Motors unveiled a new generation of Camaros and Firebirds, complete with a 5.0-litre (302-ci) fuel-injected V8 option which made 165bhp, slightly more than that of the remuscled Mustang; but the latter stuck with a relatively simple carburettor at first, instead of electronic injection, making it the favourite of hot-rodders. In fact, that would be the

hallmark of the 1980s Mustang V8: almost alone in the U.S. market it offered good performance from a fairly low-tech engine with plenty of tuning potential. It was also cheaper than the opposition; in other words, it provided just a taste of the original muscle-car concept. Maybe the *Hot Car* journalist had it right after all.

So what was all the fuss about? Oddly enough, the full-powered 5.0-litre wasn't radically different from the old one. A new camshaft (sourced, with some lateral thinking, from Ford's shelf of marine engine parts) gave more valve lift, duration and opening time. Slightly tougher valve springs allowed the V8 to rev to 6,000rpm, when it had previously run out of breath at 4,000, with maximum power coming in at just 3,600. To cope with oil control at high revs there were large valve-stem oil seals (nylon, as before), while valve-train control was assured with a double-row roller timing chain (the standard 302 used a standard-link silent chain). Ford fitted a bigger 356-cfm carburettor as well, and turned up the pressure on the fuel pump. There was also a low-restriction air cleaner.

It seems hard to credit now that these few modifications, a modest 14 per cent more power and 6 per cent more torque, should have caused such a stir. But behind those peak figures (which are only ever half the story in real-world engine performance)

897 · TNP
COLORADO

was a wider, fatter torque curve. Allowing the engine to rev out also did wonders for acceleration times and the use of a standard four-speed manual gearbox did little to harm them either.

The results were spectacular. Most magazine tests recorded a 0–60 time in the low/mid-sevens; *Hot Rod* and *Motor Trend* actually managed 6.9, while 15/16-seconds was the norm for standing quarters. Top speeds varied, even on the standard 3.08:1 axle, but over 120mph (193km/h) was almost guaranteed, making it about as quick as the much more expensive L83 Corvette and Porsche 928. Naturally, a motoring press starved of muscle cars loved it. *Motor Trend* made that sub-7-second 0–60 time into a headline, and many of them reckoned that the flagship V8 Mustang was the fastest car on the market. Was it 'the fastest car to come out of Motown in nearly a decade' (*Super Stock & Drag Illustrated*) or 'the quickest machine made in America'? (*Car and Driver*). Who cared, the point was that it was here.

All this power would have been pointless without a chassis to cope. So to go with the 302 HO (as it was known) buyers had handling suspension, P185/75R-14 radials on cast aluminium wheels, a Traction-Lok differential, power brakes and steering. On top of that, one could opt for the TR package, which brought those low-profile Michelin TRXs with matching wheels. These could be had on any Mustang along with the handling suspension.

The 302 GT hatchback, which retailed at $8,308, also brought dual black remote-control door mirrors, fog lamps, body-coloured front and rear spoilers and front grille. Inside, there was a centre console, luxury seats with black trim all over the place, four-spoke steering wheel, dashboard, all the controls, all exterior mouldings, window frames, door handles, mirrors and even the radio antenna. Traditionally, Mustang buyers had a whole range of colours to choose from, but at first, those opting for the GT had a choice of just red, black (of course) or metallic silver. If that wasn't enough, they could play the Mustang options game with items like air conditioning and Recaro seats, while an AM/FM cassette was available to bump the top Mustang into five-figure price-tag territory.

The return of the GT tag, which had been a sporty option pack on 1965–69 Mustangs, was symbolic. There was a Mercury equivalent, also the Capri RS, which was mechanically identical. *Motor Trend* spent three days testing a GT302 HO, finding 'awesome acceleration, consistently short and powerful stopping, and flat, cat-quick handling … And at a price that mere mortals can afford. For our money. It's the best-balanced, most capable Mustang ever'.

Meanwhile, what was happening to the rest of the range? All Mustangs received a mild makeover that year as the range was rejigged into L, GL, GLX and GT to mirror the Escort. The GLX replaced the luxury Ghia, the first time there had been no Mustang Ghia for eight years, and prices were up all round: the entry-level coupé L cost $6,345 in four-cylinder form, $7,032 with the 3.3-litre straight six. That included full wheel covers, wraparound body side mouldings and an AM radio. All Mustangs now had seatbelts with tension relievers, a remote-control left-hand door mirror, headlight flasher, screw-on gas cap and a larger 15.4-gallon (70-litre) tank. Hatchbacks commanded a premium of over $100; there was no L model, so the cheapest three-door Mustang was the $6,979 GL, which was the most popular single model.

Any of these could be had with the 302 HO engine and the four-speed manual transmission that came with it, so it was possible to have the GT's impressive performance with none of the sporty black bits that shouted its purpose, while following that option made the TRX handling/tyres package a must as well; together these two items added nearly $1,000 to the price of any Mustang. Those with fond memories of the Cobra II and King Cobra could order the hatchback GT with the detuned 4.2-litre (255-ci) V8. Do that, and Ford would knock $57 off the price, while owners could revel in the 1970s Mustang tradition of show in place of go. Was this so strange? A 4.2-powered GT offered all the glamour of the full-powered V8 with lower fuel bills and a less intimidating insurance premium. Whatever the case, Ford continued to offer the throttled-down 120-bhp V8 for 1982; its better fuel figures must have given a welcome boost to the CAFE fleet average. But most buyers stuck with the basic 2.3-litre four (marginally less powerful this year at 86bhp) or the ancient 3.3-litre six. The latter was in its final year with the Mustang, having been brought out of retirement when

Ford had problems securing supplies of the German 2.8-litre V6, but would be replaced by a U.S.-built V6 for 1983.

All in all, it was an optimistic year for the Mustang, though the reality was a slump in sales to little more than 130,000. This was down nearly 30 per cent on the previous year; in a still sluggish market, the U.S. motor industry couldn't afford to celebrate just yet. But behind the overall Mustang figure there was one piece of good news for Ford – over 25 per cent of Mustang buyers paid extra for a V8, a massive increase over the 3 per cent of 1981. That was over 30,000 cars, and according to one source, over 23,000 GT Mustangs were ordered, with more expensive, optioned-up Mustangs bringing bigger profits. It looked as though the 302 HO came along at just the right time.

PRODUCTION

Coupé L/GL	45,316
Hatchback GL	45,901
Coupé GLX	5,828
Hatchback GLX	9,926
Hatchback GT	23,447
TOTAL	130,418

ENGINE LINE-UP
2.3-litre four

Type	Water-cooled cast-iron, ohc
Bore x stroke	3.78 x 3.13in (96 x 79.5mm)
Capacity	140ci (2.3 litres)
Compression ratio	9.0:1
Fuelling	Two-barrel carburettor
Power	86bhp @ 4,600rpm

3.3-litre six

Type	Water-cooled cast-iron, ohc
Bore x stroke	3.68 x 3.13in (93.5 x 79.5mm)
Capacity	200ci (3.3 litres)
Compression ratio	8.6:1
Fuelling	One-barrel carburettor
Power	87bhp @ 3,800rpm

4.2-litre V8

Type	Water-cooled cast-iron, ohv
Bore x stroke	3.68 x 3.00in (93.5 x 76.2mm)
Capacity	255ci (4.2 litres)
Compression ratio	8.2:1
Fuelling	Two-barrel carburettor
Power	120bhp @ 3,400rpm

5.0-litre HO V8

Type	Water-cooled cast-iron, ohv
Bore x stroke	4.00 x 3.00in (102 x 76.2mm)
Capacity	302ci (5.0 litres)
Compression ratio	8.3:1
Fuelling	Two-barrel carburettor
Power	157bhp @ 4,200rpm

1983:
THE RETURN OF THE RAGTOP

For the Mustang, the big news for 1983 was the return of a full-blown convertible. Ten years earlier, commentators had lamented the fact that both the muscle car and the traditional ragtop would never be seen again. In 1982, the Mustang 302 GT (and its home-grown rivals) put paid to the first part of that prediction, while a year later, the new Mustang convertible took care of the second.

As it happened, Ford had insufficient confidence in the market to begin churning out convertibles just yet. Instead, it

subcontracted the work to Cars & Concepts of Brighton, Michigan. Finished coupés were shipped to Brighton where their roofs were cut off and the ragtop added. In theory, the convertible was available in all levels of trim, but in practice only GLX coupés were converted at first, with GTs following later.

The GLX package brought an electric top (in black or white) and a glass rear window; of course, there was also room for four, this being no two-seater sports car. Power came from the 5.0-litre HO V8 or the newly-introduced 3.8-litre V6. In GT trim, it was the V8 or nothing, plus a Borg Warner T-5 five-speed transmission and 3.27:1 Traction-Lok differential. GT convertibles also had the TRX package, air conditioning (in a convertible?), speed-control, centre console, power windows, tinted glass and various other luxury items. No wonder the convertible GT commanded a $4,000 premium over the equivalent hatchback; at $13,479 it was the most expensive factory Mustang ever.

There must have been a suppressed demand for an open-top Mustang – after all, the T-Roof was very nice, but to fresh-air fanatics it was not the same as a 'proper' convertible. But the new ragtop was an instant hit; Ford sold over 23,000 of them in the first year, only 1,000 of which were GTs. Most of these early convertibles were in

Black, Polar White or Bright Red.

Meanwhile, a horsepower war had been brewing between Ford and General Motors. It was just like the old days, as if the late-1960s muscle-car heyday was being repeated all over again. The year before, the 157-bhp Mustang GT was pitted against the 165-bhp Camaro, though the consensus was that Ford had the straight-line performance edge, thanks to the Mustang's lower weight. For 1983, Chevrolet announced a 190-bhp version of its fuel-injected V8, surely enough to outdrag a Mustang. Ford, however, had an answer ready and waiting.

Instead of resorting to the new-fangled electronic injection, it bolted a a 600-cfm Motorcraft/Holley four-barrel carburettor onto the 5.0 HO. A massive 17-inch (43-cm) air cleaner, with twin inlets, supplied great gulps of fresh air to this big carburettor. It was the first four-barrel seen on a factory Mustang for over a decade; add an aluminium air cleaner and strengthened valve train and it really could have been 1968 all over again.

The 5.0-litre may have had a catalyst and EGR but still had no electronic control, and was being tuned in the old muscle-car fashion; Ford actually made a virtue of this low-tech approach, maintaining that it was easier for owners to work on their cars and tune them themselves. In any case, the low-

BELOW
1983 Mustang 5-litre GLX convertible.

OPPOSITE
1983 Mustang 5-litre GT T-top.

tech approach didn't appear to be holding back power – the latest 5.0-litre produced a claimed 175bhp and 245lb ft. Remembering that those 1960s power figures had been inflated by a different measurement system, this returned the 1983 Mustang to true muscle-car territory. To back up the HO, a five-speed manual option came later in the year, with Borg-Warner's close-ratio T-5, a

great improvement on the wide-ratio four-speeder that all 1982 5.0-litres used.

This wasn't the only performance option for Mustang buyers as the 2.3-litre turbo was back. It was a very different engine from the underdeveloped motor that had made its appearance in 1979. Instead of a turbocharger bolted onto an existing motor, the package as a whole had now been reworked. The

carburettor was ditched in favour of Bosch fuel injection, while the turbo now sat upstream of the induction system rather than downstream; inside, the 2.3 was beefed up to cope with the extra strains of a turbocharged life. There were forged-aluminium pistons, the valves were made of a high-tech alloy, there was an oil cooler for more consistent temperature control, and a lighter flywheel. Despite its low 8.0:1 compression ratio, the reborn turbo produced 145bhp and 180lb ft of torque.

Sceptics were quick to point out that the little four-pot turbo was slower than the upgraded V8 and cost $250 more into the bargain. It took nearly 10 seconds to reach 60mph (97km/h), for example, where the V8 drivers could rely on less than 7 seconds. Of course, it used less fuel than the big 5.0-litre, but this was 1983; the OPEC crisis was over, oil was flowing again, gas prices had come down and queues were a thing of the past, so who cared? Such was, and is, the short-sightedness of the affluent Western world.

It is the opinion of Brad Bowling (*Standard Catalog of Mustang*) that Ford persevered with the turbo as an insurance policy in case of a third oil crisis, when it would have been well placed to clean up as unsold V8s sat in showrooms gathering dust. But that didn't happen; less than 500 customers bought turbo GTs in 1983, but nearly one in three of all Mustang buyers decided that the time was right to order a V8. Only 25 per cent opted for a four-cylinder Mustang, so in the space of two short years the Mustang's engine mix had been virtually turned on its head. The four-pot Mustang,

OPPOSITE

The European Mustang. Ford's Capri was just as popular in Britain and Germany as the pony car was in the U.S. This is an RS at the Goodwood Festival of Speed.

which had been the buyer's favourite for a decade of rising gas prices, had temporarily fallen out of favour.

Engines and soft tops aside, all 1983 Mustangs had a new front end with deeply recessed headlights (still quad rectangular units, as in 1979) and narrower grille, all of which were slightly more aerodynamic than before. There were wider tyres across the range, and new options included cloth-covered low-backed bucket seats, though the Recaro option was deleted. Also available was that fake convertible top, the Carriage roof (with a real one on offer, who needed it?), the rear wiper/washer and hatchback louvres. Even the basic L coupé was quite well-equipped these days, with reclining bucket seats, fake wood trim on the dashboard, four-spoke steering wheel, AM radio and halogen headlights all standard. The GL mostly added appearance items such as black panels, pinstripes and sports steering wheel. GLX owners had bright trim where the GL's was black, map pockets and a light group, among other things.

All these models could be had with the new 3.8-litre (232-ci) V6, which finally replaced the tired old 3.3-litre straight six for 1983. It was usefully more powerful (105bhp against 89bhp) and was without doubt the cruiser's choice among Mustang engines, especially when coupled with the automatic transmission. The V8, of course, was still manual only, though an auto option was on the way. Automatic was still popular, with just over half of buyers (56 per cent) making that choice in 1983. The V6 did well too, making up nearly 45 per cent of all sales; it was the most popular Mustang power unit,

representing a compromise between the economy-first four and fearsome V8. Mustang sales were down again that year, to less than 121,000, but Ford could take comfort from the fact that the more expensive models were now making the running.

Given the new popularity of the V8, and its delighted press reception the year before, one could be forgiven for thinking that the V8 GT was a true world-beater. But read the tests more closely, especially those of 1983, when the competition had moved on, and a less rosy picture emerges. 'Crude' is a word that comes up quite a lot, though everyone agreed that the V8 was fast. It could almost keep up with the 190-bhp Camaro in its latest 175-bhp form. It was smaller and lighter, and felt it. But more than one test concluded that the two cars had completely different characters. The Camaro was high-tech, poised and well-balanced, its handling responsive and neutral. By contrast, the Mustang bucked and roared. Fast in a straight line, it suffered from understeer and lifeless steering around corners, while the rear axle hopped and banged in protest. In short, it was just like the old days of uncomplicated, unsophisticated muscle cars, which in essence the Mustang GT had recreated for the 1980s. *Car and Driver* was adamant that the Camaro Z28 was a much better car. So what would Ford do next?

PRODUCTION

Coupé	33,201
Hatchback	64,234
Convertible	23,438
TOTAL	120,873

ENGINE LINE-UP

2.3-litre four

Type	Water-cooled cast-iron, ohc
Bore x stroke	3.78 x 3.13in (96 x 79.5mm)
Capacity	140ci (2.3 litres)
Compression ratio	9.0:1
Fuelling	Single-barrel carburettor
Power	90bhp @ 4,600rpm

2.3-litre four turbo

Type	Water-cooled cast-iron, ohc
Bore x stroke	3.78 x 3.13in
Capacity	140ci (2.3 litres)
Compression ratio	8.0:1
Fuelling	Electronic injection
Power	145bhp @ 5,000rpm

3.8-litre V6

Type	Water-cooled cast-iron, ohc
Bore x stroke	3.80 x 3.40in (96.5 x 86.4mm)
Capacity	232ci (3.8 litres)
Compression ratio	8.7:1
Fuelling	Two-barrel carburettor
Power	105bhp @ 4,000rpm

5.0-litre HO V8

Type	Water-cooled cast-iron, ohv
Bore x stroke	4.00 x 3.00in (102 x 76.2mm)
Capacity	302ci (5.0 litres)
Compression ratio	8.3:1
Fuelling	Four-barrel carburettor
Power	175bhp @ 4,000rpm

Mustang writ small: the Capri offered everything from a 1.3-litre four to a 3-litre V6; it was in production for nearly 20 years.

Capri: The European Mustang

The huge success of Lee Iacocca's Mustang hadn't gone unnoticed in Ford's European operations, though there was no serious attempt to sell the Mustang in Europe. By Euro standards it was far from being a compact pony car; it was too big, too heavy and too thirsty. The answer was simple: Europe would have its own Mustang: the Capri.

Launched in 1969 and produced in both England and Germany, the Capri's antecedents were obvious. The long hood and short deck were of the classic Mustang proportions, and even the fake air intakes in front of the rear wheels were there. Instead of

the Falcon, it was based on mid-sized European sedans, the British Cortina and German Taunus, and like the Mustang used existing parts, cutting both cost and development time in the process.

The Capri was a simple, conventional coupé (there was never a factory convertible), with independent front suspension and a live rear axle. Under the hood (or bonnet, as the British would say) was a whole range of four- and six-cylinder engines – no V8, of course. The smallest 1.3-litre four would have seemed like a lawnmower engine to many Americans, but the 1.6- and 2.0-litre fours, especially in hopped-up GT form, gave the Capri sprightly

performance. The closest things to a Capri muscle car were the V6s, a 2.6-litre for Germany and torquey 3.0-litre for Britain. When American magazines tried the Capri, they liked it. It was smaller and sportier than any Mustang, and in 1974 when the Mustang II appeared, *Road & Track* lamented the fact that the Capri had not been Americanized.

The Capri received a substantial update in 1975 as the hatchback Capri II, with a similar range of engines, and was later re-engined with a German-built fuel-injected 2.8-litre V6. It actually soldiered on into the late 1980s, though its days of mass sales were over. But it was still the European Mustang.

1984:
LITIGATION

Twenty years and several-million Mustangs on from the original 1964 launch, and Ford was in the mood to celebrate. Performance was back. The convertible was back. The Mustang V8 GT may have been regarded as rather crude when compared with younger muscle cars, but for many that was part of its appeal.

A good proportion of American car buyers, it seems, had never really been convinced by the talk of lightweight, efficient four-cylinder fun cars. They had bought them, when gas prices dictated, but gas was relatively cheap once more, and apparently plentiful. For enthusiasts, the old faith in sheer cubic inches and horsepower in preference to sophistication still held true. And for them, the down-to-earth Mustang GT, red in tooth and claw, was the perfect antidote to the cautious 1970s.

The plan for 1984 was to offer a 20th-anniversary special, and follow it up later in the year with the most powerful 1980s Mustang yet, an uprated 205-bhp GT. This actually received its press launch, but last-minute engine problems led to it being hastily withdrawn before it went on sale. The 200+bhp Mustang would return for 1985, however, and with even more power.

In the meantime, the 20th-anniversary Mustang did make an appearance, though it was the subject of a lawsuit. Ford named and badged the cars GT350, in memory of Carroll Shelby's legendary Mustangs of 1965 and '66. The trouble was, Shelby now worked for Chrysler (with none other than Lee Iacocca) and no one had asked his permission. A furious Shelby sued Ford but lost the ruling, since the GT350 designation had been out of use since 1970 and was held to have returned to the public domain.

The now-legal GT350s were based on GT hatchbacks and convertibles and came only in Oxford White. The grille was body-coloured, as were the fenders, and the convertible had a white or black top. Authentic GT350 stripes ran along the sides.

Inside, there was special Canyon Red interior trim, with Lear-Siegler articulated sports seats, a three-spoke steering wheel and other items that would become standard Mustang fitments the following year, plus a specially-inscribed plaque. Mechanically, most of the GT350s were V8 HO-powered, though around 10 per cent used the 2.3 turbo motor. Just over 5,000 were built in all, over 3,000 of which were hatchbacks. At least one magazine ran a comparison with the original Shelby GT, concluding that the 1960s car was faster and more raucous but that the modern-day equivalent was quicker around corners.

Just as Ford was paying homage to the most famous aftermarket Mustang of all time, so a new one was born: the Saleen. Steve Saleen was a business-school graduate with a background in SCCA Formula Atlantic and Trans Am racing. He had owned several Shelby Mustangs, and as a knowledgeable and enthusiastic engineer was perfectly placed to do for the Mustang something like Carrol Shelby had done for it 20 years earlier.

The first special Mustangs to emerge from Saleen Autosport were all based on 175-bhp hatchbacks and were very exclusive, with only three being built in

1984 Mustang SVO turbo. Ford persevered with the turbo as a V8 alternative.

1984 Mustang SVO.

1984. However, Saleen made no attempt to tune the engine on any of them. This was a wise move as it meant the Saleen Mustangs did not have to be entered for expensive and time-consuming tests for emissions, fuel consumption and warranty standards.

Instead, Saleen concentrated on aerodynamics, on the brakes, chassis and suspension. So the first Saleen Mustangs had his own suspension components (such as the springs, a front G-load brace and urethane anti-roll bar bushes), the widest tyres available (Goodyear Eagle GTs, at 215/60-15), with wheels to suit, plus an aerodynamic body kit. Together with various graphics and a few interior parts to spruce them up, they constituted the first Saleen Mustangs, which would be produced right into the 21st

century. It looked as though the Mustang had found its next Carroll Shelby.

Meanwhile, back at Dearborn, the 205-hp Mustang may have been aborted but the 175-bhp four-barrel V8 carried on. By this time, the V8 Mustang had so impressed the California Highway Patrol that no less than 400 were ordered as patrol cars, the Patrol having discovered that its standard Dodge and Chevrolet sedans (top speed around 85mph/137km/h) were quite inadequate to the task of catching speeding drivers in Porsches, Ferraris and Nissan ZXs. A new set of performance criteria for police cars was laid down, requiring 0–100mph in 30 seconds or less, reaching 120 in less than two minutes. The Mustang met them all and soon the V8s were cruising the California

blacktops, looking for Porsches to apprehend.

CHiPS might also have considered the new SVO version of the 2.3 turbo, but the $15,000+ price would probably have been too much for the public purse. As has been seen, the 2.3 turbo Mustang was something of a flop, even in its reworked, reliable fuel-injected form. So Special Vehicle Operations sought to revive interest by adding an air-to-air intercooler, boosting peak power to 175bhp and beefing up the bottom end of the power curve into the bargain. With the same power as the V8, and slightly less weight, the SVO turbo was about as fast: Ford claimed 134mph (216km/h) top speed and 0–60 in 7.5 seconds.

This was actually the first complete car to come out of SVO, and the occasion was marked by fitting just about every possible option to the turbo intercooled Mustang. The motor was backed up by Borg-Warner's T-5 five-speed manual gearbox with Hurst linkage, plus disc brakes all round, performance suspension with Koni adjustable gas-filled shocks and ultra-wide ultra-low-profile Goodyear NCTs (P225/50BR-16) on cast-aluminium 7-in (18-cm) wide wheels.

That was just the start, for inside were multi-adjustable leather seats, air conditioning, power windows and door locks, a sunroof, cassette player, leather-bound steering wheel, gearknob and handbrake, plus other details. The SVO Mustang cost $15,596, ready to roll, which made it a whole $6,000 more than the V8 GT and twice the price of the basic four-cylinder hatchback. Yet it sold in far greater numbers than the 'ordinary' turbo GT, with 4,500 finding buyers in the first year and nearly 10,000 sold by the time production ended in 1986, multi-adjust leather seats and all.

Meanwhile, Ford was not neglecting the standard engines. For all the talk concerning the benefits of simple, tuneable carburettors that every shade-tree mechanic could understand, this was pure corporate hogwash. It sought to hide the fact that Ford didn't yet have a fuel-injection system to suit the muscle-car Mustangs. The cruisers were a different matter, however, and throttle body electronic injection was added to the 3.8-litre V6 for 1984, increasing power to 120bhp and improving driveability. The same system was also applied to the 5.0-litre V8 to produce a softer 165-bhp alternative of the full-powered engine, with a strong 205lb ft. This V8 was also used in Ford sedans such as the Fairmont-based LTD LX and the Mercury Grand Marquis. In the Mustang, it was mated exclusively to an automatic transmission, either a three-speed unit or a four-speed overdrive, and was aimed at the luxury cruiser end of the pony-car spectrum rather than the muscle-bound variety. These (plus the 2.3 turbo) were the only Mustang motors for 1984 with fuel injection, but every engine made use of Ford's latest EEC-IV electronic engine-control system.

With the return of multiple engine choices (there were now no less than six – three 2.3-litre fours, the 3.8-litre V6 and two V8s) the Mustang range was simplified. The base L (now available in hatchback as well as coupé form) continued, but the GL and GLX were replaced by a single LX trim level. Mustang Ls now had an upshift indicator light, which

helped drivers to change up early to save fuel, and a starter interlock which allowed the engine to start only when the clutch was depressed. The convertible came in LX and GT form only, the LX with the V6 as standard. It was also brought in-house to roll off the same Dearborn production lines as the coupés and hatchbacks; the success of the convertible in its debut year had convinced Ford that the soft-top Mustang was worthy of mass-production.

All in all, 141,480 Mustangs were built that year, which hardly set the world alight but was a real turning point, the first time Mustang sales had risen in five years.

PRODUCTION

Coupé	37,680
Hatchback	86,200
Convertible	17,600
TOTAL	141,480

ENGINE LINE-UP
2.3-litre four
Type	Water-cooled cast-iron, ohc
Bore x stroke	3.78 x 3.13in (96 x 79.5mm)
Capacity	140ci (2.3 litres)
Compression ratio	9.0:1
Fuelling	Single-barrel carburettor
Power	88bhp @ 4,000rpm

2.3-litre four turbo
Type	Water-cooled cast-iron, ohc
Bore x stroke	3.78 x 3.13in
Capacity	140ci (2.3 litres)
Compression ratio	8.0:1
Fuelling	Electronic injection
Power	145bhp @ 4,600rpm

2.3-litre four turbo SVO
Type	Water-cooled cast-iron, ohc
Bore x stroke	3.78 x 3.13in
Capacity	140ci (2.3 litres)
Compression ratio	8.0:1
Fuelling	Electronic injection
Power	175bhp @ 4,400rpm

3.8-litre EFI V6
Type	Water-cooled cast-iron, ohc
Bore x stroke	3.80 x 3.40in (96.5 x 86.4mm)
Capacity	232ci (3.8 litres)
Compression ratio	8.7:1
Fuelling	Electronic injection
Power	120bhp @ 3,600rpm

5.0-litre EFI V8
Type	Water-cooled cast-iron, ohv
Bore x stroke	4.00 x 3.00in (102 x 76.2mm)
Capacity	302ci (5.0 litres)
Compression ratio	8.3:1
Fuelling	Electronic injection
Power	165bhp @ 3,800rpm

5.0-litre HO V8
Type	Water-cooled cast-iron, ohv
Bore x stroke	4.00 x 3.00in
Capacity	5.0 litres (302ci)
Compression ratio	8.3:1
Fuelling	Four-barrel carburettor
Power	175bhp @ 4,000rpm

1985:
YET MORE POWER

BELOW, OPPOSITE and OVERLEAF 210-bhp-carburettor V8 or 205-bhp injection turbo four. Those were the Mustang performance choices for 1985.

Once Ford engineers realized that tyre-smoking power was back, it seemed that there was no stopping them. Year by year, the V8 Mustang's peak bhp figure was creeping up, though maybe step change would be a more accurate description. Starting out with 140bhp, the 5.0 disappeared

for a couple of years but made a loud and proud comeback in 1982 with 157bhp and with 175bhp the following year, which would have been 205bhp had last-minute engine problems not held it back. But for 1985, the 200+ horsepower Mustang was at last finally on sale.

It seems odd that just as CAFE regulations demanded a fleet average of 22.5mpg (7.9km/litre), Ford should have announced its most muscular Mustang for 15 years. But the 1980s generation of muscle cars was more efficient than its 1960s predecessors, thanks to ultra-accurate electronic ignition and tall gearing; at 70mph (113km/h) the 1985 Mustang GT was barely ticking over at 2,000rpm. Utilize all that power and consumption could plunge to 15mpg (5.3km/litre) or less, while out on the highway the mid-20s could be expected. It should be remembered that CAFE never actually banned any car, merely slapped a gas-guzzler tax on those that failed to measure up. Moreover, performance freaks were more than happy to pay for their pleasure in an affluent U.S.A.

For the Mustang V8, 1985 marked the end of an era. It was the last year for a carburettor on the top-powered Mustang before it followed the fuel-injection route, long-since taken by most rivals. Carburettors, especially big, throaty, four-barrel Holleys,

played a key role in American muscle-car culture. Consequently the Mustang, as the only carb-fed car left, could be seen as a lone upholder of traditional values. It was a card that Ford was well aware it held and it played it strongly.

So how did this last carburettor Mustang make its 210bhp? In keeping with the hot-rod image, the extra 35 horsepower came from age-old hot-rodding techniques. There was a peakier camshaft, high-flow stainless-steel headers, plus low-friction roller tappets, and of course that big four-barrel Holley. One high-tech technique was a new accessory drive that reduced the air-conditioning compressor, the power steering pump and alternator to half speed, thus reducing losses.

The end result was 210bhp at 4,400rpm, 265lb ft at 3,400 – less power than the latest fuel-injected IROC-Z Camaro but more torque. There was more acceleration too; magazine tests recorded 6–7 seconds for the 0–60 time, and 14–15-second standing quarters. This was performance that wouldn't have disgraced an early Shelby, so the Mustang really was back where it started.

To keep up, the SVO turbo was also boosted, this time to 205bhp, but one still had to be a turbo enthusiast to buy one. It was well-equipped, offered about the same performance as the V8 and was better balanced, thanks to the weight advantage,

and also used less fuel. But it cost $4,600 more, and while in 1985 less than 2,000 people bought Mustang turbos, nearly 50,000 bought V8s of one sort or another. Put another way, for every Mustang turbo sold, there were 25 V8s – little wonder that the turbo was dropped the following year.

Of course, one alternative was to order a V8 with the full Steve Saleen treatment, which still worked out at around $300

cheaper than the SVO. Saleen was now in full production (a relative term, as he built 132 Mustangs that year) and was given a big boost when Ford agreed to sell his cars through its dealer network. Better still, all the unmodified parts came with an unaffected Ford warranty, confirming that the Saleen Mustangs were no backyard specials but had the official seal of approval. The 1985 Saleens had a very similar specification to the 1984 prototypes; consequently there were no mechanical differences, apart from bodywork and suspension changes.

Of the Mustang V8s bought in standard Dearborn trim, most were the full-powered variety, but if one wanted a Mustang to cruise behind a hassle-free automatic, then the fuel-injected 5.0-litre was still available. In fact, it was given a power boost later in the year, with 180bhp now on offer. A bigger, less restrictive exhaust with dual tailpipes, plus a full-throttle air-conditioning cut-off did the business, while the faithful four-cylinder non-turbo and the fuel-injected V6 continued unchanged. Four-cylinder sales bounced back in 1985, in spite of all the ballyhoo over the V8, to just over half of all sales, while one in three Mustang buyers went for the V8 that same year.

All Mustangs had a smoother front end this year, with a small four-hole front spoiler and parking lamps, the front grille shrinking to a single slot, as on the SVO. Meanwhile, the range was juggled again and the basic Mustang L was dropped. LX equipment included power brakes and steering, remote-control right-hand mirror, an AM/FM radio, centre console and low-backed bucket seats.

The cheapest Mustang was now the four-cylinder LX coupé at $6,885, which was actually a lower price than that of the 1984 L.

In fact, the base LX was a route to cheap performance if the GT (now not far short of $10,000) seemed too expensive. Late in the model year, Ford brought back the Boss as a stripped-out, low-priced Mustang V8. There was no air conditioning, power windows or fancy stereo, but it did have the same 210-bhp V8 as the top-range GT, and it weighed about 125lb (57kg) less.

No one would have known the Boss was back, as Ford applied no badging to the effect, but maybe that was deliberate; the LX V8 appeared no different from the humblest 2.3 four-cylinder Mustang. *Car Craft*, which drove the Boss in the summer of 1985, remarked that anyone could put together a similar car, merely by ticking the right option box for a basic LX coupé (cheapest in the range) plus the 5.0-litre V8, 5-speed transmission, a 2.73:1 Traction Lok differential and 15-in (38-cm) Goodyear Gatorback tyres with alloy wheels. The result would cost around $9,300, saving nearly $600 on the GT. Considering the GT itself was judged good value next to an IROC-Z Camaro, the Boss LX must have seemed a bargain indeed.

Most road tests, however, concentrated on the full-house GT, which even now was becoming something of an institution, especially as this was the final year for carburettors, of which all the magazines seemed aware. Remember those tests of the 1983 175-bhp GT, when the word 'crude' appeared depressingly often? Well the word now seemed to be 'fun'. One would have expected that all the extra power would have thrown the GT's handling problems into even sharper relief, but it seemed to have finally been tamed, at least partially. Vertical gas-filled shocks, plus an extra set of horizontal shocks to dampen axle movement and stem wind-up, did a great deal to help, as did the latest low-profile Goodyears, 225/60VR15 on 7-in (18-cm) cast-aluminum wheels. The axle tended to misbehave now and again (*Road & Track* reckoned the Camaro still had better handling and balance), but the GT's behaviour was transformed.

The whole car was still rather rough around the edges, but that's exactly what some road testers (maybe all road testers) loved. 'Here's a package that still offers that lovely axle-creaking torque reminiscent of another time (*Motor Trend*).' Or how about this from *Car and Driver*: 'This is not a driver's car. This is an *enthusiast's* car. Stab it and steer it, and laugh like a fool when the secondaries open and the trees get all blurred.'

Not everyone was impressed, however. Writing in *Motor* magazine in December 1984, English journalist Russell Bulgin didn't like the styling of the GT convertible, seeing it as 'a slightly awkward amalgam of American and European influences', with 'lame-brain' décor. As for the steering, it was 'as horrible as Bruce Springsteen's dress sense'. He concluded that the Mustang 'belongs to another age'. Drivers on different sides of the Atlantic had very different expectations, and Bulgin's remarks

underline just how American the Mustang V8 was. For U.S. drivers, a slight waywardness and sloppy steering was more than made up for by a beefy, revvy V8 that roared and throbbed and reminded them (for those who could remember) of the Boss 302 and 429, the Shelbys and Cobra Jets – the good old days.

PRODUCTION

Coupé	56,781
Hatchback	84,623
Convertible	15,110
TOTAL	156,514

ENGINE LINE-UP
2.3-litre four

Type	Water-cooled cast-iron, ohc
Bore x stroke	3.78 x 3.13in (96 x 79.5mm)
Capacity	140ci (2.3 litres)
Compression ratio	9.0:1
Fuelling	Single-barrel carburettor
Power	88bhp @ 4,000rpm

2.3-litre four turbo SVO

Type	Water-cooled cast-iron, ohc
Bore x stroke	3.78 x 3.13in
Capacity	140ci (2.3 litres)
Compression ratio	8.0:1
Fuelling	Electronic injection
Power	205bhp @ 5,000rpm

3.8-litre EFI V6

Type	Water-cooled cast-iron, ohc
Bore x stroke	3.80 x 3.40in (96.5 x 86.4mm)
Capacity	232ci (3.8 litres)
Compression ratio	8.7:1
Fuelling	Electronic injection
Power	120bhp @ 3,600rpm

5.0-litre EFI V8

Type	Water-cooled cast-iron, ohv
Bore x stroke	4.00 x 3.00in (102 x 76.2mm)
Capacity	302ci (5.0 litres)
Compression ratio	8.3:1
Fuelling	Electronic injection
Power	165bhp @ 3,800rpm (late 180bhp)

5.0-litre HO V8

Type	Water-cooled cast-iron, ohv
Bore x stroke	4.00 x 3.00in
Capacity	302ci (5.0 litres)
Compression ratio	8.3:1
Fuelling	Four-barrel carburettor
Power	210bhp @ 4,000rpm

1986:
GOODBYE, CARBURETTOR

Nineteen-eighty-six was a year of goodbyes. The Mercury Capri, that upmarket, luxury version of the 1980s Mustang, was reaching its final year. After a good start in 1979, it had sold in diminishing numbers year on year, and in 1985 just over 15,000 found homes. This was only one-tenth of the Mustang figure, and in terms of Ford mass-production not worth pressing the

'Go' button on the assembly line for. In the 1986 model year, its final, just over 12,600 were sold. There had been a Mercury Capri in the 1960s too, mirroring the Mustang technically but with plusher interior trim, but now the Mustang was on its own.

It was farewell too, to the SVO turbo, which made an exit in 1986; this was the 205-bhp 2.3-litre turbo Mustang, the 145-bhp

GT turbo option having been dropped the previous year. Ford finally let go of the four-cylinder turbo experiment with which it had persevered for seven years in the Mustang. It had tried hard with the concept, despite minimal sales, especially when compared with the Mustang range as a whole.

In 1979, a turbocharged four-cylinder Mustang made a lot of sense, promising the

power of a V8 with at least some of the fuel economy of a small four. The CAFE regulations were the motivation, with a target of 27.5mpg (9.7km/litre) set for 1985 – a poor figure by European standards but stratospheric to makers of big heavy V8 sedans and muscle cars.

But the 27.5 target never happened. In the event, it was softened to 21mpg for 1984 and 22.5mpg for 1985. These were achieveable figures, even for a Mustang V8, and still took plenty of development work to make them happen, but reducing engine friction and fitting extra-tall gearing did the trick. Consequently, the Mustang was able to avoid the gas-guzzler tax and remain affordable. As for CAFE, it failed to radically change U.S. car industrial practice and the public's buying habits. Gas was still cheap in the U.S.A., at least compared with Europe, so there was little incentive for manufacturers to

strive to better the CAFE targets. CAFE also exempted light commercial vehicles, which later allowed a flood of luxury, gas-guzzling pickups and SUVs to flout the consumption targets quite openly.

Given the choice, however, Mustang buyers invariably chose a V8 or V6 over the turbocharged four. Their preference was reinforced by the fact that the V8 remained over $4,000 cheaper than the SVO, though it has to be said that Ford deliberately positioned the top turbo as a costly flagship, loading it with every conceivable option. But loaded or not, who would pay extra for a revvy, fussy, four-cylinder turbo when he or she could have a V8, a 'proper' Mustang in the muscle-car tradition, especially with the 1979 oil crisis a distant memory; gas prices had by now come down and queues were a thing of the past.

For keen drivers, the 2.3 four was lighter

than the block-busting V8, less nose-heavy and better balanced, but drivers who really cared about such things (enough to pay a $4,000 premium) were in a tiny minority, which was reflected in tiny sales. The SVO did recover slightly, achieving 3,382 in its final year, which came to less than 10,000 in its three-year production run. So maybe the Mustang turbo wasn't right for 1980s America; as to the future, we live in a world of uncertain oil supplies, global warming and increasing environmental concern – who's to say when a fuel-saving Mustang might be back on the agenda?

The year 1986 was of far more relevance to traditional muscle-car enthusiasts than the demise of a high-tech turbo or luxury Capri. The full-powered V8 Mustang finally ditched its four-barrel carburettor in favour of fuel injection. Today, when every car, even the cheapest, has precise, reliable fuel injection, this doesn't seem such a big deal. But for V8 muscle cars it was. They had always used carburettors, big four-barrels from Holley or Rochester. They had been an easy route to extra power, as almost anyone could buy a bigger carburettor and manifold to suit and bolt it on. CFM (cubic feet per minute, which measured the carb's breathing capacity) become one of those key figures in muscle-car culture, alongside brake horsepower and standing quarter-mile times.

The Mustang had actually held out against fuel injection for quite some time, though the basic V6 and V8 had already adopted it. Now, keeping up with the CAFE target (even the less ambitious one that became law) made it essential, and by 1987

all Mustangs would be injected. The system used was sequential multi-point injection as opposed to the simpler throttle body type used in the 180-bhp Mustang V8 and the V6. Computer-controlled, with speed density management, it changed the underhood look of the 5.0-litre V8 as well as improving efficiency. As some magazines had already predicted, power was down slightly (by 5 per cent to 200bhp), but torque was boosted to 285lb ft, a 7.5 per cent increase.

With a fatter torque curve, acceleration was actually improved, with at least one road test recording 0–60mph in 6 seconds dead. An added benefit of injection was that it made the Mustang smoother and easier to drive at low speeds. But injection wasn't the only change to the V8 for 1986. There was a concerted effort to cut friction (again, with the CAFE target in mind). All V8s now had roller tappets (said to reduce friction by 7 per cent), and the water pump was revised to reduce drag and increase the cooling system efficiency by 11 per cent. Piston skirts were redesigned and low-tension rings were fitted to cut friction further still.

Despite all these changes, *Hot Rod* declared that the latest Camaro, in top-spec IROC Z28 guise, was finally a better car all round than the Mustang GT. For years, road testers had been praising the injected Camaro as better balanced and more sophisticated than the relatively crude Mustang. But it was heavier and slower and maybe slightly too competent for its own good. With the option now of a 230-bhp Corvette tuned-port injection V8, it could finally outdrag the Mustang. What the Ford

had in its favour, of course, was price. At $10,691 for the hatchback GT (and several hundred less if one didn't mind slumming it in an LX) the Mustang remained the bargain muscle car of the 1980s.

Apart from the big step (in Mustang terms) of fuel injection, there were few other changes for 1986. All cars now had a third high-mounted stop lamp (a mandatory requirement) mounted on the spoiler on LX hatchbacks, GTs and SVOs. On convertibles, a baggage rack was added on which to mount the light. There was extra sound-deadening and a longer anti-corrosion warranty – hardly radical stuff – but perhaps the arrival of fuel injection had been shock enough for one year! It did no harm to sales at all; the Mustang had its best year since the 1979 debut, with sales rocketing by over 50per cent to 244,410. If anyone was shedding tears over the demise of the Holley four-barrel V8, they were in a distinct minority.

PRODUCTION

Coupé	84,774
Hatchback	117,690
Convertible	22,946
TOTAL	244,410

ENGINE LINE-UP

2.3-litre four

Type	Water-cooled cast-iron, ohc
Bore x stroke	3.78 x 3.13in (96 x 79.5mm)
Capacity	140ci (2.3 litres)
Compression ratio	9.5:1
Fuelling	Single-barrel carburettor
Power	88bhp @ 4,000rpm

2.3-litre four turbo SVO

Type	Water-cooled cast-iron, ohc
Bore x stroke	3.78 x 3.13in
Capacity	140ci (2.3 litres)
Compression ratio	8.0:1
Fuelling	Electronic injection
Power	205bhp @ 5,000rpm

3.8-litre EFI V6

Type	Water-cooled cast-iron, ohc
Bore x stroke	3.80 x 3.40in (96.5 x 86.4mm)
Capacity	232ci (3.8 litres)
Compression ratio	8.7:1
Fuelling	Electronic injection
Power	120bhp @ 3,600rpm

5.0-litre HO V8

Type	Water-cooled cast-iron, ohv
Bore x stroke	4.00 x 3.00in (102 x 76.2mm)
Capacity	302ci (5.0 litres)
Compression ratio	9.2:1
Fuelling	Electronic injection
Power	200bhp @ 4,400rpm

OPPOSITE
1986 Mustang 302-ci SVO.

1987:
NEW NOSE, MORE POWER

As it turned out, the Fox-bodied pony car was the longest-lived Mustang of all. Take a look at the history. The original Mustang had been updated every two to three years, in 1967, '69 and '71. These were not modest facelifts but new bodies, and often consisted of substantial engineering changes under the skin, mainly to accommodate ever larger V8s. The back to basics Mustang II had no major revisions or restyles, but it was replaced after only five years.

As for the Fox Mustang, it was finally given a facelift after seven years (not a new body, merely a new nose and some tweaks here and there), and the car wasn't finally replaced until the 1994 model year, a full 15 years after it was first unveiled. Well before the end of the 1980s, the Mustang had already been written off by some observers as an outdated rear-wheel-drive, a muscle-car throwback that had no place in the modern world. How and why did Ford manage to string it out for so long?

A radically new, modern Mustang would have been expensive, and may not have been acceptable in any case. There were, however, well-founded rumours that the company was considering just such a car. In the early 1980s, the SN8 (for Sporty North American car No.8) was a serious project. If it had come to fruition, the new Mustang would have been a small, high-tech car with a nimble chassis in the European tradition; in the event, however, it failed to get the green light.

The SN8 would have been substantially new and thus very costly and time-consuming to develop, but in the mid-1980s a much cheaper alternative presented itself. Ford now had a large stake in the Japanese manufacturer Mazda. Surely it made sense, the argument went, for the small-car expert to develop a replacement for the Mustang, using a front-wheel-drive platform which could be used by both companies. The car would be built in Flat Rock, Michigan, thus hopefully side-stepping objections to a Japanese-imported Mustang, and would be sold with both Ford and Mazda badges. As an all-new, high-tech up-to-the-minute replacement of the ageing Mustang, and at relatively little cost to Ford, it sounded too good to be true.

It was. Ford was horrified by the public outcry when news of the plan leaked out to the motoring press. American buyers wanted a Mustang that was traditional, and they let Ford know it in no uncertain terms. That meant rear-wheel-drive, a V8 engine and all-American designed and built. Ford capitulated, and the Mustang remained as it was. The joint project continued, however, finally unveiled as the Ford Probe, a four-seater coupé that was as it appeared – svelte, sleek and modern, but not a Mustang.

The second tranche of reasons for keeping the Fox Mustang going was very simple. The car was still selling in large numbers and making good profits. From a low point in 1983, when a still-respectable 120,000

Mustangs were built, sales had increased year on year to 141,000 (1984), 156,000 (1985) and 224,000 (1986). Riding the back of a renewed wave of enthusiasm for grunting V8 motors, backed by relatively good economy from the 2.3-litre four-cylinder, plus low prices, the Mustang just kept on selling. It was by no means sophisticated, but this, of course, was part of its appeal. Moreover, although the Fox Mustang had cost millions of dollars to develop, this had been repaid with interest seven times down the line, with every Mustang Ford now sold turning a profit.

So in 1987 there were good reasons for Ford not to replace the Mustang with a rebadged Mazda but to give it a quick facelift and carry on business as usual. For 1987 the Mustang was given its first (and only) makeover, when a new nose in the SVO style brought a smoother look, with just a small grille left on the LX and nothing at all on GTs. There were big single rectangular headlamps, while the C-pillars on the hatchbacks were made to look slimmer by a combination of blacking them out and extending the rear quarter-window glass; the GT hatchback and convertible got more cues to differentiate them from the base LXs. A ground-effect body kit included big front and rear spoilers, sill extensions and fender trims. Even the tail lights were different, hidden behind a lattice cover.

There were changes inside too, with a softer, more rounded dashboard designed by

Trevor Creed. Minor controls were now sited on wing extensions near to the driver's hands; there was a new two-spoke steering wheel (tiltable on the GTs) and a centre console. The pedals on manual-gearbox Mustangs were finally positioned on the same plane to allow for heel and toe changes. Side-window demisters were a new practical touch, and there was better-quality fabric, plus cloth inserts in the door trims. New storage bins were useful, and the optional AM/FM stereo was now tuned electronically rather than manually.

Performance freaks were not disappointed, though the 250-bhp 351-ci Mustang (as at least one magazine had speculated) didn't appear. But Ford really couldn't ignore the challenge of Chevrolet's 230-bhp 1986 Camaro, so the fuel-injected 5.0-litre GT was boosted to 225bhp (hopefully enough to outdrag the GM, which was still heavier than the Mustang). Most of the extra 25 horsepower came from a bigger air intake, 60-mm throttle body and freer-flowing cylinder heads. The full-powered 5.0-litre was already available with both four-speed automatic as well as the faithful Borg Warner T-5 manual and had been since the 'cruising' detuned 5.0-litre had been dropped the previous year.

To cope with the extra power, there were larger brakes, now 10.84-in (27.5-cm) ventilated discs on the front, while four-cylinder Mustangs continued with the 10.6-in (27-cm) discs. The suspension had to be modified to suit the big rotors with repositioned lower arm pickup points, which also lowered the car's roll centre. Damping rates were also revised to suit the higher tyre pressures recommended for the standard Goodyear Gatorbacks.

What was surprising this year was the success of the convertible. Sales had been sliding during its first couple of years before bouncing back in 1986, when all Mustangs did well. Even the following year, when sales as a whole slipped by nearly 30 per cent, Ford still sold over 20,000 ragtops. In 1988, the figure was over 35,000, the open-top Fox Mustang's best year so far. Price had something to do with it: at less than $13,000, the convertible LX was beginning to seem like good value; moreover, in 1987 it had little competition. In fact, so successful was the convertible that Ford dropped the T-Roof option in early 1988.

Dearborn also seemed to have latched on to the concept of the LX Mustang V8 as a bargain-basement muscle car. To save buyers the trouble of wading through the long options list in search of all the right boxes to tick, a 5.0-litre V8 package was devised, which brought everything together. For $1,885 one could have an identical mechanical set-up to the show-off GT: 225-bhp 5.0-litre V8, T-5 manual gearbox, well tied-down suspension (Quadra Shock rear end, anti-roll bars at both ends), 11-in (28-cm) front discs, 7-in (18-cm) aluminium wheels (though not turbines) and low-profile Goodyear Gatorback tyres.

What was not provided was the GT's show-off parts, notably the look-at-me body kit, turbine-style aluminium wheels and various other bits and pieces. So an LX with the 5.0-litre package was subtle muscle indeed. Look hard and you might spot the little '5.0L' badges that Ford fitted as part of the package, but that was about it. Otherwise, the V8 LX was almost identical to the 2.3-litre four-cylinder car on which it was based.

Even if one didn't go for the street

sleeper look, there was another good reason for buying an LX instead of a GT. It weighed over 300-lb (136-kg) less, so it was quicker to both 60mph and over the quarter-mile (sub-six and 13 seconds respectively, according to *Hot Rod*, if one fitted a pair of slicks). It was also better balanced on twisty roads as well as $1,500 cheaper; for not much more than $10,000, American buyers could have one of the fastest cars on the market. Next to the plush GT it looked a little stripped-out, but one couldn't get much closer to the original muscle-car concept than that.

PRODUCTION

Coupé	64,704
Hatchback	94,441
Convertible	21,447
TOTAL	180,592*
*Some sources say	159,145

ENGINE LINE-UP
2.3-litre four

Type	Water-cooled cast-iron, ohc
Bore x stroke	3.78 x 3.13in (96 x 79.5mm)
Capacity	140ci (2.3 litres)
Compression ratio	9.5:1
Fuelling	Electronic injection
Power	90bhp @ 3,800rpm

5.0-litre HO V8

Type	Water-cooled cast-iron, ohv
Bore x stroke	4.00 x 3.00in (102 x 76.2mm)
Capacity	302ci (5.0 litres)
Compression ratio	9.2:1
Fuelling	Electronic injection
Power	225bhp @ 4,000rpm

1988:
TWIN TURBO PLANS

Nineteen-eighty-eight was a quiet year for the Mustang in terms of model changes. There were bigger batteries all round (75 ampere in the V8s, 58 in the fours) and a new injection system for California-bound V8s, but that was about it, apart from four new paint colours. It was as though Ford felt the need of a rest after giving a facelift to the Fox Mustang the previous year (the first in seven years). Part of those changes involved dropping the 3.8-litre V6 motor, as well as the cruising V8 and SVO turbo. So from 1987 onwards, the Mustang was back to just two engine choices, the 90-bhp 2.3-litre four (now with fuel injection) and the 225-bhp V8, with nothing in between.

Ford did increase prices, however, by around $700 for hatchbacks and coupés and $1,100 for convertibles. In spite of this, however, 1988 turned out to be one of the Mustang's boom years. Only five times in its 15-year production run did the Fox Mustang break through the 200,000 barrier: on its debut in 1979 (a massive 369,000), in 1980, and again in '86, '88 and 1989, when over 214,000 Mustangs were produced. These particular Ford figures refer to the U.S. market only, with relatively few Mustangs built for export.

Once again, the hatchback was the buyers' favourite, as it always had been, with over 125,000 built. It cost around $500 more than the sedan, but the liftback gave it added practicality and it looked a little more sporty than the sedan-like notchback coupé. Only 53,000 of those found buyers. But the real surprise was the convertible, which continued its relative success with over 35,000 built, making 1988 its best year so far.

Meanwhile, Steve Saleen had been getting into his stride as the Carroll Shelby of the 1980s. Saleen stuck to his original philosophy of steering clear of engine or transmission modifications, which enabled him to carry on offering the standard Ford warranty on most Saleen Mustangs, and to sell them through Ford dealers. Instead, they majored on suspension changes, with the company's own Racecraft set-up fitted as standard. This included the coil springs,

Monroe shocks, special strut-mounting bearings, a urethane anti-roll bar pivot and different alignment figures.

As well as the revised suspension, there was a Saleen only body kit (all the usual paraphernalia of spoilers, skirts and extensions) and 225/50VR-16 General XP-2000V tyres. The Saleen Mustang was never promoted as a luxury upgrade but part of the 1988 package was a six-speaker AM/FM stereo with graphic equalizer (did anyone ever learn how to use a graphic equalizer; did they ever need one?), FloFit sports seats and three-spoke Momo steering wheel.

More functional was the Hurst quick-ratio gear shift, though the 170-mph speedo was really there as a brag. The latter was a Saleen face stuck over the standard 85-mph speedometer – not really relevant at the time of the double-nickel speed limit, but it looked serious, and that's partly what customers were paying an extra $10,000 for. That was another change: the cost of the Saleen conversion had increased a little since the original $4,000 premium of 1985; not that it put many people off, as over 700 Saleen Mustangs were sold in 1988.

Options were few, with a lower 3.55:1 rear axle the only regular choice, though as a special order one could have an automatic transmission, sunroof or aftermarket tuning parts. All Saleens were based on the LX hatchback, coupé or convertible, with the 5.0-litre V8 Custom Equipment Group and rear window demister, shipped direct from Dearborn to Saleen without a radio. By now Saleen had a thriving business; however, he allowed himself a quiet time each year when Ford made its Mustang model-year switchover. In 1988, he attempted to fill this gap with the Sportruck, based on the Ford Ranger pickup, but uncertain parts supply killed the project off after only 24 had been built. ·

Of course, most of the Saleen Mustangs stuck with the standard 225-bhp V8, but Ford itself was thinking how it could upgrade the Mustang in this area to enable it to meet and beat the upcoming Corvette ZR-1. So it commissioned the famous Jack Roush to build something suitable, to which he responded with a twin-turbo 5.7-litre (351-ci) car with around 400bhp. It failed to get the nod, however, when Ford management decided to squeeze more power out of the existing 5.0-litre.

But that wasn't the end of the story. The V8 Mustang had already become something of a hot-rod legend of the 1980s, and there were plenty of specialists ready and willing to do what Dearborn would not. Chris Kaufmann was one such, offering a 5.7-litre Mustang, though in Stage 3 form this was for track use only (or for those with access to very long, traffic-free private roads). More typical of road-legal Mustangs was the 280-bhp 5.0-litre run by James J. Bittle, who happened to be Saleen's parts manager.

Road & Track gave both of these cars a blast at the Firebird International Raceway in the summer of 1988. A special big-block Camaro was there too, with just short of 500bhp, which not surprisingly was decisively quicker than the two Mustangs; but the 330-bhp Kaufmann car ('a real point and squirt car') shot throught the quarter-mile in 13.5 seconds at 105.5mph (169.8km/h). It generated 0.92g of lateral force and whipped through the test slalom at 65.8mph (105.9km/h). The Bittle (with a mere 280bhp), actually quicker through the slalom, managed 0.91g and a 13.9-second standing quarter. And the Camaro? With nitrous button pressed it was on a 12.2-second quarter, at over 127mph (204.4km/h).

That was all very well for the minority of enthusiasts prepared to spend extra cash and void the official warranty by adding aftermarket parts. Most buyers wanted to do neither, and in any case Ford had by now taken the decision not to build a 351 Mustang. The shadow of two oil crises simply wouldn't go away and CAFE was here to stay, so although the V8 Mustang had sparked a new generation of muscle cars, a rerun of the 1960s was not to be. The sky wasn't the limit on power any more: safety, emissions and insurance ratings were the new criteria.

This was why the ageing Mustang V8 was beginning to stand out, like a sweating full-back fresh from the game turning up at a polite cocktail party. Nowhere was this distinction plainer than when the Fox was compared side by side with the Ford Probe. The Probe was the Mustang that might have been, the Mazda-based coupé that at one time

Ford executives hoped would be a fourth-generation Mustang.

Healthy sales and the V8 revival caused them to think again, but the Probe was launched anyway, as Ford needed something to equal the sophisticated Japanese coupés that were making an impression on U.S. buyers. The Mustang was popular with its own clientele, but was just too uncouth, too hairy-chested and too loud to cater for folk who preferred a quiet and comfortable coupé like the Toyota Celica.

Obligingly, *Road & Track* placed a Mustang GT and Probe GT side by side in early 1988 and predictably found two very different cars appealing to very different customers; how the course of history would have changed if the Probe had been a

ABOVE
Mustang Saleen 405 coupé.

OPPOSITE
1988 Mustang 5-litre GT convertible.

OPPOSITE and LEFT
The 1988 Mustang 2.3-litre automatic.
All eyes were on the glamorous V8s,
but the bargain-priced fours were still
selling in reasonable numbers.

OPPOSITE and LEFT
1988 Mustang 5-litre LX automatic.

LEFT
1988 Mustang 5-litre GT five-speed,
here in convertible form.

*BELOW and OPPOSITE
1988 Mustang 351 convertible. Note
the stripes – a homage to Carroll
Shelby.*

Mustang. In place of the familiar rip-roaring 225-bhp V8 there was a four-cylinder sohc unit of 145bhp (turbocharged in GT guise). There was independent suspension at both ends, anonymous blob-like styling, and a convenient, well-appointed interior. Two very different cars, but on paper they seemed to perform quite similarly. Despite its huge power disadvantage, the Probe wasn't that

far behind: 7.3 seconds 0–60 (Mustang, 6.4), only a second adrift to 100mph and just 0.6 seconds slower over the standing quarter. It even made almost the same cornering force as the old stager – 0.80g against 0.81g.

But this was only half the story. The Mustang remained a short-wheelbased car with great gobs of torque (to use an old motoring adjective), which needed some

skill to drive it fast without spinning it into the undergrowth. The Probe understeered in a mild and safe manner – it would not bite back. It was comfortable, practical, easy to drive, and fast when required. On weekday commutes or trips to the stores, moreover, the Probe was like any other Japanese-designed hatchback. But the Mustang made no such concessions, and that's what made it a Mustang.

PRODUCTION

Coupé	53,221
Hatchback	125,930
Convertible	35,500
TOTAL	214,651*
(U.S. market only).	
*Some sources say	211,225

ENGINE LINE-UP
2.3-litre four

Type	Water-cooled cast-iron, ohc
Bore x stroke	3.78 x 3.13in (96 x 79.5mm)
Capacity	140ci (2.3 litres)
Compression ratio	9.5:1
Fuelling	Electronic injection
Power	90bhp @ 3,800rpm

5.0-litre HO V8

Type	Water-cooled cast-iron, ohv
Bore x stroke	4.00 x 3.00in (102 x 76.2mm)
Capacity	302ci (5.0 litres)
Compression ratio	9.2:1
Fuelling	Electronic injection
Power	225bhp @ 4,000rpm

1989:
BIRTHDAY, WHAT BIRTHDAY?

RIGHT and OPPOSITE
Steve Saleen continued to build his
tweaked Mustangs in small numbers.

Ford, as car makers go, is no more aware of its heritage than any other. But one might have expected it to make a bit of a splash when the Mustang's 25th anniversary came around. After all, the name had developed into what modern marketing-speak called a brand with added value.

It was not only a badge on a car. To a couple of generations of Americans, 'Mustang' also conjured up a host of nostalgic images. Those fearsome early Shelby GTs (before they became mere badge and paint jobs); watching hard-fought Trans Ams at a twisty raceway; street racing

around the local town or cruising down to the beach. Many people learned to drive in a Mustang, or bought one as their first car. And although many middle-aged middle Americans bought Mustangs as well, it remained indelibly associated with youth and having a good time.

It was a survivor, too. In the 25 years since a proud Lee Iacocca revealed the world's first pony car, the U.S.A. had been through a lot: the Vietnam War, race riots and Watergate, not to mention two oil crises and the first realization that one day the gas pumps might actually run dry. These were decades of uncertainty, of rapidly changing values in a fast-moving world. In the world of cars, there had been times when it seemed as though the muscle car, or any kind of fun car, was on the way out. And yet the Mustang, the car that many Americans grew up with, was still around. For many people, this was strangely comforting.

So when the Mustang, the first, original and most enduring pony car reached its 25th anniversary, many enthusiasts were excitedly contemplating what Ford would do. Perhaps Dearborn would produce the most horsepower-laden Mustang of all: that twin-turbo 400-bhp car that Jack Roush built at Ford's request (see 1988) was the prototype for just such a car. In the event, Ford decided against it; the super-Mustang would have attracted huge publicity, but maybe not all of the right kind for a company that was mindful of America's dependence on imported oil. Not only would such a car have been hugely expensive to develop (not counting the work needed to meet all the emissions and safety legislation), but it would have sent the wrong message – that Ford as a company had learned nothing from two oil crises.

This was quite understandable, but it is surprising that there was no other special edition: no loaded convertible in bright red or a luxury coupé with all the options, or maybe another attempt to ape the early Shelbys, big fat racing stripes and all. Actually, it didn't take a genius to realize why Ford was making no attempt to exploit the Shelby connection. Remember the GT350 convertible and the way it had been used to commemorate the Mustang's 20th anniversary? Ford may have won the court case when Carroll Shelby sued for misuse of his model name, but Ford had no wish to risk going through all that again.

There was no other attempt to make anything of the 25th (quite a landmark for any model) until halfway through the model year. From April 1989, Ford began to fix

little 25th-anniversary plaques onto dashboards, and went on doing so for a year. The official explanation was that this was the true anniversary, since that April was exactly 25 years since the original launch, in which case it would have made the GT350 convertible a 19th-anniversary model, it having been available from September 1983, the start of the 1984 model year. Another possible reason for Ford's apparent reluctance

to make much of the Mustang's 25th was that it was thinking of killing the car off once the 1989 model year had run its course.

Whatever the true reason, 1989 was a fairly uneventful model year, though there was another milestone when the six-millionth Mustang rolled off the line. It was a good time for the LX, however, with the GT's articulated highback sports seats now standard equipment (though not in the sedan) and power windows,

power door locks and power mirrors on the LX convertible. To make the LX V8 even more of a muscle-car bargain, Ford finally dsignated it a model in its own right, as the LX 5.0L Sport.

Like the previous Boss and V8 option packages, this was mechanically identical to the GT, except that it lacked some of its trim and all the flashy bodywork. Along with the 225-bhp V8 and T-5 manual gearbox there

OPPOSITE, ABOVE and OVERLEAF
1989 Mustang 5-litre LX with body kit.

were sports seats and interior trim, cast-aluminium wheels with P225/V-rated tyres, constant-ratio power steering, a Traction-Lok rear axle, GT-specification suspension and a beefier 75-amp alternator.

Available in all three body styles, the LX 5.0L Sport cost $11,410 as the notchback coupé, $12,265 in popular hatchback form and a little over $17,000 as a convertible, saving around $500 over the equivalent GT. However, its weight advantage over the GT was down to around 80lb (36kg), thanks to extra equipment for the Sport, so it wasn't quite the stripped-out lightweight bargain that the original LX V8 had been; it still cost less than some four-cylinder Japanese coupés yet offered supercar performance in a straight line. And for those attracted to the idea of a muscle car that whispered rather than shouted, the Sport looked almost identical to the base four-cylinder LX.

The Saleen Mustangs were LX-based too, as there was no point in paying extra for the GT body kit which Saleen would simply unbolt and replace with his own. For the first few years of producing special Mustangs, Steve Saleen also steered clear of engine tuning, preferring to concentrate on appearance, suspension modifications and the interior. As already seen, this had the substantial benefit of enabling him to sell his hopped-up Mustangs through Ford dealers with a Ford warranty still intact.

But for 1989, Saleen finally introduced Mustang SSC (which modestly stood for 'Saleen Super Car'). There were no radical changes to the 5.0-litre V8, but Saleen did fit a larger 65-mm throttle body and revised intake

plenum. The cylinder-head intake ports were enlarged and polished, and the rocker-arm ratios were changed to increase valve lift. Bigger stainless-steel headers replaced the standard exhaust manifold, with new mufflers to reduce back pressure to an absolute minimum. Even so, without extra cubic inches and wild cams, Saleen claimed a near 30 per cent power boost to 292bhp.

Car and Driver was sceptical when it tested the SSC. It measured a 0–60 time of 5.9 seconds, a standing quarter of 14.2 (at 98mph/158km/h), with the Mustang running out of breath in its tall top gear at 4,500rpm (149mph/240km/h). It was fast, but maybe not 292-bhp fast; *Car and Driver* estimated that it was more like 270. This being a Saleen, the suspension came in for attention, notably because of Monroe shocks (adjustable from the cockpit to soft, normal or hard) and Saleen's own springs, which *Car and Driver* drily described as 'firm'.

A drawback of the Fox Mustang, when compared with more modern muscle cars, was the flexibility of its shell, which the SSC sought to cure with a 'Chassis Support System'. This was a triangular tube structure that braced the two front strut towers to one another and the engine bulkhead. In the back, a similar arrangement did the same in the hatch area and there was a K-member beneath the front box section.

The result underlined the effect of stiff suspension, though it did reduce body flex; *Car and Driver* decided that, at 0.82g, the SSC's ultimate grip was disappointing, little better than the standard Mustang. The difference was that it was very stable at the

limit, so more drivers could use more of the performance envelope more of the time. Inside, the custom-built leather seats and trim indicated where some of the car's $35,000 asking price had gone, as did the 120-watt ten-speaker stereo. Being a Saleen, there was a full body kit so that everyone would know that it was a hot Mustang. Stiff, bumpy, fast and rip-roaringly noisy, the Saleen SSC Mustang left no one in any doubt that the aftermarket hot rod was alive and well.

PRODUCTION

Coupé	50,560
Hatchback	116,965
Convertible	42,244
TOTAL	209,769

(U.S. market only)

ENGINE LINE-UP

2.3-litre four

Type	Water-cooled cast-iron, ohc
Bore x stroke	3.78 x 3.13in (96 x 79.5mm)
Capacity	140ci (2.3 litres)
Compression ratio	9.5:1
Fuelling	Electronic injection
Power	90bhp @ 3,800rpm

5.0-litre HO V8

Type	Water-cooled cast-iron, ohv
Bore x stroke	4.00 x 3.00in (102 x 76.2mm)
Capacity	302ci (5.0 litres)
Compression ratio	9.2:1
Fuelling	Electronic injection
Power	225bhp @ 4,000rpm

1990:
THE QUIET SURVIVOR

In the 1990 model year, Ford finally recognized that the Mustang had been around for 25 years, though in a very low-key kind of way. 'Mustang, the first pony car,' read one brochure, 'brought affordable sporty car performance and styling to every street and highway in America. And what it did best 25 years ago, it still does the best today.' But it still wasn't shouting the Mustang's heritage from the rooftops. Blink, and one might have missed it altogether.

The same understatement was attached to the closest thing Ford had to a 25th-anniversary Mustang, a special edition of the convertible. Based on the 5.0-litre LX ragtop in Deep Emerald Jewel Green, this sported a white leather interior and matching white soft top. There were Sport seats and body colour for the mirrors and body side mouldings. Turbine-style aluminium was fitted (previously for GTs only) and instead of a spoiler there was a luggage rack. No other Mustang had ever used the all-white interior, so in this it was unique. There was also a 25th-anniversary plaque on the dashboard, making it a celebration of a quarter-century of Mustangs at last.

On the other hand, maybe not. All Mustangs built between March/April 1989 and the middle of the 1990 model year had a similar plaque. And while some maintain that the Emerald convertible really was the silver-anniversary Mustang, there could be other explanations. Some say that the green and white colour scheme was part of a regional promotion programme in conjunction with the 7-Up Bottling Company or a promotion allied to the National Basketball Association, or maybe with the NCAA, a college sports

administration body in the U.S.A. Al Kirschenbaum (*Official Mustang 5.0 Technical Reference & Performance Handbook*) suggests that the deep-green convertible was simply a response by Ford to many specialist tuners and body builders who were offering special versions of the Mustang convertible, and making money out of doing so. Ford simply wanted a slice of the cake.

Whatever its *raison d'être*, the convertible emerald Mustang was popular, as special editions go. Ford initially planned on building around 3,800 of them, but due to excessive demand, 4,301 rolled out of Dearborn between January and April 1990; all but 10 per cent were automatics.

For 1990, all Mustangs came with an airbag on the driver's side which necessitated a new steering wheel and obviated the need for tilt adjustment. In the rear, three-point seatbelts with shoulder harnesses were another standard safety feature. A 140-mph speedometer had replaced the double-nickel one for 55mph the previous year, and leather seats were a new option for hatchbacks, while all Mustangs now had map pockets. An interesting aside is that the centre console armrest was deleted early in the year, then reintroduced eight months later. This was reportedly an attempt by Ford to trim weight from the car to prevent EPA reclassification. Losing the armrest saved 7lb (3.2kg).

Mechanical changes amounted to almost nil for 1990, with engine, transmission, brakes and wheels/tyres all unchanged from 1989. There were two minor changes,

however: the tops of the front suspension struts were moved slightly back towards the cowl to reduce understeer and improve tyre wear, while the lower control arms were repositioned.

Meanwhile, the 5.0-litre LX was quietly becoming something of a success story. It had taken a while for the public and press to realize that an LX with an optional V8 and handling suspension was really a Mustang GT without the body kit and a few luxury items. Consequently, it was just as fast, offered the same thrill, and actually handled slightly better due to its lower weight. And of course it was much cheaper. The hatchback was $1,000 less in 1990, and the LX V8 also came in even lower-priced coupé form. If one could live with its subdued looks, it was even more of a performance bargain than the GT.

Sales reflected this. In 1982, only 4,646 non-GT Mustangs were ordered with a V8. Four years later, the first year of the LX, there were just 6,674. This rocketed to over 16,000 in 1987 and over 30,000 in '88, then nearly 46,000. In 1990, although sales were down slightly, the LX 5.0-litre outsold the GT for the first time, repeating the trick the following year. During the Fox Mustang's final couple of years – 1992 and '93 – it wasn't far behind. Maybe the LX's plain-Jane looks were attractive in themselves and it was no longer cool to shout 'performance', muscle-car revival or not.

Although the enthusiast press concentrated on the V8 Mustang in all its forms, sales figures reveal that around half of Mustang buyers were still opting for the

2.3-litre four. The actual figure varied, but in the second half of the Fox Mustang's life it fluctuated between 38 and 62 per cent of production. Ninety horsepower, it seems, was quite enough for some people, especially while the 55-mph limit was in force. For them, the four-cylinder Mustang LX in coupé, hatchback or convertible form made for well-equipped and relatively economical transportation. In any case, this too was part of the original Mustang concept: modest power (by U.S. standards) in a cheap-to-run but sporty-looking car.

Options had always been part of the Mustang story, and for 1990 Ford changed tack a little. The four-cylinder LX received a Special Value Package, with power locks, electric mirrors, power windows, styled wheels, upgraded radio and a cruise control; worth $835 on the official list, Ford threw it

OPPOSITE

Even though it couldn't be called a Shelby, the 1990 Mustang GT appeared in Shelby colours.

in free on 2.3 coupés, hatchbacks and convertibles. Buyers of the LX V8 Sport had to pay extra for some of these that year: its own Special Value Group cost $1,003 on the coupé or hatchback, just under $500 for the ragtop.

There was still a lot for the money: the electric mirrors, ugraded radio, styled wheels, cruise control and power windows were all as fitted to the four, but the V8's package added a Power Lock Group, Custom Equipment Group, air conditioning and illuminated vanity mirrors. A four-speed automatic transmission at $539 was available with either four or V8, and there were many other options ranging from an engine-block heater ($20) to clearcoat paintwork ($91). Californians still had to pay $100 extra for their emissions package.

Meanwhile, it was business as usual in the world of magazines. By now, the Mustang was such a familiar part of the scenery that most features concentrated on modified and tuned cars. However, Dean Batchelor of *Road & Track* did take the time to drive a GT convertible and ended up comparing it favourably with his 1932 Ford Roadster. Both 1990 and 1932 Fords were good-value V8 ragtops, and both were among the fastest cars available in America in their time. They even had similar power to weight ratios, and the Mustang's live rear axle certainly provided echoes of the 1930s on bumpy, twisty roads. Moreover, they were both bright red.

Meanwhile, Steve Saleen was aiming at a different market: the police. By this time, U.S. police forces were running around

5,000 Mustangs, having discovered that they actually made good patrol cars, being fast and relatively cheap. But even the V8 could sometimes be embarrassed by law-breakers in Porsches, so Saleen came up with a very special law-enforcement Mustang for the city of Seal Beach in California.

This came with all the usual accoutrements of a Saleen Mustang: low-profile General XP200 radials on wide wheels, stiffer springs, the usual bodywork bracing and body kit, plus an SVO rear axle with disc brakes. The latter was a real boon to the police, who had found the standard drums not always up to pursuit work. In addition, the four-speed automatic transmission was bolstered to cope with the rigours of police work, with a heavy-duty clutch pack, revised valve body and hydraulics. Monroe adjustable shocks, a low 3.55:1 rear axle (for faster getaways) and a roll cage were also fitted to the 'SB/S' ('Seal Beach Special'). The Seal Beach police liked it, but would ideally have had ABS anti-lock brakes as well. There was no pleasing some people.

PRODUCTION

Coupé	22,503
Hatchback	78,728
Convertible	26,958
TOTAL	128,189

ENGINE LINE-UP

2.3-litre four

Type	Water-cooled cast-iron, ohc
Bore x stroke	3.78 x 3.13in (96 x 79.5mm)
Capacity	140ci (2.3 litres)
Compression ratio	9.0:1
Fuelling	Electronic injection
Power	90bhp @ 3,800rpm

5.0-litre HO V8

Type	Water-cooled cast-iron, ohv
Bore x stroke	4.00 x 3.00in (102 x 76.2mm)
Capacity	302ci (5.0 litres)
Compression ratio	9.2:1
Fuelling	Electronic injection
Power	225bhp @ 4,200rpm

1991:
THE 203mph MUSTANG

The year 1991 saw another Mustang landmark, though not the kind that deserved much in the way of celebration. For the first time ever, the base-model pony car broached the $10,000 barrier. The cheapest Mustang available was still the LX coupé, but now it cost $10,157, due to a price increase of around 3 per cent across the range.

This came with the four-cylinder 2.3-litre engine, also fitted to the LX hatchback ($10,663) and LX convertible ($16,222). The price of V8 power had risen too, and upgrading to an LX 5.0-litre cost around $3,000, making it $13,270 for the coupé, just over $14,000 for the more popular hatchback and well over $19,000 for the ragtop. Go for a top-line GT and over $600 was added to the price of a convertible, nearly $1,000 on the hatchback.

On the face of it, these look like steep prices, especially when compared with those of the original Mustang. Back then, Ford made a big thing of the low sticker price: just $2,368 for the basic hardtop, $2,614 for the convertible. Of course, not many people actually kept to those prices, quickly succumbing to the temptations of a long and luscious options list; but the 1964 Mustang, in basic stripped-out form, was cheap indeed.

Despite that $10,000+ price tag, however, this still applied to its 1991

descendant. America had suffered a great deal of inflation in the intervening quarter-century, so everything (not only Mustangs) was more expensive than ever. Thirteen thousand dollars did not buy a huge amount of car in 1991, but it did allow one to drive away from the local Ford dealer in something with supercar performance, proving that some things never change and that the V8 Mustang was as much of a bargain as it had always been.

Despite price increase, few changes were made to the Mustang for 1991; it's worth reiterating that after its 1987 facelift, the Fox Mustang ran right through to 1993 with no major revisions at all. The 5.0-litre V8, now well-proven in its fuel-injected full-power form, still put out an impressive 225bhp at 4,200rpm and 300lb ft at 3,200. Related to that original 289 of the 1960s, it remained the personification of an uncomplicated American V8, even with fuel injection.

However, the four-cylinder motor was updated in the form of a twin-plug cylinder head. This encouraged more complete burning of the fuel/air mixture, which was good news for emissions and also boosted power to 105bhp at 4,600rpm, with compression ratio up to 9.5:1. These changes also affected economy; a 2.3-litre Mustang with the four-speed automatic transmission recorded 30mpg (10.6km/litre) on the official

highway figures, and 22mpg (7.7km/litre) on the city cycle. Oddly, the five-speed manual was slightly thirstier at 21/28mpg, but even the V8 manual could manage 25mpg out on the open road (the auto made 24) but dipped to 18mpg in the city.

Once again, these open-road figures were mediocre by European standards though respectable for an American car. The economy was slowing down in the early 1990s but there was no sign of a third oil crisis, so nearly two-thirds of Mustang buyers opted for the V8; even so, Mustang sales dipped to a new low of 98,737 that year. This was the worst sales year yet, not only for the Fox but also for any Mustang, lower even than in the dark days of the early 1970s. The car market in general was down too, but not to this extent, and the Mustang's share slumped to 1.7 per cent.

But a few parts were added to spruce up the car to keep it looking fresh, even though fewer people were actually buying it. There were new 16-in (41-cm) five-spoke alloy wheels for both GT and the 5.0 LX, coupled with new P225/55ZR-16 tyres (the latter standard on the LX, optional on the GT). The convertible top linkage was changed to make the roof sit 4in (10cm) lower when it was folded, making the ragtop look cleaner and sleeker with the top down. A brief road test of the GT convertible praised the power-operated top (just 15 seconds to fold it down into its new slimline shape), loved the highly-effective heating/air conditioning, and reckoned that the Mustang was only 2dBA noisier than a Mercedes 500SL convertible. But in one respect the 1991 Mustang had something in common with more elderly convertibles; cross railroad tracks, or even big bumps and the cowl would shake and the steering column shimmy. The open top was undeniably less rigid than the steel-topped Mustangs, which themselves were hardly paragons of strength.

But in 1991 the real interest, at least as far as the magazines were concerned, lay not in standard Mustangs but in tuned ones. Turbocharged, supercharged and nitrous oxide-injected, they kept on cropping up year after year, with specialists promising to give any new Mustang V8 Porsche-equalling performance for just a few extra thousand dollars. Actually, make that Porsche-beating, if the Cartech turbocharged car (featured in *Sports Cars of the World*) was any guide. This was turbocharging 1990s style, with no pretence that the turbo was there to combine performance with reasonable mileage (as with Ford's own 2.3 turbo in the 1980s). It was pure performance, full stop.

The V8 responded well to either turbo or supercharging. With a 9.0:1 compression ratio it could take reasonable levels of boost without the need to lower the ratio, which made conversion a whole lot simpler. The engine's internals were well-proven, strong and reliable, likewise the transmission, which would happily take more power; both Borg Warner T-5 and the 8.8-in (22.3-cm)

differential were unchanged on the Cartech turbo, though a Centerforce II clutch and pressure plate were part of the conversion. The effect of the Cartech conversion was astounding, producing 392bhp at 5,000rpm and no less than 550lb ft at 4,200. The Cartech Mustang was fully street-legal, right down to its catalytic converters.

Even with a street-friendly 2.73:1 rear axle, it managed a 0–60 time of 4.9 seconds, and reached 100mph (161km/h) in exactly 11; the standing quarter came up a couple of seconds later. Given the 225-horsepower Mustang's less than perfect handling, the effect of nearly 400 can only be imagined. So the standard tyres were ditched in favour of 16-inch (41-cm) Z-rated 2250/50 and 245/50s Goodyears. To suit, there were 7-

The 1991 standard Mustang was a fast car, but not fast enough for some.

and 8-inch wide MSW modular wheels. Suspension Techniques springs were 30 per cent stiffer than standard and lowered the car by an inch and a half. There were stronger anti-roll bars, plus Tokico Illimina low-pressure struts and rear shocks. Journalist Ro McGonegal reckoned that one could fit all the parts in one's driveway in the course of a long weekend, though they doubled the price of a Mustang GT to around $26,000.

The question was, how fast was it, and did it have the potential to go faster in a straight line? Corky Bell, the man behind Cartech, was determined to build the first 200-mph Mustang. So a Haltech fuel-injection system was added, with a separate injector for each cylinder and laptop adjustability for fine-tuning. This would deliver enough fuel to support 15psi of turbo boost; in other words, 36.6-ci (600-cc) per minute or 54 gallons (245 litres) per hour. The standard V8 wouldn't have been able to process that amount of fuel, so bigger valves went in (1.84-in intake, 1.65-in exhaust), along with high-tension valve springs and retainers, plus polished intake and exhaust ports – nothing too radical.

The result was 371bhp at the rear wheels (which translates into well over 400 at the flywheel), and the car was taken along to Fort Stockton, Texas, and to Phoenix, Arizona, to see what it would do. With a rollcage fitted (as much to stiffen the chassis for ultra-high speeds as for any safety consideration) and a 6psi boost, the Cartech Mustang ran to 183mph (294.5km/h) over the Arizona desert. Later, at Stockton, and increased to 10psi, it recorded an official 203mph (326.7km/h). Was this the fastest road-legal Mustang of all time?

PRODUCTION

Coupé	19,447
Hatchback	57,777
Convertible	21,513
TOTAL	98,737

ENGINE LINE-UP
2.3-litre four

Type	Water-cooled cast-iron, ohc
Bore x stroke	3.78 x 3.13in (96 x 79.5mm)
Capacity	140ci (2.3 litres)
Compression ratio	9.5:1
Fuelling	Electronic injection
Power	105bhp @ 4,600rpm

5.0-litre HO V8

Type	Water-cooled cast-iron, ohv
Bore x stroke	4.00 x 3.00in (102 x 76.2mm)
Capacity	302ci (5.0 litres)
Compression ratio	9.0:1
Fuelling	Electronic injection
Power	225bhp @ 4,200rpm

1992:
BRAND-NEW RETRO

In the 26 years that the Mustang had been on sale in the 20th century, what had been the sales low point? Surely not the 1960s, when Ford's pony car broke all the Detroit records, when queues – even crowds – invaded Ford dealerships and no one else had anything remotely to equal it.

Maybe it was the 1970s, when there were two oil crises, spiralling prices and the death of the muscle car was imminent. Then, the Mustang was downsized into a four-cylinder runabout and Chevrolet came close to dropping the Camaro altogether. No, it was not the 1970s; in fact, Mustang II actually sold very well as the 'right car at the right time'.

Could it have been the 1980s? Hardly; the four-cylinder Mustang was still selling in sizeable numbers to people coveting a sporty image without shelling out too many dollars, while the V8 was riding the waves as a reborn muscle car. In fact, 1992 turned out to be the worst year of the 20th century for the Mustang, with a sales figure of just 79,280. Why?

By now, it was an open secret that a new Mustang was on the way for 1994, so it is possible that buyers were waiting for that or purchasing something else in the meantime. It was the old dilemma of car manufacturers the world over; once customers got wind of a new model on the horizon they were less

inclined to fork out on an existing one. Mustang sales did recover in 1993, its final year, due partly to the extra interest engendered by the Cobra (page 328 et seq.) and partly through the realization that this really was the last chance to buy a basic V8 Mustang, the performance bargain of the 1980s and early '90s.

Of the 80,000-odd that did commit to a 1992 Mustang, around half bought hatchbacks. As ever, the practical three-door layout was the most popular Mustang of all, and the split between four-cylinder and V8 (across all three body styles) was almost exactly 50/50, suggesting that Ford was

offering the right choice of engines and catering for two very different types of owner. It is an interesting to note that coupé sales had slumped to less than 16,000 and that the notchback Mustang was now being comprehensively outsold by its convertible cousin, over 23,000 of which found homes that same year. Meanwhile, the ragtop had actually been outnumbering the coupé since 1990.

The open-top Mustang, perhaps even more than the others, personified an older type of car. More to the point, an older type that could still be bought brand new in 1992. In a road test of the GT, *Road & Track*

Fox was the longest-lived Mustang of all, but 1992 saw sales slump as buyers anticipated the next generation.

Now showing its age, the 5-litre Fox Mustang GT had become a real live retromobile.

described it as a 'rorty retro rocket'. (Would you rather send a letter than fax one? Do you hate computers? If the answer is 'yes', then needless to say, the Mustang GT convertible is your kind of car.) Despite the advances that had taken place over the years – the fuel injection, air bags and electronic ignition – the convertible was an outdated piece of kit in some ways. It still used a live rear axle with drum brakes. There was no ABS, let alone the option of four-wheel-drive or four-wheel-steering, which some high-tech Japanese coupés were offering. Instead, the Mustang

buyer had just two-wheel-drive (the rear pair, naturally) driven by a traditional pushrod V8.

Of course, this was exactly what some customers liked about it. Martin Peters liked the V8's instant low-down grunt and the heaviness of the five-speed manual gearchange ('in keeping with the heavy metal character'.). He liked the 'traditional V8 rumble … and some old-fashioned whine from some big, Yankee gears. It sounds that much better with the top down'. This was the reason for its appeal. The Mustang V8, especially as a convertible, felt distinctively

American at a time when most cars did not. For the patriotic, with stars 'n' stripes hanging from their front porches, that was all it needed to be. It was the Harley-Davidson phenomenon all over again, but this time on four wheels. (These all-American motorcycles had almost died in the 1970s and early '80s, but now were riding the crest of a wave in a cloud of nostalgia and patriotism that some high-income Americans could afford to indulge.)

Like the equivalent Harley, a 1992 Mustang was as traditional as it could be,

without looking actually old, but it was easy to live with beneath the surface. To close the top, for example, one only had to release two levers at the top of the windshield, push a button, and the ragtop folded neatly back into its space behind the rear seat. Once stowed, there was a neat trunk to cover it up. Top up, there was a little buffeting over 60mph, but as earlier road tests showed, the ragtop Mustang was relatively quiet and had efficient air conditioning. Unless one was a hard driver who liked to push things to the limit (in which case the Fox Mustang's live rear axle would still let it down), few sacrifices were needed to purchase this rolling piece of Americana.

Laid-back cruisers, for whom an automatic convertible was the ultimate type of pony car, had always been part of Mustang history. But there was another element – the sort of hard-driving enthusiasts who had bought Shelby Mustangs in the mid-1960s, a Boss Mustang in the late-'60s/early '70s and something else until the mid-1980s, when the full-powered V8 Mustang began to tempt them back. Most dedicated of all was the SAAC – the Shelby Automobile Club – an owner's club catering for those for whom the ultimate American supercar would always be the original GT350.

There was no chance that another Mustang would appear bearing a Shelby badge; remember the hooha when 'GT350' badges appeared on the side of the 20th-anniversary convertible? Carroll Shelby himself took Ford to court for misuse of a famous name. He lost, but Ford was unlikely to repeat the experience.

The SAAC was a different matter, and was on good terms with Shelby himself (still working for Chrysler and Lee Iacocca at the time). He agreed to lend his name to a reincarnation of the GT350, a limited-run Mustang financed and organized by the SAAC. In the event, the Shelby badges were considered misleading by SAAC leading light Rick Kopec, and were soon replaced by the club's snake logo. Still, the 'Shelby' SAAC Mustangs did go ahead, and with Carroll's blessing.

The 'Shelby AAC Mk1 Mustang', to give it its full title, sought to recreate the spirit of the first GT350, using off-the-shelf tuning parts to create a rough-edged road car that might also be competitive on track. It also came in white with big blue stripes, just like the real one. The V8 (there was no chance of it being a 2.3 four-cylinder Shelby) used SVO cylinder heads with improved airflow, bigger valves and tighter tolerances than the standard one. There was a larger 65-mm throttle body too, contributing to 296bhp at 5,500rpm and 326lb ft at 4,200. No turbos, no nitrous oxide, no tweaking with the electronics, just tried and tested hot rodding. This was accompanied by two braces to stiffen the car up, one between the front shock towers, another inside the car, plus, of course, stiffer springs, a lower ride height and Koni shocks all round. There were fat low-profile Goodyears and SVO disc brakes all round.

According to *Motor Trend*, the result offered great fun in small doses, but try to take the SAAC Mustang for a long haul and its charm began to wane. The souped-up V8 bellowed and roared; the car banged its uncomfortable occupants over bumps; the brakes were either full-on or full-off, while the steering seemed 'numb'. At $40,000, *Motor Trend* concluded that the SAAC Mustang made a standard $18,000 Fox look very good indeed. So in one way, the SAAC had succeeded in emulating the rip-roaring original Shelby – unforgettable to hard drivers, unforgiveable to just about everyone else.

PRODUCTION

Coupé	15,717
Hatchback	40,093
Convertible	23,470
TOTAL	79,280

ENGINE LINE-UP
2.3-litre four

Type	Water-cooled cast-iron, ohc
Bore x stroke	3.78 x 3.13in (96 x 79.5mm)
Capacity	140ci (2.3 litres)
Compression ratio	9.5:1
Fuelling	Electronic injection
Power	105bhp @ 4,600rpm

5.0-litre HO V8

Type	Water-cooled cast-iron, ohv
Bore x stroke	4.00 x 3.00in (102 x 76.2mm)
Capacity	302ci (5.0 litres)
Compression ratio	9.2:1
Fuelling	Electronic injection
Power	225bhp @ 4,200rpm

1993:
FAREWELL TO FOX

1993 Mustang 5-litre limited-edition LX.

This was the final year for the Fox Mustang, the longest-lived Mustang of them all. Since 1979, Ford had sold two-and-a-half million of them and decided that it should go out with a bang. There was talk of Mustang III, a no-compromise concept sports car that Ford hinted might just go into production. The Mustang Cobra was a hopped-up hot-rod version of the standard car, with 235bhp, and there was a limited edition convertible loaded with extras.

However, not all this activity was to mark the end of the Fox Mustang's long production run. It was also an attempt to deflect interest from the new F-body Camaro/Firebird, which made its debut that year. With up to 275bhp in curvy modern bodywork, these were truly modern muscle cars, and threatened to make the Fox seem like a dinosaur.

Let's take that convertible first. It was actually a Ford collaboration with Creative Industries, and offically a 1993$^{1}/_{2}$ car introduced later in the model year. Available only in Canary Yellow Clearcoat or Oxford White, the 1993 Limited Edition (it had no official name) was a follow-up of a Vibrant Red special-edition convertible of the previous year. The white car cost $976 more than standard, bringing with it a white interior and white 16-in (41-cm) five-spoke aluminium wheels. The Canary car was similar, but with chrome five-spokes and an interior in a choice of black or white to match the top.

Both '93$^{1}/_{2}$ convertibles had body colour side mouldings, windshield surround, door mirrors and rear spoiler, which replaced the LX convertible's luggage rack and was unique to this special edition. There were galloping pony logos embossed on the headrests and embroidered floor mats. One thousand five hundred Oxford Whites left the

328

production line and 1,503 Canary cars. All Mustangs had some detail changes for this final year, but only the dedicated Mustang watcher would spot them. The optional cassette player gave way to a CD player and the standard AM/FM radio was given an easier to read display, plus 24-watt power; but a graphic equalizer was no longer available. The front seats on the LX 5.0-litre were actually downgraded and buyers now had to pay extra for articulated sports seats.

The V8 was also downgraded that year, from 225 to 205bhp. Torque was now also quoted at a lower figure, at 275lb ft at 3,000rpm. This was odd, because there had been no engine changes for 1993 to justify it. However, there are several explanations. One is that the lower power figure reflected incremental changes that had been made over the last seven years which, if true, meant that Ford's 225-bhp claim had been hogwash, at least towards the end. Others are that the company wished to align the older 5.0-litre's power rating with that of its newer modular engines or that it was a response to the concerns of insurance companies or that it was meant to take the heat out of the environmental debate (which hadn't gone away).

There is another explanation: the Mustang Cobra. This last hurrah for the Fox Mustang produced a claimed 235bhp, which was not bad, but a mere 10bhp more than the claim for the old GT, and hardly enough to tempt buyers into laying out extra cash. But the Cobra was no warmed-up GT: it may have looked similar, but there was a whole list of changes under the skin. Remember

SVO (Special Vehicle Operations), Ford's specialist department that designed and produced cars like the 205-bhp Mustang Turbo? The SVT (Special Vehicle Team) and SVE (Special Vehicle Engineering) were formed in 1991 to do much the same job – to produce limited-edition hopped-up versions of standard Fords. The Cobra was their first.

Actually, that's not quite true. Alongside it was the SVT F-150 pickup with a 240-hp 351-ci (5.75-litre) V8 making it one of the first performance trucks. But the Mustang still got plenty of attention. Available as a hatchback V8 only, its extra 30bhp came via a new cast-aluminium intake manifold, GT-40 cylinder heads (still cast iron) with bigger intake and exhaust ports, larger valves and modified rocker arms. The throttle body was bigger too, now up to 70mm, and a new cam sought to make the most of this deeper-breathing capacity. Finally, the crank and water pump pulleys were 12 per cent smaller than standard to make them lighter and the V8 more revvy and responsive. Sure enough, the red line was at 6,000rpm, with a fuel shut-off at 6,250rpm

But that wasn't the end of it. The faithful, long-serving Borg Warner T-5 sat behind the V8, now with phosphate-coated gears and stronger bearings. There was a shorter-throw gearchange as well, while the driveshaft yoke was hardened. Differential was the standard 8.8-inch, in this case with a 3.08:1 ratio. The Cobra was also the first factory Mustang (SVOs apart) to have disc brakes all round. Both pairs were vented – 10.84-inch rotors front, 10.07-inch rear. The Goodyear rubber was now down to a 45 aspect ratio, uni-

directional Eagles measuring 245/45ZR-17, while the 17-inch (43-cm) seven-blade alloy wheels, 7.5 in (19-cm) wide, were unique to the Cobra.

The traditional means of making a Mustang handle was to fit stiffer springs, but SVT's philosophy was different. They called it 'controlled compliance', which in plain English meant softer springs but with good damping to keep them under control. Those at the front were variable-rate (400/505lb/in), while the rears were plain constant-rate 160lb/in (far softer than the GT).

Inside was a standard Mustang interior, but with white dials which would become a Cobra trademark, plus articulated sports seats, a Premium sound system, the Power Equipment Group, air conditioning and cruise control – this was no stripped-down special. Options included leather seats, four-way power adjustment for the driver's perch, a sunroof, CD player and California emissions equipment. What the Cobra didn't have was the extrovert body kits that typified earlier Mustang Cobras – the Mustang II, Cobra II and King Cobra II, or the very early Fox Cobras. There were front and rear spoilers, but no stripes, badges or hood-size emblems.

The question was, did this final incarnation of the Fox Mustang measure up to the first F-body Camaro/Firebird which was launched the same year? *Car and Driver* tested all three together to find out, and the short answer was 'no' – the Mustang was placed third out of three. Next to the sleek and aerodynamic GM F-cars, the Mustang looked slightly absurd, as if someone had inadvertently pitted a hotted-up sedan

against a pair of genuine sports cars.

However, *C/D* made it plain that SVT had done a good job, and the Cobra certainly wasn't a rocky, bellowing hot-rod Mustang of the old school. It considered the ride to be even a little too soft, but the Goodyears gave an excellent 0.85g on the skidpan. But the rear-drive, unsophisticated Mustang chassis still needed skilful handling near its limits, when it was necessary to shift from strong understeer to oversteer very quickly indeed. It loved the engine in its latest 235-bhp guise and the car's good manners when not being driven at nine-tenths. But it still came third.

But what of 'Mustang III', the two-seater concept car that also appeared in 1993; was this really a preview of the next Mustang? It wasn't, of course, but the Porsche-like roadster did give a hint of what the 1994 Mustang would be like. Ford cheerfully admitted that it was based on a shortened version of the new platform, with MacPherson strut front suspension and a live rear axle with a four-shock set-up.

So there wouldn't be any suspension surprises in the new Mustang. It would also be rear-wheel-drive, as was the Mustang III, with an open-front grille (like the III), air intakes in front of the rear wheels, and three-bar rear lights. It would also be powered by a supercharged V8, the same 4.6-litre quad-cam alloy unit already fitted to the Lincoln Mark VIII; there were no promises, though, that this would be driving the fourth-generation Mustang as well. The same went for the Borg Warner T56 six-speed manual gearbox.

With the supercharger and ethyl

injection, the Mustang III made the desired impression on the handful of journalists who were permitted to drive it at a private test track. Ford reckoned 0–60 in less than 4.5 seconds and *American Car World* thought that the handling was 'balanced, predictable and agile'. Not that anyone took liberties with the car, which was said to be worth half a million dollars. Ford played the usual PR trick by saying that the Mustang III might well go into production at around $65,000 if there was enough public demand. It never did, but the show car served its purpose, taking some of the steam out of the Camaro/Firebird launch and underlining the fact that – just a few months away – the fourth-generation Mustang would be let loose.

PRODUCTION

Coupé	24,851
Hatchback	62,077
Convertible	27,300
TOTAL	114,228

ENGINE LINE-UP

2.3 litre four

Type	Water-cooled cast-iron, ohc
Bore x stroke	3.78 x 3.13in (96 x 79.5mm)
Capacity	140ci (2.3 litres)
Compression ratio	9.5:1
Fuelling	Electronic injection
Power	105bhp @ 4,600rpm

5.0-litre HO V8

Type	Water-cooled cast-iron, ohv
Bore x stroke	4.00 x 3.00in (102 x 76.2mm)
Capacity	302ci (5.0 litres)
Compression ratio	9.0:1
Fuelling	Electronic injection
Power	205bhp @ 4,200rpm

5.0-litre Cobra V8

Type	Water-cooled cast-iron, ohv
Bore x stroke	4.00 x 3.00in
Capacity	302ci (5.0 litres)
Compression ratio	9.0:1
Fuelling	Electronic injection
Power	235bhp @ 4,600rpm

OPPOSITE
1993 Mustang SVT Cobra.

BELOW
1993 Mustang 5-litre GT.

1994:
FOX 4 – THE 1990s MUSTANG

Since 1964, and not counting the updates of the original in 1967 and '71, there had been four Mustangs, which were really just bigger, fatter versions of the same thing. The first truly new Mustang was Lee Iacocca's second-generation Mustang of 1974, radically downsized and downgraded to cope with a brave new world where it had been accepted that gas was a finite resource.

The 1979 Fox Mustang (generation three) developed the same theme, being lighter and more aerodynamic than the car it replaced. But as the 1980s progressed, Fox found itself at the centre of a muscle-car revival, selling as many V8s as four-cylinder economy coupés. It was starting to look a little tired and old-fashioned, but Ford managed to make a virtue out of necessity, promoting the Mustang as the last of the traditional V8 rear-drive muscle cars. As such, the V8 Fox Mustang found its own niche, and only towards the end of its 15-year production run did sales begin to flag. One could only take the good ol' boy analogy so far, and by the early 1990s emphasis was clearly on the 'old'.

Work on a successor started in 1990, when a group named Team Mustang settled into an old Montgomery Ward warehouse south of Dearborn. The new car was codenamed SN-95 (Sporty North American car, project No. 95) and was masterminded by John Coletti, Ford's product planning manager, later known as the project's godfather. There was also help from none other than ex-Formula One driver Jackie Stewart, who had been a consultant to Ford for many years.

The new Mustang was gradually taking shape, but Ford didn't want the general public to see what it looked like while the prototype was being road-tested. Prototype parts were bolted into a Fox Mustang for the purpose, while outwardly it was identical to the thousands of other Mustangs seen on North American roads. Or was it? One of the things that made this such an easy ploy was that the fourth-generation was actually based on a modified Fox Mustang platform. It was called Fox 4, a reference to the 1994 model year launch date. Nowadays it is hard to credit that the 2004 model had its roots in the 1979 Mustang, which in turn owed much to the 1978 Ford Fairmont sedan. In the event, over 500 of the new Mustang's 1,850 parts were carried over from Fox. It still used MacPherson strut front suspension, a live rear axle and rack-and-pinion steering. Even the venerable all-iron V8 was still there. Was this really a new Mustang or simply a quick restyle?

However, these bare figures tell only half the story. Most of the reused components were simple floorpan parts and non-structural brackets, while the important stuff really was all new. This was just as well, as Team Mustang was given a daunting list of goals to meet. The new car had to have better ride, handling and steering than the old one. Powertrain performance, brakes, climate control, comfort and NVH (noise/vibration/harshness) all had to be superior. It had four years in which to complete the task (not that long for a substantially new car) and a tight budget.

But it succeeded, the first and most obvious change being the styling. It was

hardly surprising that the new Mustang followed the trends of the time and had a rounded, more organic look than the 1980s Fox. Yet many of the 30-year-old Mustang styling cues remained: the long hood/short rear deck, the sculpted sides and air intakes. It was even very close in size to the original: apart from extra width (4 inches/10cm added) it was just a couple of inches taller, and almost identical in length. However, Ford resisted the temptation to turn the Mustang into an out-and-out sports car, which is what General Motors had done with the 1993 Camaro/Firebird; next to them, the new Mustang was taller, more upright and more practical.

Once the basics were in place, clinics were held to decide the final look, when customers were given three variations on the same theme from which to choose. Each styling proposal was named after a movie star, to underline its different character. There was a sleek and sophisticated 'Bruce Jenner', an aggressive 'Rambo' and a muscle-bound 'Arnold Schwarzenegger'. Arnie got the decisive nod.

There were two rectangular headlamps flanking a curved grille opening with a large chrome galloping pony (this had made its first appearance on the 1993 Cobra), which was an instant hit. The rear lights were in three horizontal bars, which gave the car a distinctive look and emphasized its extra width.

In spite of its practicality, the useful hatchback had gone. Remember how the Mustang II designers had wanted to produce a hatchback or a coupé but not both? It would

have saved a lot of money to have had just one body style, but unfortunately customer clinics showed a 50/50 split, so in the end both were built. Things were different for the 1994 Mustang: with a narrower range, and no cheap four-cylinder model, the new car was

unlikely to sell in the same numbers as its predecessors. So the Mustang came as a coupé only, though to keep the hatchback buyers happy it had a distinct fastback appearance rather than that of a sedan-like notchback.

There had to be a convertible, however.

The ragtop had done much to bolster Fox Mustang sales towards the end, so Fox 4 was designed from the start to come in roofless form. This meant it had to be far stiffer and more rigid than its predecessor, whose chassis flexibility had been a serious weakness. This was especially true of the convertible, which had been an afterthought conversion rather than designed-in from the start.

Consequently, a great deal of effort went into making the new Mustang stronger than the old one. On GT V8s, a bolt-in brace was added between the front strut towers and engine bulkhead, an old tuning trick popular on the Fox V8. All cars had bigger box sections in the rocker panels and roof rails, while both front and rear screens were bonded into place with a rigid urethane adhesive. This did the trick, and the new coupé proved to be 44 per cent stiffer in torsion than the old and 56 per cent more resistant to bending; the lack of a hatchback also made the body stronger. As for the convertible, that was a whole 80 per cent stiffer torsionally and 40 per cent less bendable. It also had thicker-gauge rocker panels and other stress-bearing panels, while a 25-lb (11-kg) tuned mass damper was fitted inside the right fender as well.

Inside, the Fox Mustang's rather bland interior (an aspect that really dated the car) was ditched in favour of a twin-cowl set-up that was retro and modern at the same time. There was a full set of instruments, of course, but the same level of convenience found in modern Fords, such as the Mazda-built Probe. And naturally, it was still an occasional four-seater, proving that some things didn't change.

The LX was dropped, though it was still possible to choose between base and GT Mustangs, both available as coupés or convertibles. Prices started at $13,355 for the V6 coupé, rising to $21,960 for the V8 GT convertible. It was more expensive than the Fox Mustang, certainly, but the V8s in particular remained good value, costing about the same as Japanese coupés like the Toyota Celica and the Honda Prelude or for that matter the Ford Probe. Clever and sophisticated these may have been, but for some the alternative of a genuine American-made V8 pony car, with all the historical baggage that came with it, was the only choice.

New Bottle, Old Wine

Despite many nods to the past (especially a Mustang past), Fox 4 looked entirely new, as if nothing beneath its façade had appeared in any of its predecessors. But this was far from the truth. As well as the hidden body parts (and despite the 275-bhp Camaro), the Mustang's familiar 5.0-litre V8 was back. (To be precise, it was actually closer to a 4.9 (4942cc), but Ford always listed it as the more impressive-sounding 5.0.) Still with a cast-iron block, pushrods and two valves per cylinder, it looked positively ancient for a modern performance car engine, at least on paper. In practice, and for 90 per cent of drivers, the smooth, strong and flexible V8 was plenty of engine, though in the eternal war of horsepower tech spec and image it was somewhat lagging behind.

There was a modest power boost to 215bhp at 4,200rpm, thanks to a low-profile intake manifold and new pistons. But pleasant as the familiar 5.0-litre was, it was no match for a full-powered Camaro, which in Z28 form offered 28 per cent more power and a meaty 325lb ft, peaking at a nice, low 2,400rpm. It was clear that the Mustang's power deficit was untenable for a muscle car; even at the launch, Ford promised that its new 4.6-litre modular engine would soon find its way into the Mustang – quite when was a matter of debate. Describing the new car in late 1993, *Car and Driver* confidently predicted that it would be ready for 1995, while according to Brad Bowling (*Standard Catalog of Mustang*), Ford itself promised the re-engined Mustang in 1997, as much as four years away. (In the event, both were wrong – it turned out to be the 1996 model year). In any case, it was known that a 240-bhp Cobra was also on the way, so it was a case of picking one's dream-engined Mustang and being prepared to wait.

But the traditional V8 was not alone. For the first time in 20 years there was no four-cylinder Mustang. Instead, the base model came with Ford's 3.8-litre V6, a smooth and well-proven motor of 145bhp that was already powering the Taurus, Thunderbird and Lincoln Continental. Hugely more torquey and powerful than the 2.3-litre four it replaced, the V6 Mustang turned out to be little faster; there was a penalty in all that body-stiffening, not to mention dual air bags and super-strong side impact protectors, which had given the new base Mustang 300lb (136kg) more weight than the old one. It was also at a disadvantage in that it had taller gearing than the four-cylinder Fox Mustang – in fact, a massive 30 per cent – which had been necessary to meet the CAFE regulations and succeeded with a highway figure of 30mpg (10.6km/litre) for the Mustang V6.

Both V6 and V8 came with a choice of five-speed manual or four-speed automatic transmissions, while there were disc brakes all round for all cars with ABS an option. The suspension and steering looked suspiciously similar to that of the old Mustang, but Ford confirmed that much effort had gone into making the former more comfortable and compliant.

And so it turned out to be. Early road tests revealed that the Mustang had been transformed from the rocky, bucking, untamed muscle car of the 1980s into something altogether more calm and sophisticated. When the inevitable comparisons with the Camaro were made, it seemed that the Mustang was the safe option.

It had calmer steering and more compliant suspension, according to *Car and Driver*. Push it hard into a corner and the reaction was safe, speed-scrubbing understeer, with no tendency to suddenly snap the tail round under provocation. The Camaro was a different matter, with sharper steering and higher limits, plus edgier handling that a skilled driver would have fun exploiting. Compared with a Mustang GT, the Camaro Z28 was noisy and bumpy, a more serious sports car. Both still had live axles, and on poor surfaces their handling had a tendency to deteriorate sharply; but the good news was that Team Mustang had transformed the Mustang's behaviour while keeping the same basic layout. Most tests

made a point of commenting on how much more solid and together the new Mustang felt compared with its predecessor, the flexible Fox.

That was the good news. The bad news for Ford performance freaks was indicated by the stopwatch. Magazine comparisons majored on the Mustang GT versus Camaro Z28, the hottest version of each car – not that this was unfair to the Ford, as the pair were quite close on price. This left the Mustang with its 60-horsepower deficit and trailing acceleration times. It was by no means slow, at 6.1 seconds 0–60 and with a 14.9-second standing-quarter, but the Z28 managed 5.4 and 14.1. General Motors's car made the most of its closer-ratio six-speed gearbox, though in any case its superior torque made it quicker than the Mustang in top-gear roll-ons as well.

Car and Driver's verdict would have made unsettling reading for Ford executives, or indeed for anyone who still saw Mustang as the ultimate muscle pony. In all the attributes that had made the Mustang what it was the Camaro scored higher: in engine, brakes, handling, value, styling and (horror of horrors) fun-to-drive rating, *C/D* awarded it more points. Meanwhile, the Mustang narrowly beat the Chevy on sensible things like comfort, ride and utility. In *C/D*'s overall ratings it scored 74 points against the Z28's 85. Clearly there was work to be done.

PRODUCTION

Coupé	42,883
Coupé GT	30,592
Convertible	18,333
Convertible GT	25,381
Cobra coupé	5,009
Cobra convertible	1,000
TOTAL	123,198

ENGINE LINE-UP
3.8-litre V6

Type	Water-cooled cast-iron, ohv
Bore x stroke	3.80 x 3.40in (96.5 x 86.4mm)
Capacity	232ci (3.8 litres)
Compression ratio	9.0:1
Fuelling	Electronic injection
Power	145bhp @ 4,000rpm

5.0-litre V8

Type	Water-cooled cast-iron, ohv
Bore x stroke	4.00 x 3.00in (102 x 76.2mm)
Capacity	302ci (5.0 litres)
Compression ratio	9.0:1
Fuelling	Electronic injection
Power	215bhp @ 4,200rpm

5.0-litre Cobra V8

Type	Water-cooled cast-iron, ohv
Bore x stroke	4.00 x 3.00in
Capacity	302ci (5.0 litres)
Compression ratio	9.0:1
Fuelling	Electronic injection
Power	240bhp @ 4,800rpm

1995:
COBRAS, SALEENS &
SUPERCHARGING

BELOW
1995 5-litre Mustang Cobra. It was
the last year of production for the old
5-litre V8 engine.

OPPOSITE
1995 Mustang Cobra.

Once the sales figures had been published it was clear that the fourth-generation Mustang was the first not to have recorded huge sales in its first year. This was to be expected, with just two models available and no bargain-basement four-cylinder coupé. Moreover, U.S. buyers were aware that a whole raft of other good-looking sporty cars were competing for their hard-earned dollars. The 1964 Mustang had no real rival to speak of, while the 1974 had plenty on its home ground but few anywhere else. By 1979, the third generation was having to face foreign competition in the form of Japanese coupés like the Toyota Celica and Honda Prelude. By 1994 there was a myriad of high-tech, attractive coupés from Detroit, Japan and Europe, which ensured that Mustang no longer had everything its own way.

In spite of this, Ford still managed to sell more 1994 Mustangs than '93s, in fact 123,198 in total against 114,228. As ever, the base models proved more popular than the GTs, though not by much (61,216 sold against just under 56,000), while convertibles now formed a substantial chunk of production with 36 per cent of the total, which incidentally included just over 6,000 SVT Cobras.

If anyone was disappointed by those early Mustang road tests, which made it clear that Ford's pony car was now the safe, comfortable and sensible choice, they were in a minority. In the 1995 model year, sales rocketed to over 185,000, with coupés again the best-sellers, which may have been helped by the GTS coupé. In 1994, there was a $4,000 price gap between the V6 coupé and V8 GT, which left something of hiatus in the range. Then Ford seemed to remember the old LX V8 and how successful it had been in offering V8 performance in a cheaper non-GT package.

The GTS did the same job. It was really a GT, right down to the familiar 5.0-litre V8

and the five-spoke alloy wheels that came with it. All it lacked was the GT's rear spoiler, fog lights and sports seats, which saved almost $1,000 on the sticker price. The GTS came as a separate model because, for the first time, engines were not included in the Mustang's options list.

In the old days, upgrading a new pony car from a six to a V8, with all the sporty accoutrements, was simply a matter of ticking the right box on the order form. The options list was still lengthy in 1995, but was now restricted to convenience (four-speed automatic, $815), comfort (air conditioning, $855), safety (ABS, $565) and appearance (15-inch aluminium wheels, $265). If all these big-ticket items seemed a little pricey, one could still have an optional rear-axle ratio on the GT and GTS coupé for just 45 bucks. At the other end of the scale, option pack 250C brought air conditioning, rear-window defroster, front floor mats, cruise control, remote keyless illuminated entry, AM/FM stereo Mach 460 radio/cassette, CD player and leather bucket seats. The cost? $2,755.

Another option listed for 1995 was a hardtop for the convertible, complete with glass rear screen, a proper headliner and even an interior light. It was a two-person job to fit it, being heavy and awkward, the idea being that convertible owners would keep it in the back of the garage during summer and use it in the winter months to make their Mustang

OPPOSITE
The 1995 supercharged Mustang 5-litre GT.

BELOW
The 1995 Mustang GT. Air conditioning was now on the options list.

The 1995 Mustang GT 302. Ford made the most of that familiar pony car badge.

quieter, easier to heat and safer in a roll-over crash. But it wasn't a success: less than 500 hardtops were actually sold, all of them on the SVT Cobra convertible.

Like the final-year Fox Mustang, the new one had its SVT Cobra equivalent, which at least went part of the way to address the standard GT's power deficit when compared with the Camaro Z28. Quoted figures were 240bhp at 4,800rpm and 285lb ft at 4,000, so it seemed like a peakier motor than the Camaro's; moreover, the Cobra weighed 100lb

(45kg) less, so would go some way towards closing the performance gap.

As before, SVT's compliant suspension philosophy meant that the Cobra had softer springs than the GT, though the front springs now had a linear rate (not variable) of 400lb/in, the rear springs still being 160 linears. The front anti-roll bar was smaller than the GT's (25- vs 30-mm) but the 27-mm rear bar was bigger. There were disc brakes all round, of course, like the GT, but this time with larger 13-in (33-cm) vented front rotors and 11.65-in (29.6-cm) vented rotors to the rear. Bosch three-channel, four-sensor ABS (an option on the GT) came as standard. The Goodyears were larger too, now 255/45ZR-17s on 17 x 8-in (43 x 20-cm) alloy rims. All of these specifications were the same for 1994 as well as 1995 (the Cobra made its debut later in new Mustang's first year).

It also fell to the Cobra to uphold another old Mustang tradition. The car was chosen to pace the 1994 Indianapolis 500, a great honour for any muscle car; as in previous years, Ford sought to make the most of it by offering pace-car replicas. These were very different from the three real pace cars, each one having been specially modified by Jack Roush. These had modified four-speed automatics, 15-gallon (68-litre) racing fuel cells, stiffer rear springs (to cope with the weight of TV camera equipment), a fire extinguisher and 50,000-watt strobe lights.

The 1,000 replicas were all Rio Red convertibles, with saddle-leather interiors and saddle ragtops. There were all the usual decals and badges too, but again (and here too, history was repeating itelf) these were shipped

to dealers inside the cars so that customers could choose whether to use them or not. Either way, they paid for them (pace-car replica ragtops cost over $6,000 more than the standard Cobra coupé).

Meanwhile, Ford did not have the monopoly of hopped-up Mustangs. Steve Saleen had wasted no time in building his own version of the fourth-generation pony car. As with the Cobra, there were very few changes for the second year, so the following specifications apply to both 1994 and '95 Saleens.

Times had changed since Saleen Mustangs were suspension and body-kit specials. At first, Steve Saleen, lacking the resources to certify hot engines in particular, steered clear of modifying any major components in order to keep the Ford warranty intact. But now his Mustangs were big business; for 1994 and '95 he offered two, both with major changes beneath the hood. The V6 Sport was seen as an entry-level car, built out of the base V6 but with the 3.8-litre engine supercharged to produce 220bhp. There were also Racecraft suspension parts, 8-in (20-cm) wide wheels and the usual Saleen body kit. At less than $22,000, it cost about the same as a fully-optioned GT, but made slightly more power and was lighter, so should have been quicker. It was also in a lower insurance bracket.

More popular (though still selling in tiny numbers) was the S-351. This too was based on the Mustang V6, examples of which were delivered to Saleen's new California factory to have every mechanical part stripped out. In place of the V6 came a 5.75-litre (351-ci) V8 built by Saleen Performance and fully certified by the EPA. But it wasn't only a cubic-inch conversion; the 351 also had bigger valves than the standard 5.0-litre, hydraulic roller camshaft and lifters, plus a 65-mm throttle body, 77-mm mass air sensor and the latest EEC-IV engine management system. The result was 371bhp and enough oomph to decisively outdrag any Camaro Z28. If by any chance it couldn't, a Vortech supercharger was optional, as was a 3.55:1 rear axle for quicker acceleration.

Each Saleen S-351 Mustang took 120 man-hours to convert, which was why it cost $34,990 in coupé form or $40,990 in convertible. It also came in racing form as the SR ('Supercharged Racer'), with 480-bhp FIA Group A competition bodywork, dual-plane rear wing, carbonfibre hood, a roll bar, Recaro racing seats and four-point racing harness – all for $45,990. It seemed as though Camaro would have to look to its laurels.

PRODUCTION

Coupé	137,722
Convertible	48,264
Cobra coupé	4,005
Cobra convertible	1,003
Cobra R	250
TOTAL	185,986

ENGINE LINE-UP
3.8-litre V6

Type	Water-cooled cast-iron, ohv
Bore x stroke	3.80 x 3.40in (96.5 x 86.4mm)
Capacity	232ci (3.8 litres)
Compression ratio	9.0:1
Fuelling	Electronic injection
Power	145bhp @ 4,000rpm

5.0-litre V8

Type	Water-cooled cast-iron, ohv
Bore x stroke	4.00 x 3.00in (102 x 76.2mm)
Capacity	302ci (5.0 litres)
Compression ratio	9.0:1
Fuelling	Electronic injection
Power	215bhp @ 4,200rpm

5.0-litre Cobra V8

Type	Water-cooled cast-iron, ohv
Bore x stroke	4.00 x 3.00in
Capacity	302ci (5.0 litres)
Compression ratio	9.0:1
Fuelling	Electronic injection
Power	240bhp @ 4,800rpm

The 1995 24 hours of Daytona, Florida, where a Mustang belonging to Kendall, Newman, Martin and Brocham can be seen in action.

1996:
A NEW V8

There was big news for 1996 when the fourth-generation Mustang was finally given a high-tech engine to match its 1990s looks. Even at a launch in late 1993, Ford had admitted that a replacement for the venerable 5.0-litre V8 wouldn't be long coming. And now, here it was.

Not that the 4.6-litre V8, which had made its debut in the GT coupé and convertible, was genuinely new. It was already seeing service in Lincoln sedans, having come from a family of modular engines that had first seen the inside of a Ford showroom back in 1991. The 'modular' tag referred to a whole family of power units with many components in common, making them cheaper and easier to build. In a Lincoln sedan, the 4.6-litre V8 had already proven itself to be smooth and efficient; but did that make it the right choice for a Mustang?

Some had their doubts. The muscle-car market still hadn't recovered from its love affair with cubic inches, but the new V8 had less of them than the old (21 fewer, in fact). Moreover, the paper specification didn't seem that exotic: still two valves per cylinder (rather than four), and just one overhead camshaft per bank of cylinders, mounted on a cast-iron block.

In any case, the 5.0-litre was a tough act to follow – just look at its lineage. It had first appeared in 1968 in the Boss 302 Mustang, a revvy, track-bound sportster built in small numbers. Then it became the entry-level V8, a relatively cheap way of upgrading the basic six-cylinder Mustang. Unavailable in early Mustang IIs, it was the most powerful option right through the 1970s, the closest thing Ford had to a muscle car in those straitened times.

In the 1979 Fox Mustang, the 302 (now deemed a '5.0-litre' by Ford) was at first a soft cruising option, then dropped out altogether for a couple of years as the second oil crisis began to bite. But its real glory days were from 1982, when it returned in the manual-gearbox Mustang GT to spearhead a second generation of reborn muscle cars. An uncomplicated, pushrod, carburettor-fed V8 in a world of fuel-injected sophistication, the 5.0-litre V8 supplied the Fox Mustang with instant muscle-car street credibility as well as all the history to back it up.

So dropping the faithful 5.0-litre, and all the baggage that came with it, was a momentous step to take. Maybe it explains why Ford was careful to quote exactly the same power for the new V8 – 215bhp and 285lb ft. The peaks of these power/torque curves were no higher than before, though the new engine was red-lined at 6,000rpm.

But the point about the 4.6-litre V8 wasn't its power (one must look to the 305-bhp Cobra for that) but the fact that it was thoroughly modern. There was an integral oil-cooling system, using coolant water, for which Ford claimed a longer engine life. Lightweight pistons and connecting-rods helped to raise that rev ceiling, while platinum-tipped spark plugs and the accessory belt drive were both good for a claimed 100,000 miles (161000km). The alternator, air-conditioning compressor and power-steering pump were all mounted directly on the block, which made for a neater underhood space. There was electronic ignition, fuel injection and a new diagnostic system.

This was all most impressive; even those who bemoaned the lack of cubic inches could find comfort in the fact that the 4.6 had lots of tuning potential. Overhead cams aided the higher rev ceiling, and unique cylinder-head bolts and spacing gave the engine plenty of strength for high-horsepower applications.

One would have expected the 4.6 to have slipped straight under the Mustang's hood without a hitch, the two having been destined to match up before the car was even launched. But some changes were necessary since the overhead-cam V8 was taller than the old one. The engine cross-member was redesigned to suit, the steering gear and suspension arms lowered, and a more compact brake pump was fitted.

At the same time, the base V6 was upgraded to 150bhp and adopted the stiffer cylinder-block from the Thunderbird Super

ABOVE
1996 Mustang Cobra convertible.

OPPOSITE
1996 Mustang GT V8. Ford claimed the same power for the new 4.6- as the old 5-litre engine.

Coupé. Neither this nor the V8 came with a Camaro-rivalling six-speed transmission, but the old Borg Warner T-5 was finally pensioned off in favour of the stronger T-45, which housed the transmission casing and bellhousing in one unit for extra rigidity. The automatic transmission was also new, making far more use of electronic control than the old four-speed. There were larger anti-roll bars for the GT, as well as retuned shocks and progressive spring rates. All GTs and Cobras

were fitted with Ford's Passive Anti-Theft System, which meant they couldn't be hot-wired without the specially-coded ignition key. And in case anyone missed the new engine under the hood, 1996 Mustangs had vertical tail lights and came in four new colours: Moonlight Blue, Deep Violet, Pacific Green and Bright Tangerine.

If doubts concerning the 4.6-litre modular V8 still lingered, they were surely dispelled by the SVT Mustang Cobra for 1996. Instead

of mildly tweaking the standard engine, as in previous Cobras, this latest version used a radically-different 4.6, with double-overhead camshafts, four valves per cylinder and an aluminium block. Moreover, this special 4.6 was not even built on the Dearborn production line.

Instead, the cylinder-block was cast in Italy by a company named Tremec, then shipped to Ford's Romeo, Michigan plant. Here, 12 two-person teams were solely

GT convertible buyers had the standard two-valve 4.6 V8, but for the special four-valve dohc unit it was necessary to pay extra for a Cobra.

responsible for assembling the dohc 4.6s. They fitted the 32-valve heads, the twin 57-mm throttle bodies and 80-mm mass air sensor, and the German-built crankshaft. Six bolts were used to retain each bearing cap; when it was finished, the two workers who had built it signed a plate on the cam cover!

It all sounded very special and limited-production, but buyers loved the idea of a high-tech, hand-built Mustang, and over 10,000 Cobras were built for 1996. They

wouldn't have been disappointed either, as Ford claimed 305bhp for it, and 300lb ft at 4,800rpm; the engine had a rev ceiling of 6,800 but a fuel cut-off ensured that it would never break the 7,000 barrier.

However, some may well have been disappointed. When driven hard on a hot day, the Cobra 4.6 had a tendency to overheat; Ford had to issue a cooling upgrade kit to cure the fault. And that wasn't the only problem. The accessory belt drive was prone to terrible

squealing and could even fly off altogether, though later belts were rectified. The new Borg Warner T-45 transmission wasn't trouble-free either. This had a 320lb ft torque capacity, but the Cobra's 300 was liable to prove too much for it, with bent shifter forks and rapid wear of synchronizer cogs reported. The problem was solved when Tremec began to make the T-45 under licence in 1998.

Yet despite the problems and a hefty price increase – to $24,810 for the coupé and over $27,000 for the convertible – this was the most popular SVT Cobra yet, with Ford selling over 2,500 ragtop Cobras and nearly 7,500 coupés. It was also the most powerful yet, but only just. The previous year, a limited run of 5.7-litre cars had been built using a bigger-block version of the standard 5.0-litre. The actual block had been sourced from a Ford marine engine, with aluminium-alloy pistons added, a special camshaft, forged-steel connecting rods, GT-40 heads and special intake manifolds. It pushed out 300bhp and a monstrous 365lb ft of torque. Wisely, SVT eschewed the standard T-5 transmission, substituting a stronger Tremec five-speed unit instead.

To maximize the benefit of all that urge, the Cobra R was stripped of its luxury equipment: no air conditioning, radio, rear seat – some of the soundproofing was even ditched. With a 3.27:1 axle it could rocket off the line but had no hope of meeting CAFE regulations, so on top of the $35,499 sticker price went a $2,100 gas-guzzler tax. However, that didn't prevent all 250 Cobra Rs from being pre-sold.

Meanwhile, what did Steve Saleen make

of the high-tech 4.6-litre Mustang? In a way it was back to business as usual. Being a new engine and an unknown quantity, the 4.6 received only minor changes. Instead, the 1996 S-281 was big on suspension and body kit, so it was just like old times. Available on both standard Mustang and Cobra, the Saleen added ultra-low-profile BF Goodrich tyres (245/40-18s) on 18-inch (46-cm) alloy wheels. Magnesium wheels were optional, as were Recaro seats, a carbonfibre hood and 3.55:1 rear axle. On convertibles, one could pay extra for the Speedster package, which included a hard tonneau cover for the back seat and a padded roll bar. The 1996 Saleen could be had supercharged, but only if fitted by dealers or aftermarket tuners.

It turned out to be the most popular Saleen yet, with over 400 S-281s built that year. Most were coupés, though Saleen did complete an order for 30 convertibles for the Budget rental car company, just as Hertz had ordered Shelby Mustangs all those years ago; the Budget Saleens, however, were restricted to 'premium' outlets such as Las Vegas. If the S-281 had too few cubic inches and too many camshafts, traditionalists were still able to order the S-351, and Saleen shipped out 20 of them in the 1996 model year. This could now be ordered with a Vortech supercharger for a 500-bhp Mustang missile. Sometimes, cubic inches really did matter.

PRODUCTION

Coupé	61,187
Coupe GT	31,624
Convertible	15,246
Convertible GT	17,917

Cobra coupé	7,496
Cobra convertible	2,510
TOTAL	135,620

ENGINE LINE-UP

3.8-litre V6

Type	Water-cooled cast-iron, ohv
Bore x stroke	3.80 x 3.40in (96.5 x 86.4mm)
Capacity	232ci (3.8 litres)
Compression ratio	9.0:1
Fuelling	Electronic injection
Power	150bhp @ 4,000rpm

4.6-litre V8

Type	Water-cooled cast-iron, sohc
Bore x stroke	3.60 x 3.60in (91.4 x 91.4mm)
Capacity	281ci (4.6 litres)
Compression ratio	9.0:1
Fuelling	Electronic injection
Power	215bhp @ 4,400rpm

5.0-litre Cobra V8

Type	Water-cooled aluminium, DOHC
Bore x stroke	3.60 x 3.60in
Capacity	281ci (4.6 litres)
Compression ratio	9.8:1
Fuelling	Electronic injection
Power	305bhp @ 5,800rpm

The St. Petersburg SCCA Race, Florida, 1996. Jan Gooding is in action in his Mustang Cobra.

1997:
LOW POINT

BELOW AND OPPOSITE
1997 Mustang 4.7-litre SVT Cobra.

In 1997 the Mustang was due for a quiet time after all the double-overhead-cam 4.6-litre V8 excitement of the previous year. Maybe it was a little too quiet from Ford's point of view, as sales dropped by 20 per cent. That was after an even bigger fall in 1996; moreover, only 108,344 1997 model-year Mustangs had found owners, a far cry from the 185,000 that had rolled out of Ford showrooms in 1995.

This was despite another good year for the Cobra, of which just over 10,000 had been sold. It was reportedly only the handbuilt nature of the Cobra's engine that was holding back production; apparently, Ford could have sold thousands more. The best-seller of the entire range was the base-model coupé, making up over one half the

OPPOSITE and LEFT
1997 Mustang 4.6-litre SVT Cobra.
Cobras were a success story, even
though Mustang sales were down
overall.

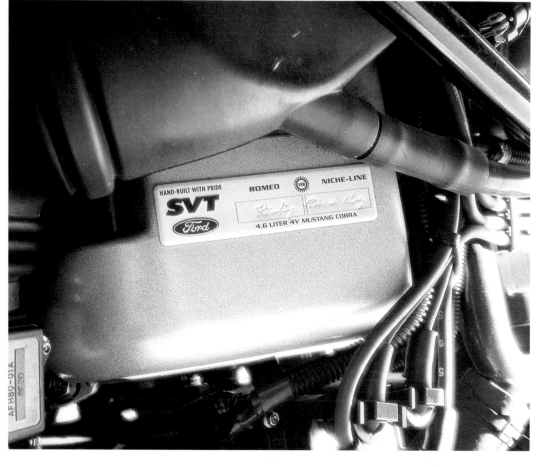

ABOVE
The 1997 Mustang 4.6-litre SVT Cobra
logo indicated the dohc V8.

ABOVE RIGHT
A 1997 Mustang SVT Cobra with a
hand-built engine which has been
signed by the mechanics.

total at 56,812. Compared with that, the 18,464 GT coupés seem relatively puny (little more than half the 1996 figure), with both base and GT convertibles selling just over 11,000 apiece. The GTS coupé, incidentally, had been dropped, and prices now ranged from $15,880 (base coupé) to $28,135 (Cobra convertible).

All-in-all, there were few changes for 1997. The PATS anti-theft system became standard across the range, utilizing an encoded ignition key with 72-billion transponder codes. There were also new

17-in (43-cm) wheels with dark-grey metallic centres, optional on the GT, while efforts to fix the Cobra's cooling led to a bigger radiator for all Mustangs; the mesh grille in front of it was deleted. The auto transmission shifter was made thicker (more ergonomic, according to Ford) and the optional leather on a V6 Mustang now came in grey instead of white. Finally, there were two new colours: Autumn Orange and Aztec Gold.

So if Cobra was the Mustang's success story of 1997, what was all the fuss about? It

must have been quite a car, as sales were apparently unaffected by the troubles with overheating, escaping accessory drive-belts and fast-wearing gearboxes. *Road & Track* tested a Cobra convertible in 1997, headlining it as the 'No Apology Pony', and wondered if it had been Ford's intention to build a 'European-style grand tourer', which came as something of a surprise to those who saw it as a modern interpretation of the hotted-up muscle car.

It still came with an exotic-looking spec sheet for the V8: aluminium block (from

LEFT
Four valves per cylinder and dohc made the SVT Cobra V8 very different from the standard 4.6.

PAGE 358
A 1997 Mustang 4.6-litre Saleen.

PAGE 359
1997 Mustang 4.6-litre Saleen speedster GT S281.

Italy), forged-steel crankshaft (from Germany), topped with dohc 32-valve heads and backed up by a super-strong bottom end with six-bolt bearing caps (it needed the extra strength to cope with a 6,800-rpm red

line). The inlet arrangement was also special: as well as the 80-mm mass air sensor, twin 57-mm throttle bodies and low-restriction conical air cleaner, there was an extra butterfly valve in each secondary intake tract.

This was closed at low rpm, so intake charge was diverted through the primary tract only, encouraging a high-velocity swirl (hence better mixing and burning) in the combustion chamber. At 3,250rpm, the secondary

OPPOSITE, LEFT and PAGES 362–364
1997 Mustang 4.6-litre Saleen Speedster GT S281.

butterflies were designed to click open, allowing the maximum volume of charge to surge through both intake tracts.

Road & Track thought it gave the best of both worlds – good torque at low revs plus extra power up high, with a zest for revs. Well, maybe not as good as all that. Even the paper figures revealed that the Cobra's dohc 4.6 V8 had a bare 15lb ft advantage over the base Mustang GT. More to the point, it peaked way up the rev range at 4,800rpm instead of at the GT's 3,500. *Road & Track* considered it a little soft at the base of the rev range, secondary butterflies notwithstanding, though it couldn't help but point out that it still made 275lb ft at 2,000rpm, so the top 4.6 wasn't exactly a gutless wonder.

But despite all the technical ingenuity, a Cobra convertible was no European grand tourer but 'as American as a John Wayne film festival'. The look, weight, feel and sound of the car all shouted 'Detroit', even after all these years and the extra refinement taken on board in 1994. This included the live rear axle which, refined though it was these days, was still upset by bumpy corners when cornering on the limit (Ford's independent rear suspension set-up, promised in 1964, still hadn't materialized!). *R & T* thought that this latest Mustang convertible, which Ford had tried so hard to stiffen up, when compared with the flexible Fox, still flexed and twisted when driven hard on bumpy roads – but only enough to worry racers and keen drivers who could in any case opt for the stronger coupé.

If the Cobra still wasn't quite as

sophisticated as an Audi or BMW, the road testers thought that its classic Mustang virtues more than made up for it: it could out-accelerate most European exotics and was a whole lot cheaper than any of them. The blue oval added to a Mustang badge may not have had the snob value of a Porsche or Jaguar, but it still represented value-for-money performance.

But if a Cobra really was too run-of-the-mill, and one still yearned for a Mustang, a brand-new Saleen could well have been the answer. The company claimed slightly more power than the Dearborn Mustangs – 220bhp for the Mustang GT-powered S281, or 310bhp if it was based on a Cobra. The S351 was still available in limited numbers (just 40 were built this year), now with a six-speed manual transmission and standard supercharger. One new option on the 351 was 'Widebody' front end, fenders, rear quarter panels, rear valance, dual-plane rear wing and carbonfibre hood, which made the Saleen look like a racer for the road, hot from Indianapolis, which of course was the whole idea. But one would have had to be quite committed (or wealthy) to go the Saleen route. The cheapest S281 coupé cost $29,500, and a full-house S351 convertible came in at just short of $58,000 – sufficient for two Mustang GT convertibles, with enough change to pay for a luxury cruise. Maybe a Porsche wasn't such poor value after all.

PRODUCTION

Coupé	56,812
Coupe GT	18,464
Convertible	11,606
Convertible GT	11,413
Cobra coupé	6,961
Cobra convertible	3,088
TOTAL	108,344

ENGINE LINE-UP
3.8-litre V6
Type	Water-cooled cast-iron, ohv
Bore x stroke	3.80 x 3.40in (96.5 x 86.4mm)
Capacity	232ci (3.8 litres)
Compression ratio	9.0:1
Fuelling	Electronic injection
Power	150bhp @ 4,000rpm

4.6-litre V8
Type	Water-cooled cast-iron, sohc
Bore x stroke	3.60 x 3.60in (91.4 x 91.4mm)
Capacity	281ci (4.6 litres)
Compression ratio	9.0:1
Fuelling	Electronic injection
Power	215bhp @ 5,000rpm

5.0-litre Cobra V8
Type	Water-cooled aluminium, dohc
Bore x stroke	3.60 x 3.60in
Capacity	281ci (4.6 litres)
Compression ratio	9.8:1
Fuelling	Electronic injection
Power	305bhp @ 5,800rpm

1998:
FALLING BEHIND

Could it be true that only a couple of years after its launch the sophisticated Mustang 4.6 was already falling behind? Despite the autographed cam cover, the 32 valves and Italian-cast block, an SVT Mustang Cobra was decisively slower than a Camaro Z28. More seriously, however, the Camaro's V8 used old-fashioned pushrods instead of overhead cams, and derived its extra urge from sheer cubic inches!

How the tables had turned. Throughout the 1980s and early '90s, Ford had promoted the Mustang as the back-to-basics supercar – pushrods, cast-iron block, four-barrel carburettor and all. But its newly sophisticated Mustang was now being overtaken by a Camaro of the old school.

Compare power outputs on paper and the Cobra and Z28 seemed very evenly matched, both producing 305bhp. In fact, a glance further down the spec sheet and the Mustang appeared to have a slight advantage, with nearly 100lb (46kg) less weight to haul around. Yet another look and one would discover that the Camaro's extra litre of engine capacity gave it 35lb ft more torque, peaking at 4,000rpm, 800rpm lower than that of the Mustang.

In practice, this turned into a slight but decisive advantage on acceleration. The Mustang achieved the 0–60 time in 5.4 seconds, 0.3 seconds quicker than the

Camaro, and scorched through the standing quarter in 13.9 with the same advantage. Subjectively too, it felt quicker when running up through the gears; in fact Kim Reynolds, testing the two cars side by side for a *Road & Track* special, thought it was just as smooth.

The Z28's small-block V8 had come straight out of the Corvette the previous year, though it wasn't quite as low-tech as the pushrods implied. Of all-alloy construction, and with fuel-injection, it used lightweight pushrods, roller tappets and harder valve springs to allow a 6,000-rpm red line. It even outperformed the Corvette's exotic Lotus-developed LS1 V8, which had gone the same 32-valve dohc route as the Mustang Cobra.

To add salt to the wound, the Camaro cornered better too. It had more grip and less body roll, was easier to balance between understeer and oversteer and even felt more solid. The Mustang was 'a hopeless understeerer' at the limit, and less compliant on bumpy tarmac. And there was one more thing: in Cobra guise, the Mustang cost almost $5,000 more than a Z28, while a standard Mustang GT was about $500 cheaper than the Z28 but was way behind on performance.

In spite of this, victory still went to Ford's pony car. Kim Reynolds ended up

preferring it, pronouncing that the Mustang was more fun, less serious. It felt more nimble and had bigger windows. Mind you, he also admitted to having something of a Mustang bias – his dad had run a 1964 Mustang while Reynolds Jnr. was still in short pants.

But none of this really mattered. The bottom line was that the Mustang was still outselling both Camaro and Firebird combined. In fact, rumours were circulating that General Motors was thinking of dropping the F-cars altogether because of poor sales, indicating that dynamic excellence and serious sports-car looks were not what the buying public wanted, while Mustang had the magic ingredient in abundance.

There were a few changes for 1998. The standard Mustang GT gained 10bhp, to 225bhp at 4,750rpm, from cleaned-up and revised exhaust ports. Torque was up as well, to 290lb ft. The 150-bhp V6 was unchanged, but there were some appearance changes. The base V6 cars now had polished aluminium wheels and a premium sound system (with cassette and CD player). By now, air conditioning was part of the basic package, as were power windows, door locks and decklid release, plus remote keyless illuminated entry. The GT also received an upgraded sound system, plus

OPPOSITE

1999 Mustang Cobra SVT.

sports seats and a spoiler. The separate clock pod disappeared on all the Mustangs and one was now obliged to peer at the radio display to see what time it was.

All this extra equipment came at very little extra cost. A Mustang Cobra may have seemed pricey next to a Camaro, but the run-of-the mill Mustangs were better value if one liked interior goodies. Despite all the newly standard luxuries, the 1998 base coupé cost only $90 more than the 1997. The GT coupé did rise substantially, but both convertibles enjoyed a price cut of several hundred dollars apiece!

The ragtop Mustangs were a genuine success, making second place in the U.S. convertible sales chart – only the Chrysler Sebring convertible sold in greater numbers. Reflecting this, 1998 was another good year for the Mustang, when sales recovered sharply from the low of 1997. Over 175,000 were sold, with base V6 coupés again the most popular by far. Ford sold nearly 100,000 of them that year, though it couldn't complain about moving over 28,000 GT coupés, or for that matter over 40,000 convertibles of all types.

Along with all the extra standard equipment, the Mustang's options list was radically shortened and simplified, with many items organized into groups. The Convenience Group, for example (on base cars only), included front floor mats, rear window demister, cruise control and a power driver's seat, all for $495. GT buyers could pay $595 extra for the GT Sport Group: 17-in (43-cm) five-spoke aluminium wheels, hood stripe and fender stripes, leather shift

knob and engine oil cooler. Base V6 owners could go a similar route with the Sport Appearance Group at $345, when they could expect 16-in (41-cm) aluminium wheels, rear spoiler, leather-bound steering wheel and side stripes.

PRODUCTION

Coupé	99,801
Coupé GT	28,789
Convertible	21,254
Convertible GT	17,024
Cobra coupé	5,174
Cobra convertible	3,480
TOTAL	175,522

ENGINE LINE-UP
3.8-litre V6

Type	Water-cooled cast-iron, ohv
Bore x stroke	3.80 x 3.40in (96.5 x 86.4mm)
Capacity	232ci (3.8 litres)
Compression ratio	9.0:1
Fuelling	Electronic injection
Power	150bhp @ 4,000rpm

4.6-litre V8

Type	Water-cooled cast-iron, sohc
Bore x stroke	3.60 x 3.60in (91.4 x 91.4mm)
Capacity	281ci (4.6 litres)
Compression ratio	9.0:1
Fuelling	Electronic injection
Power	225bhp @ 4,750rpm

5.0-litre Cobra V8

Type	Water-cooled aluminium, DOHC
Bore x stroke	3.60 x 3.60in
Capacity	281ci (4.6 litres)
Compression ratio	9.8:1
Fuelling	Electronic injection
Power	305bhp @ 5,800rpm

1999:
NEW EDGE, NEW POWER

Nineteen-ninety-nine was a highly-significant model year for the Mustang. More power, New Edge styling – even that fabled independent rear suspension finally made it into production, keeping a 35-year-old promise at last.

Ford had no intention of repeating the fiasco of its pony car's 25th birthday, which in corporate terms went almost unnoticed. The 30th had been celebrated with the new fourth-generation Mustang, and now three of the car's major flaws were being addressed at the same time.

Not everyone had liked the 1994 Mustang's styling, deeming it too rounded, too soft and too bland, especially when compared with a Camaro or Firebird. So for 1999, Mustang's first major facelift of the 1990s, it was given what Ford called New Edge styling. As suggested, it was sharpened up and given more muscle. Sharper edges on the front fenders and hood gave it more presence, while the old car's sculptured concave sides gave way to a no-nonsense flatness, ending in a narrow but tall air intake. There was a non-functional air scoop on GT hoods, and all Mustangs had a larger front grille, with the galloping pony emblem emphasized by a chrome surround, while at the back, the rear lights were big and square instead of small and curvy. So while the 1999 Mustang was clearly an update on the

'94, its appearance had been transformed.

Under the hood, all Mustangs received a substantial boost. The 3.8-litre V6 saw power rise by over 25 per cent to 190bhp at 5,250rpm, thanks to a new intake manifold, better air flow in the heads and lower friction pistons. Torque was up too, but by a more marginal 5lb ft to 220lb ft, now peaking at 2,750rpm.

Meanwhile, the GT V8 also benefited from better airflow, plus bigger valves, a higher lift camshaft, revised combustion chambers and a new ignition system with individual coils for each cylinder. The result was 260bhp at 5,250rpm, with torque boosted to 300lb ft (as with the V6, Ford engineers were concentrating on power figures instead of torque). They were clearly also working on emissions, as the V8 now qualified as a TLEV (Transitional Low Emission Vehicle) and the V6 as an LEV (Low Emission Vehicle). SVT engineers had also been at work coaxing 320bhp out of the dohc 4.6-litre V8, with the same set of changes wrought on its less complex cousin. Torque was now rated at 317lb ft.

To cope with all this extra power and torque, Mustang owners could pay $230 extra for TCS – traction control – which worked in synchronization with the ABS. When the ABS sensors detected wheelspin, the TCS cut power slightly and braked the

appropriate wheels, though street racers would no doubt have been relieved to note the on/off switch on the centre console, making it still possible to burn rubber if one really wanted to. Steering feel around the centre was said to be improved and Ford claimed that 3ft (0.9m) had been shaved off the turning circle. There was slightly more rear-suspension travel on base and GT

Mustangs, made possible by raising the transmission tunnel by 1.5in (3.8cm), and scuttle shake on convertibles was reduced by using new subframe connectors.

But the true innovation came from SVT, when the Mustang Cobra was finally given independent rear suspension. After 35 years, that live rear axle, which had been the bane of so many hard-driving Mustang owners'

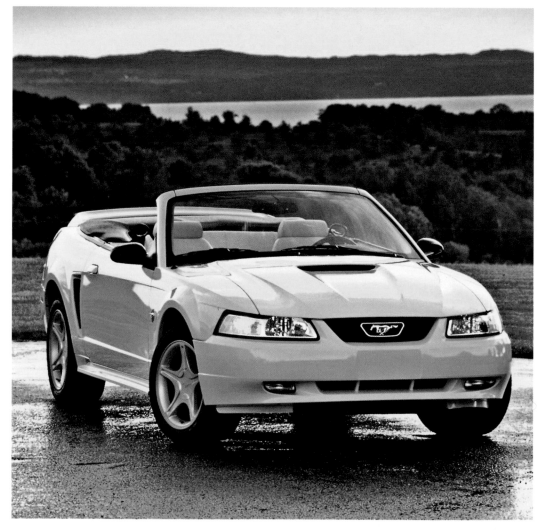

OPPOSITE
LEFT: *1999 Mustang GT.*
RIGHT: *1999 Mustang GT convertible.*

LEFT, PAGES 372 and 373
1999 Mustang Cobra convertible. All had the New Edge styling that added something special.

lives, had at last been ditched. The new system used an aluminium differential case from the Lincoln Mark VIII, but otherwise was unique to the Mustang. Upper- and lower-control arms were attached to a welded tubular subframe, with high-rate (470lb/in) linear springs and a thicker (now 26-mm) anti-roll bar. The whole set-up reduced unsprung weight by a massive 125lb (57kg) and improved weight distribution into the bargain; Ford claimed 55/45 for the Cobra against 57/43 for the old live-axle set-up. In theory, it could be bolted straight into any modern Mustang, the four mounting points being identical.

So what effect did all this have on the road? *Road & Track* made the inevitable comparison with Camaro in April 1999, pitching a new SVT Cobra against the Camaro SS, which would have made far happier reading for the Ford top brass than

the Z28 comparison of the previous year. The Cobra still didn't make quite as much torque as the Chevy small-block, and didn't have that motor's instant response, especially at low revs (the Camaro, remember, had an extra litre of capacity at its disposal). But the acceleration gap was closing. The Cobra was actually quicker off the mark (R&T considered the independent suspension helped here) and equalled the Camaro's 0–60 time of 5.5 seconds. Thereafter, the General Motors car's extra torque began to tell as it pulled ahead, with a 3-second advantage over the quarter-mile.

OPPOSITE and BELOW
1999 Mustang GT 4.6 convertible, the 35th-anniversary edition.

But the true revelation was on twisty roads. For decades, the Mustang had been hampered by a rear suspension that wasn't even the equal of other live-axle set-ups, let alone a good independent system. The new

Mustang changed all that. Here was a Cobra that offered both good ride and fine handling, backed up by revised steering that gave just the right amount of feedback. No longer would the car hop and skip over mid-

OPPOSITE
This 1999 Mustang has a 4.6-litre Cobra V8.

corner bumps. Set up for mild understeer, it would power oversteer if asked, though the TCS still kept everything under control. Cobra whipped through *R&T*'s standard test slalom at 64.5mph (103.8km/h), while the live-axle Camaro could only manage 60, and that with some steering correction.

According to writer Matt DeLorenzo, the new Cobra finally put to rest the notion that muscle-bound pony cars were good only for tyre-smoking, straight-line starts. The Camaro still has something of that – it was edgier and less sophisticated – but the Cobra came out on top. The Mustang's transformation was complete (at least in Cobra form), from the hairiest car on the block to one of the most competent.

For many Mustang fans, such road-test results would have been enough to celebrate the car's 35th birthday, but Ford had other ideas. It wished to avoid the accusation of ignoring its pony-car heritage, which had happened 10 years previously, and built 5,000 limited-edition GTs. As with all such cars, the changes were cosmetic; for $2,695 the 35th-anniversary package bought a raised hood scoop, rear spoiler, side scoops, black panels, Midnight Black leather interior with silver leather inserts, floor mats with 35th-anniversary script, and an aluminium gear-shift knob for the manual cars. Unlike some special editions there was a choice of colours: Black, Silver, Crystal White and Performance Red. Roll on the 40th.

PRODUCTION

Coupé	73,180
Coupé GT	19,634
Convertible	19,244
Convertible GT	13,699
Cobra coupé	4,040
Cobra convertible	4,055
TOTAL	133,637

ENGINE LINE-UP

3.8-litre V6

Type	Water-cooled cast-iron, ohv
Bore x stroke	3.80 x 3.40in (96.5 x 86.4mm)
Capacity	232ci (3.8 litres)
Compression ratio	9.4:1
Fuelling	Electronic injection
Power	190bhp @ 5,250rpm

4.6-litre V8

Type	Water-cooled cast-iron, sohc
Bore x stroke	3.60 x 3.60in (91.4 x 91.4mm)
Capacity	281ci (4.6 litres)
Compression ratio	9.0:1
Fuelling	Electronic injection
Power	260bhp @ 5,250rpm

4.6-litre Cobra V8

Type	Water-cooled aluminium, dohc
Bore x stroke	3.60 x 3.60in
Capacity	281ci (4.6 litres)
Compression ratio	9.8:1
Fuelling	Electronic injection
Power	320bhp @ 6,000rpm

2000:
COBRA RECALLED

OPPOSITE
2000 Mustang GT.

BELOW
2000 Mustang Saleen S281 speedster.

America, as the 20th century drew to a close, was reputed to be one of the most crime-ridden countries on earth. How far this is down to modern-day paranoia is a matter for debate, but how else can one explain an internal trunk release on the 2000 model-year Mustang? Accessible from inside the trunk, and glow-in-the-dark, it was Ford's response to reports of carjacking in which unfortunate victims were bundled into the trunks of their own cars.

That was the most significant change to the non-Cobra Mustang for 2000, that and the fitment of child-seat anchor brackets on the rear seats. The latter was an encouraging sign, indicating that the Mustang was still popular with young families (part of the original 1964 brief), and was not just another

OPPOSITE and LEFT
2000 Mustang V6. Often overlooked,
the 3.8-litre Mustang looked just as
good as the full-house V8.

sports car masquerading as a 2+2.

The seat anchors, the trunk release and three new colours (Sunburst Gold, Performance Red and Amazon Gold) were the extent of the changes on the 2000 Mustang. After the major innovations of 1999, it seemed that the pony car was being given a quiet year in which to recover and collect itself.

At least, that was the plan, but in the meantime some serious problems had revealed themselves in the 1999 Cobra, the one that had wowed road testers with its new independent rear suspension. It was soon clear that many such Cobras were not making the claimed 320bhp; it turned out that late in the design process the exhaust system had been pinched so that it cleared the lower rear suspension arms but touched the tarmac.

So many cars were affected that there was a general recall to fit freer-flowing intake manifolds and silencers. This, said Ford, would do trick. But the recall was a major operation for SVT, involving over 8,000 cars. In a major corporate climbdown it decided not to produce any standard Cobras for 2000. 'Rather than rushing to produce a limited number of 2000 models,' went the official SVT website announcement, 'and risking production/manufacturing issues by hurrying – we're choosing to focus our efforts … on the 1999 Cobra owner notification program … [and] timely production of the 2001 SVT Mustang Cobra.' In other words, it would concentrate instead

on correcting the 1999 cars and ensuring that the 2001 would make its claimed 320bhp. A climbdown perhaps, but it was also sensible, and showed an awareness that the Cobra's credibility, not to mention that of the entire Mustang line-up, depended on it actually delivering the brake horsepower it promised.

Something else was occupying SVT engineers for 2000. This was the Cobra R, a thinly-disguised racer for the road with a specially assembled 5.4-litre V8 pushing out 385bhp and 385lb ft. It is tempting to dismiss the Cobra R as a public relations exercise, a means of distracting attention from the embarrassing recall of all those 1999 Cobras. While this may be possible, it is unlikely. The Cobra R was such a comprehensive upgrade on the basic Cobra that it could never have been knocked up in the aftermath of the recall. It was a car that had almost certainly been planned well in advance.

The reason for thinking this was that SVT didn't tune the standard 4.6-litre V8, or pluck another, beefier, Ford motor directly from the shelf. Instead, it made up its own, making use of specialist suppliers as well as the corporate parts bin. The block was actually derived from that of the modular 4.6, but in cast-iron and displacing 5.4 litres, thanks to a much longer stroke of 105.8mm. Taller than the standard 4.6, the 'Triton' was actually used in Ford trucks, but in this application was surmounted by four-valve aluminium heads with double-overhead camshafts. The truck internals were rejected in favour of Carillo connecting-rods (made of billet steel) and forged pistons giving a compression of 9.6:1. Higher-lift cams were fitted, along with a specially-made intake

manifold, tubular headers and Bassini X-pipes. The result was 385bhp at 5,700rpm and 385lb ft at 4,500. That made the Triton Cobra particularly power-efficient for its size, with 71.3bhp/litre in comparison with the 1995 Cobra R (using the old 351-ci V8), which made 51.7.

All this power was supported by Tremec six-speed manual transmission (the first six-speeder fitted to any production Mustang) and a 4-in (10-cm) aluminium driveshaft transferred power back to an 8.8-in (22.4-cm) differential, also in aluminium, with a relatively low 3.55:1 ratio inside to maximize

OPPOSITE and BELOW
The 2000 Mustang V6 with 190bhp was the entry-level Mustang.

acceleration. If SVT's boss, John Coletti, had been more honest, this was probably what the Cobra R was all about: to blow the Camaro into the drag-strip weeds once and for all.

But the R was intended to be a road-legal, almost track-ready race car, rather than a drag racer, so there were plenty of suspension changes. The Cobra's independent rear end was still there, but much stiffer Eibach coil springs were fitted at both ends, plus high-end Bilstein shocks. Brembo disc brakes were fitted all round, with four-piston calipers, while the tyres were 265/40ZR-18 BFGoodrich G-Forces.

Inside, the Cobra R's racing aspirations were characterized by Recaro racing seats and the absence of air conditioning, rear seat, sound system and various pieces of trim. Not that it was a completely stripped-out racer; Cobra Rs still came with power windows, door locks and trunk release, plus twin airbags and a full-sized spare tyre. One couldn't see the 20-gallon (91-litre) bladder fuel cell, but it was there. On the outside, there was no mistaking the Cobra R, with its massive rear wing, big front spoiler and skirt extensions. In time-honoured fashion, the front spoiler was shipped unfitted, to be added by the dealer if the customer so desired (those with steep driveways need not have applied). Even after the standard colour was changed from Grabber Orange to Performance Red, and in the absence of any stripes or badges, the R still managed to turn heads.

If the Cobra R's aim had been to topple the Camaro SS as the fastest pony car on sale, then it succeeded. *Road & Track* recorded a 0–60 time of 4.8 seconds, the test car reaching

100mph (161km/h) in 10.9 seconds and covering the standing quarter in 13.2. Revved out to the 6,600-rpm red line and gear speeds equated to 47mph/76km, 67, 97, 139 and an estimated 170 in fifth gear, 160mph/257km in top. At those speeds, the Cobra was being held back by its aerodynamics.

Not that it was all good news. The ultra-stiff suspension was fine on well-surfaced race tracks, but on the street made the Cobra R feel nervous and jumpy. *Road & Track* concluded that a Corvette was quieter, more comfortable and easier to live with day to day. It may not have had Cobra's ready-to-race appeal, but it was also more than $10,000 cheaper – SVT was asking $54,000 for the R without any options. Still, that didn't seem to bother anyone ordering one of the limited-edition Rs. SVT built 300 of them, and every one was pre-sold before the first was even delivered.

ENGINE LINE-UP
3.8-litre V6

Type	Water-cooled cast-iron, ohv
Bore x stroke	3.80 x 3.40in (96 x 86.4mm)
Capacity	232ci (3.8 litres)
Compression ratio	9.4:1
Fuelling	Electronic injection
Power	190bhp @ 5,250rpm

4.6-litre V8

Type	Water-cooled cast-iron, sohc
Bore x stroke	3.60 x 3.60in (91.4 x 91.4mm)
Capacity	281ci (4.6 litres)
Compression ratio	9.0:1
Fuelling	Electronic injection
Power	260bhp @ 5,250rpm

5.4-litre Cobra R V8

Type	Water-cooled cast-iron, dohc
Bore x stroke	3.55 x 4.2in (90.2 x 107mm)
Capacity	330ci (5.4 litres)
Compression ratio	9.6:1
Fuelling	Electronic injection
Power	385bhp @ 6,250rpm

OPPOSITE and BELOW
2000 Mustang 5.4-litre SVT Cobra R.

2001:
BULLITT

The 1968 Bullitt 3. This replica of the 1968 Mustang Fastback GT 390 (right), which co-starred with Steve McQueen in the movie, Bullitt, *retraces the route on the original San Francisco streets which featured in the famous chase scene. McQueen's son, Chad, was on hand to 'test' the new 2001 Mustang Bullitt GT (opposite) as well as the classic muscle car as they relived the movie.*

Everyone, especially Mustang lovers, remembers the 1968 movie *Bullitt*, the gritty Steve McQueen detective drama. What do we remember most about the film? Is it the way Frank Bullitt's girlfriend makes him confront the violence he must cope with day by day, to which he seems to have become inured? Or perhaps it is the final scene, where he looks at his reflection in the mirror after a particularly bloody day and thinks, 'how can I live with myself?' No, none of that emotional stuff – it's the car-chase scene, perhaps the most famous ever, in which Frank Bullitt and his Mustang fastback are pursued through the streets of San Francisco by a Dodge Charger full of baddies.

Ford knew that every car enthusiast in the Western world would remember that car chase, which is why it had the late Steve McQueen in an ad, supposedly in 1968, driving a 2002 Ford Puma. It looked real, but

Chad McQueen goes airborne in the 2001 Mustang Bullitt GT as it follows the same movie route as its predecessor.

OPPOSITE and LEFT
The 2001 Mustang Bullitt GT had
beefier power and torque curves than
the standard car.

it was all done using computer-crafted tricks. But there was nothing tricky or fake about the Mustang Bullitt, a special-edition that Ford offered for 2001 (though actually introduced later in the year as a 2002 model). At least one journalist remarked that it would have been easy for Ford merely to stick Bullitt badges on any Mustang, paint it a different colour and sell just as many; but this one was actually quite different under the skin.

This was no cosmetic special. It had a new aluminium intake (replacing the plastic one), twin 57-mm throttle bodies and a freer-flowing exhaust system. On paper, this produced just five extra horsepower over the standard GT, and three extra lb ft (the latter peaking at the same 4,000rpm). In practice, the difference was far more tangible. The GT didn't really arrive near the top of its torque curve until 3,700rpm, but the Bullitt made 283lb ft (93 per cent of the peak figure) at

RIGHT
The interior of the 2001 Mustang
Bullitt GT.

BELOW
Whichever way one looked at them,
drilled pedals were either a homage to
the past or a meaningless indulgence.

OPPOSITE
A larger throttle body and a freer-
flowing exhaust system gave the Bullitt
engine the edge over the standard
Mustangs.

just 2,200rpm. In short, it had a lot more low-down grunt.

That gave it better response, born out by slightly quicker 0–60 and quarter-mile times, making it 0.4 seconds faster over the quarter. That in turn was backed up by stiffer springs and Tokico shocks, which also lowered the ride height by three-quarters of an inch. The 13-inch (33-cm) disc brakes came straight out of the SVT Cobra, though what the Bullitt didn't have was the Cobra's independent rear suspension, sticking instead to the standard Mustang's tried and tested live axle.

It wouldn't have been a special edition worth its salt without a few cosmetic tweaks, and the Bullitt had plenty of these. The idea was to evoke the spirit of the late-1960s Mustang, and that's exactly what it did. Five-spoke alloy wheels were similar to those fitted to many of the Shelby Mustangs. There were bright-red brake calipers and a brushed-aluminium gas cap, not to mention large side and hood scoops, the latter fake but effective. The plastic dashboard was left simple and unadorned and even the stitch pattern of the seats was designed to suggest 1968 rather than 2001. In Highland Green (like Bullitt's car), black or dark blue, the Bullitt Mustang cost $3,695 more than the standard GT, which was good value considering the performance, braking and cosmetic package it had been given.

Meanwhile, the SVT Cobra was back after its 12-month sabbatical, now raring to go with a guaranteed 320bhp. *Road & Track* was able to vouch for this – its test car was actually slightly slower than the 1999

version, but the performance figures were taken in 102°F (39°C) temperatures. In 1999, it had been a chilly 60-something, when the air was colder and more dense and performance was more satisfactory. Traction control was now standard, but with a flick of the switch could be set to 'Power Start'; in other words, this turned the TCS off, allowing show-off drivers to smoke their tyres; but it didn't mean that keen but incompetent drivers were left to their own devices. The TCS would only remain off while the car was moving in a straight line. Should a sideslip be detected, the system would kick in by itself, altering the timing and fuel-air ratio and applying a little brake to get things back under control.

Steve Saleen was still producing Mustang specials and offered a supercharged S281, the S281SC in 2000 and '01, with a claimed 350bhp and 410lb ft. Sub-5-second 0–60 times were recorded and 0.93g on the skidpan, with power up to 365bhp for 2001. These Saleens started at $32,000, but if money was burning a hole in one's pocket, then the SR might well have fitted the bill at $158,000. This used the familiar 351-ci V8, in 505-bhp form with 500lb ft and driving through a six-speed gearbox. Saleen claimed 0–60 in four seconds dead, and a stomach-tightening 1.09g on the skidpan.

So much for the full-on performance

OPPOSITE and LEFT
The 2001 Mustang Bullitt GT, with the badge that meant so much.

BELOW
The Bullitt was all about feeling good – hence this brushed aluminium gear knob.

Mustangs, but as ever, far more people were opting for the standard production-line cars. These saw few changes for 2001, apart from the addition of some look-at-me body parts. The hood gained a gaping non-functional scoop, bigger side scoops, a revised spoiler and black trim around the headlights. A new option for the GT was five-spoke 17-inch (43-cm) wheels, similar to the Torq-Thrusts popular on late-1960s muscle cars. These new cosmetic features were putting the 1990s Mustang shape through a now-familiar ritual. Like earlier Mustangs, it was gaining beefier bodywork as the years went by.

There was one substantive change for 2001 and it was a real break with tradition. From the start, a central part of the Mustang philosophy had been to offer buyers a long list of options, the idea being that everyone should create their own 'personal' car, while Ford made an extra slice of profit on every option box ticked. But now the whole option set-up was simplified, with around 50 order combinations available; compare this with 2000, when it had been 2,600!

OPPOSITE
2001 Mustang Cobra convertible.

BELOW
2001 Roush Mustang.

2001 Roush Mustang.

The engine bay of the 2001 Roush showing a detail of the supercharger.

RIGHT
2001 Roush Mustang, with Jack Roush Edition graphics on rear window.

OPPOSITE
2001 Mustang GT 4.6 V8.

Most of the options were gathered into one of three packages, offered as separate models on the coupé or convertible. The Standard Equipment Package (only available on the V6 coupé) consisted of 15-in (38-cm) painted alloy wheels, P205/65 tyres, stereo CD and radio/cassette, air conditioning, twin airbags and Securilock anti-theft system. The Deluxe Equipment Group (for both base and GTs) added a rear spoiler, power driver's seat, leather-bound steering wheel, sports bucket seats (on the GT), cruise control and 17-inch painted alloy wheels. Various options could be added to these, such as automatic transmission and the Sport Appearance group. Finally, top-level factory Mustangs came with the Premium Equipment Group: automatic transmission, 16-inch bright alloy wheels, P225/55 tyres, Mach 460 sound system with six-disc CD changer, ABS with traction control and, on GTs, leather sports front bucket seats and 17-inch alloy wheels.

ENGINE LINE-UP
3.8-litre V6

Type	Water-cooled cast-iron, ohv
Bore x stroke	3.80 x 3.40in (96.5 x 86.4mm)
Capacity	232ci (3.8 litres)
Compression ratio	9.4:1
Fuelling	Electronic injection
Power	190bhp @ 5,250rpm

RIGHT
2001 Mustang GT 4.6 V8.

OPPOSITE
2001 Mustang Cobra SVT.

4.6-litre V8

Type	Water-cooled cast-iron, sohc
Bore x stroke	3.60 x 3.60in (91.4 x 91.4mm)
Capacity	281ci (4.6 litres)
Compression ratio	9.0:1
Fuelling	Electronic injection
Power	260bhp @ 5,250rpm

Bullitt 4.6-litre V8

Type	Water-cooled cast-iron, sohc
Bore x stroke	3.60 x 3.60in (91.4 x 91.4mm)
Capacity	281ci (4.6 litres)
Compression ratio	9.0:1
Fuelling	Electronic injection
Power	265bhp @ 5,000rpm

4.6-litre Cobra V8

Type	Water-cooled cast-iron, dohc
Bore x stroke	3.55 x 4.2in (90.2 x 107mm)
Capacity	281ci (4.6 litres)
Compression ratio	9.8:1
Fuelling	Electronic injection
Power	320bhp @ 6,000rpm

In 2001, Ford presented 24 show vehicles at the SEMA (Specialty Equipment Market Association) show in Las Vegas. Highlights included this special-edition Mustang Titanium, featuring Ford's 4.6-litre engine with a Vortech supercharger, JBA headers and a titanium exhaust by Borla. The interior included custom titanium trim with Mustang Bullitt pedals and shifter-knobs.

LEFT
Ford also displayed this Granatelli Motorsports/Summit Racing 2001 Mustang Cobra; Granatelli claims that this is the fastest modular-motor drag-race Mustang. Motivated by a 1400-bhp, 5.4-litre V-8, it is capable of running the quarter-mile in 7.9 seconds and reaching 190mph (306km/h).

2002:
THE MODERN RETRO

BELOW
2002 Mustang GT.

OPPOSITE
2002 Mustang GT convertible.

For 2002, the Mustang barely changed at all. Neither, from a marketing point of view, did it need to; it was still the best-selling pony car, bar none. The Cobra R had finally seen off the hottest Camaros in a straight-line battle, while all the other Cobras, with their independent rear ends, had done the same on twisty roads. The Bullitt coupé was making a great job of remembering the Mustang lineage, and back in the real world the base V6 coupé was giving 30mpg (10.6km/litre) on the EPA's highway test. Why should anything be changed?

The more critical among us would say that the standard Mustangs would have done well to adopt the Cobra's independent rear suspension. Even the most gushing road

Looks familiar? Thirty-five years on from the time that the first Mustang wore Shelby colours, here was another one. It is otherwise a standard 4.6-litre GT.

ABOVE and OPPOSITE
2002 Mustang 4.6-litre V8 GT.

the early 21st-century Mustang: it had been toughened up, compared with the original 1994 car, but had received lots of retro styling cues to evoke memories of those first Mustangs, even if the memories had come from books, magazine articles or the recollections of aged relatives.

So mechanically, there were no changes, though the 3.8-litre V6 was credited with slightly more power for 2002, with 193bhp at 5,500rpm and 225lb ft at 2,800. That year the V6 also lost its simulated side scoops and gained a new hood, while 16-inch alloy wheels were now standard; on the Sport Appearance Group (a V6 only option), there was a new tape stripe. Some may have been more excited by the Mach 1000 sound system, newly optional for 2002, which came with speed-sensitive volume control, or maybe the new four-piece two-tone leather steering wheel. But most revelled in the fact that with the GT V8 one could still buy a V8 muscle car with supercar performance at a reasonable price.

testers, much as they loved the V8 rumble and the unapologetic muscle-car sensation, couldn't help but mention this. And despite receiving many refinements over the years, the 2002 Mustang still suffered from its live axle, both in ride and ultimate handling. It was far better than earlier Mustangs, but still needed a skilled driver to test its limits on bumpy back roads.

This was irrelevant to the majority of drivers, who had been more attracted to the Mustang's retro yet modern styling. It has to be said that Ford had done a superb job on

ENGINE LINE-UP
3.8-litre V6

Type	Water-cooled cast-iron, ohv
Bore x stroke	3.80 x 3.40in (96.5 x 86.4mm)
Capacity	232ci (3.8 litres)
Compression ratio	9.4:1
Fuelling	Electronic injection
Power	193bhp @ 5,500rpm

4.6-litre V8

Type	Water-cooled cast-iron, sohc
Bore x stroke	3.60 x 3.60in (91.4 x 91.4mm)
Capacity	281ci (4.6 litres)
Compression ratio	9.0:1
Fuelling	Electronic injection
Power	260bhp @ 5,250rpm

Bullitt 4.6-litre V8

Type	Water-cooled cast-iron, sohc
Bore x stroke	3.60 x 3.60in
Capacity	281ci (4.6 litres)
Compression ratio	9.0:1
Fuelling	Electronic injection
Power	265bhp @ 5,000rpm

4.6-litre Cobra V8

Type	Water-cooled cast-iron, dohc
Bore x stroke	3.55 x 4.2in (90.2 x 105.8mm)
Capacity	281ci (4.6 litres)
Compression ratio	9.8:1
Fuelling	Electronic injection
Power	320bhp @ 6,000rpm

2003/2004:
BACK TO THE FUTURE

BELOW and OPPOSITE
The 2003 Mustang Mach 1 saw the
return of another well-known pony-
car badge.

The Mustang's retro styling, the success of the Bullitt and the V8 GT had combined to teach Ford the value of nostalgia when applied to cars – assuming it needed to be taught. So what name could be resurrected for 2003; was it possible to delve once more into the Mustang's rich history and evoke potent memories of the 1960s? Really, the company was spoilt for choice, even if it was chary of using anything connected with Carroll Shelby. The Boss had already been done, but what about the Cobra Jet or the SportsRoof, or even the Ghia or Grande? In the event, it was none of these, but 2003 did see the return of the Mach 1.

It was basically a dressed-up GT, with the emphasis on detailing taken straight from the golden age of the muscle car. First and most

obvious was the Shaker hood scoop, which had been popular in the late-1960s/early-'70s, the air scoop quivering while the big V8 idled and rumbled. There hadn't been one on a Mustang for decades, but now it was back. The scoop wasn't just for show, however, and Ford termed it a 'Ram Air' system (another old muscle-car term) to underline the fact.

Not that it added much to the Mach 1's power. Despite adopting the dohc 32-valve version of the 4.6-litre V8, the Mach 1 was listed at 305bhp at 5,800rpm and 320lb ft. The SVT Cobra offered 320bhp from the same basic engine, which hardly mattered, as the Mach 1 was all about making a statement. So along with the Shaker went loud Mach 1

stripes. There were 17-in (43-cm) bright-aluminium 'Heritage' wheels, a big rear spoiler, variable-rate sport rear suspension, and inside, a Mach 460 sound system with six-CD changer. Available with the Premium equipment group only, the Mach 1 cost $29,330, or exactly $5,000 more than the equivalent GT coupé. It was only offered as a

417

closed car, incidentally, not as a convertible.

There was still a basic unadorned Mustang for those who wanted it (or couldn't afford a Mach 1), though the V6 coupé and convertible were now very well equipped even in standard form. Coupé equipment included 16-inch alloy wheels

with 225/55 tyres, plus a Securi-Lock anti-theft system. The convertible (commanding a $5,000+ premium) came with cruise control, six-way power driver's seat and colour-keyed front mats. The GTs were little changed for 2003, still in 260-bhp form and still with the Quadrashock live axle rear end,

though there was still no sign that they would adopt the Cobra's independent rear. A Traction Lok differential was now standard and came in de-luxe or premium forms.

But the Mustang performance flagship was still the Cobra, with the SVT badge for added cachet. To put extra distance between

OPPOSITE and BELOW
2003 Mustang Mach 1.

RIGHT and OPPOSITE
This is the Mach 1 V8, but the SVT Cobra was still the most powerful option.

BELOW and OPPOSITE
2003 Mustang Mach 1.

this and the 305-bhp Mach 1, it was supercharged for 2003, boosting power to 390bhp; this made it the most powerful factory Mustang of all time, and by a huge margin, bearing in mind that the late-1960s figures were inflated by the measurement system. A six-speed gearbox was part of the deal, as was the Mach 460 sound system and leather/suede seating. The price was $38,460, without options (it's not known what Lee Iacocca would have thought of a $40,000 Mustang, but he probably wouldn't have approved). Meanwhile, the car he fathered was approaching another birthday, when hopefully life would begin at 40.

LINE-UP (2003)

Coupé V6	$18,345
Convertible V6	$24,080
Coupé GT V8	$24,330
Convertible GT V8	$28,670
Mach 1	$29,330
SVT Cobra	$38,460

SVT Cobra 2003

Engine

Type	Water-cooled 90-degree
	V8, cast-iron block, aluminium heads, dohc, 32 valves
Bore x stroke	3.55 x 3.54in (90.2 x 90mm)
Capacity	281ci (4.6 litres)
Compression ratio	8.5:1
Power	390bhp @ 6,000 rpm
Torque	390lb ft @ 3,500 rpm
Specific output	84.8 bhp/litre
Redline	6,500 rpm
Intake valves	2 per cylinder, 37-mm head diameter
Exhaust valves	2 per cylinder, 30-mm head diameter
Fuel system	Sequential electronic fuel injection
Ignition system	Distributorless coil-on-plug

Induction system	Eaton Corporation Generation IV Roots-type supercharger with water-to-air intercooler		tuned equal-length runners		3.0- in polished exhaust tips
		Throttle body :	57-mm twin bore	Transmission:	
		Mass-air sensor :	90-mm diameter	Rear axle	8.8-in ring gear with
		Exhaust manifolds:	Cast iron	3.55:1	limited-slip differential,
Boost pressure:	8.0psi max	Exhaust system:	Dual, stainless steel,		aluminum case
Intake manifold:	Cast aluminum,		2.25-in diameter;	Driveshaft	Aluminium, with

OPPOSITE and BELOW
Shaker hoods were back in the Mach 1.

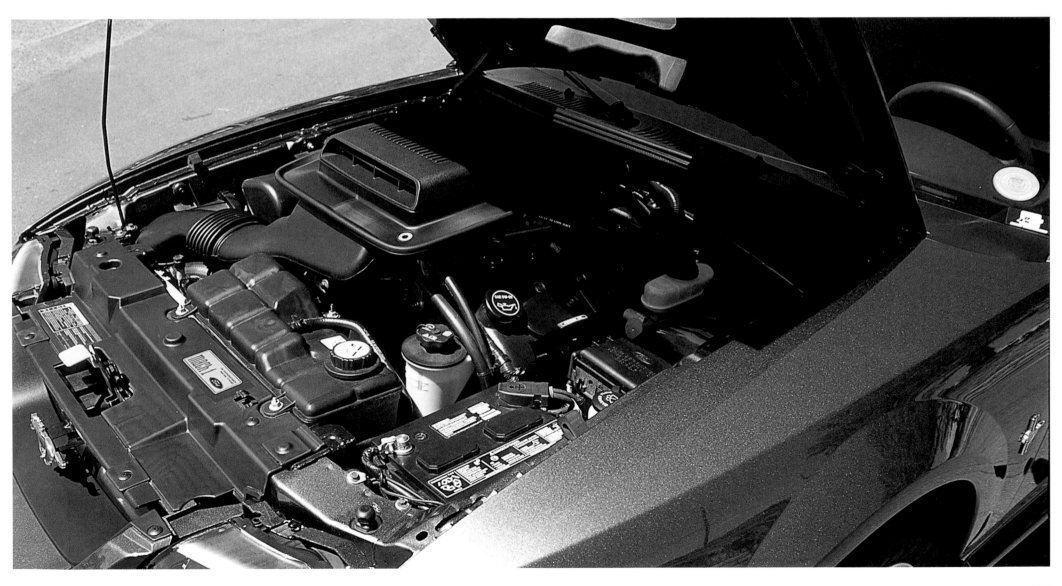

	hardened yoke and U-joints
Transmission:	TTC T-56 6-speed manual
Clutch	11.0-in single plate
Gear	Ratio
1st	2.66
2nd	1.78
3rd	1.30
4th	1.00
5th	0.80
6th	0.63
Reverse	2.90

Suspension

Front	Modified MacPherson strut system with gas-charged Bilstein™ monotube dampeners and separate 600-lb/in (500-lb/in on convertible) spring on lower arm, 29-mm tubular stabilizer bar
Rear	Multi-link independent system, cast-iron upper control arm, aluminum lower control arm, fixed toe-control tie rod, aluminum spindle, gas-charged Bilstein™ monotube shock absorber, 600lb/in (470lb/in on convertible) coil spring, 26-mm tubular stabilizer bar

OPPOSITE and LEFT
2003 Mustang Mach 1.

Steering

Brakes

Front	13.0-in (330-mm) vented Brembo™ disc, PBR™ twin-piston caliper
Rear	11.65-in (296-mm) vented disc, single-piston caliper
ABS	Four-channel, four-sensor system

Wheels/Tyres

Wheels	17 x 9in (43 x 23cm), 5-spoke cast-aluminum-alloy
Tyres	Goodyear Eagle F1, 275/40ZR-17

Dimensions and Capacities

Wheelbase	101.3in (257.3cm)
Length	183.5in (466.1cm)
Height	Coupé 52.5in (1336mm) Convertible 52.9in (134.4cm)
Width	73.1in (185.7cm)
Track, f/r	60.3in/60.3in (1530mm/1530mm)
Kerb Weight	Coupé 3,665lb (1662kg) Convertible 3,780lb (1715kg)
Fuel Capacity	15.7 gallons (71.4 litres)
Weight Distribution, f/r	57%/43%

OPPOSITE and LEFT
2003 Mustang Cobra 4.6-litre
supercharged.

RIGHT
2003 Mustang Cobra 4.6-litre supercharged engine.

OPPOSITE
2003 Mustang 4.6-litre GT.

OPPOSITE and LEFT
It was still possible to have a plain V8
without supercharger in the 2003
Mustang, as is the case with this GT.

OPPOSITE
2004 Mustang SVT Cobra.

LEFT
2003 Mustang SVT Cobra.

PAGES 436 and 437
2004 Mustang SVT Cobra convertible.

2004 Mustang SVT Cobra convertible.

LEFT
2004 Mustang SVT Cobra
Mystichrome.

PAGE 440
2004 Mustang GT convertible.

PAGE 441
2004 40th-anniversary-edition
Mustang GT.

INDEX